"Dori Berger is that rare combination of musician, scientist, and clinician. Based on her extensive research experience, she unfolds a detailed prescription of protocols, culled from Eurhythmics and the most recent science, that can lead to dramatically improved results. In doing so, she makes a clear argument for how music moves from a passive therapy to a potent intervention!"

—*Dr. Patricia Gray, Director of The BioMusic Program, University of North Carolina, Greensboro, USA*

"A professional musician and practitioner in sensorimotor treatment of autism and related diagnoses, Dorita Berger writes brilliantly to inspire therapists who help persons with disorders of intention and awareness share life with self-confidence and joy. With up-to-date brain science of intentions and feelings, this book will also be a resource for students of psychology, medicine and education. Born musical, our sense of others' rhythms and melodies of affection, invention and discovery can be enhanced to overcome confusion and anxiety."

—*Colwyn Trevarthen, PhD, FRSE, Professor (Emeritus) of Child Psychology and Psychobiology, Department of Psychology, The University of Edinburgh, UK*

"Dorita Berger's book is a gift to all individuals on the autism spectrum. As a music therapist and scientist, Dr. Berger combines cutting-edge research with a healthy dose of practical advice to show how eurhythmics in a music therapy-based clinical environment can be used to support a wide range of neurophysiologic diagnoses. This book is an outstanding resource for therapists, neuroscientists, and families."

—*Frances H. Rauscher, Professor Emerita, University of Wisconsin Oshkosh, and co-author of* Neurosciences in Music Pedagogy

"In a book like no other, Dr. Berger masterfully introduces the science behind the power of music and movement, followed by artistically presented, easy-to-implement, and practical intervention solutions for the clinician, parent, or other person to connect with individuals with autism and other neurophysiological diagnoses."

—*Stephen M. Shore, Clinical Assistant Professor of Special Education, Adelphi University*

EURHYTHMICS FOR AUTISM AND OTHER NEUROPHYSIOLOGIC DIAGNOSES

by the same author

Music Therapy, Sensory Integration and the Autistic Child
Dorita S. Berger
ISBN 978 1 84310 700 2
eISBN 978 1 84642 712 1

The Music Effect
Music Physiology and Clinical Applications
Daniel J. Schneck and Dorita S. Berger
Illustrated by Geoffrey Rowland
ISBN 978 1 84310 771 2
eISBN 978 1 84642 462 5

of related interest

Basic Anatomy and Physiology for the Music Therapist
Daniel J. Schneck
ISBN 978 1 84905 756 1
eISBN 978 0 85700 992 0

Early Childhood Music Therapy and Autism Spectrum Disorders
Developing Potential in Young Children and their Families
Edited by Petra Kern and Marcia Humpal
ISBN 978 1 84905 241 2
eISBN 978 0 85700 485 7

Autism Movement Therapy® Method
Waking up the Brain!
Joanne Lara with Keri Bowers
Foreword by Stephen M. Shore
ISBN 978 1 84905 728 8
eISBN 978 1 78450 173 0

Reframe Your Thinking Around Autism
How the Polyvagal Theory and
Brain Plasticity Help Us Make Sense of Autism
Holly Bridges
ISBN 978 1 84905 672 4
eISBN 978 1 78450 177 8

Eurhythmics for Autism

AND OTHER NEUROPHYSIOLOGIC DIAGNOSES

A Sensorimotor Music-Based Treatment Approach

Dorita S. Berger
Foreword by Stephen M. Shore

Jessica Kingsley *Publishers*
London and Philadelphia

Appendices 2 and 3 are reproduced with permission from *TEMPO* magazine.

First published in 2016
by Jessica Kingsley Publishers
73 Collier Street
London N1 9BE, UK
and
400 Market Street, Suite 400
Philadelphia, PA 19106, USA

www.jkp.com

Copyright © Dorita S. Berger 2016
Foreword © Stephen M. Shore 2016

All rights reserved. No part of this publication may be reproduced in any material form (including photocopying or storing it in any medium by electronic means and whether or not transiently or incidentally to some other use of this publication) without the written permission of the copyright owner except in accordance with the provisions of the Copyright, Designs and Patents Act 1988 or under the terms of a licence issued by the Copyright Licensing Agency Ltd, Saffron House, 6–10 Kirby Street, London EC1N 8TS. Applications for the copyright owner's written permission to reproduce any part of this publication should be addressed to the publisher.

Warning: The doing of an unauthorized act in relation to a copyright work may result in both a civil claim for damages and criminal prosecution.

Library of Congress Cataloging in Publication Data
Berger, Dorita S., author.
 Eurhythmics for autism and other neurophysiologic diagnoses : a sensorimotor music-based treatment
approach / Dorita S. Berger.
     pages cm
 Includes bibliographical references and index.
 ISBN 978-1-84905-989-3 (alk. paper)
 1. Eurythmics. 2. Music therapy. 3. Music--Psychological aspects. I. Title.
 ML3920.B425 2015
 616.89'1654--dc23
                    2015016673

British Library Cataloguing in Publication Data
A CIP catalogue record for this book is available from the British Library

ISBN 978 1 84905 989 3
eISBN 978 0 85700 905 0

*This book is dedicated
to my precious clients, who taught me
how to think clinically;
to my undergraduate and graduate students,
and colleagues who encourage me to
stand by my ideals; and
to my family and friends who endure my panic and
anxieties with returning love.
Thank you all.*

CONTENTS

Foreword by Stephen M. Shore	13
ACKNOWLEDGEMENTS	16
Prelude	19
About music training, and Eurhythmics as treatment	22
Objectives and organization of this book	24
About this book	27
A note about the terminology in this book	29

Part One: The Theory
Human Adaptive Function—Making Sense of the Environment

1. Coming to Our Senses	32
We are our physiology	32
Making sense of the environment	34
Proprioception	36
The vestibular sensory system	42
The visual, tactile, and auditory senses	46
Summary	55
2. This is Your Brain on Sensations!	59
What about emotion?	61
Emotion and survival-anxiety (fear)	63
Survival-anxiety, stress, and sensory processing	64
Information processing and the brain	64
What happens if information is deemed unsafe?	69
Survival-anxiety and the HPA axis	70
What does this all mean?	74

3. **Interpreting Autism and Sensory Characteristics** 77
   Hypothesis 1: Focused Eurhythmics-based music treatment can reduce pervasive survival-anxiety (HPA-driven fear factor) driven by sensory misinterpretation to yield functional coping skills 79
   Hypothesis 2: Movement, and motor planning timing deficits, often unaddressed in music-based treatment, can be improved with Eurhythmics-based music and movement interventions 84
   A look at typical autism behaviors 89
   Summary 91
   Further Reading 93

Part Two: The Practice
COPING: Calming—Organizing—Pacing—INtegrating—Growing. Reaching for Functional Adaptation

4. **What is This Thing Called Eurhythmics?** 96
   What is music? 97
   What is Eurhythmics? 100
   What does sensorimotor mean? 104
   A quick overview of music energies in clinical work 105
   Summary 109

5. **Eurhythmics in Music-Based Clinical Work** 111
   Treatment structure—Goal: COPING 114
   Summary 128

6. **Sensory Organization Through Quick Response Movement** 130
   Module 2: Seated 134
   Transitions 138
   Module 3: Fully-body movement gross-motor movements in and across space: Upper-/Lower-body organization 143
   Summary 152

7. Free To Be Me 154
   Module 4: Instrumental and rhythm improvisations, seated or moving. Drumming and/or various rhythmic instrumental and movement interactions 156
   Module 5: Closing the session, seated 173
   A word about solfeggio 173
   Summary 177

8. Observing With a Clinical Eye 179
   Case example analysis 184
   Conclusion 194

Part Three: Putting It All Together

9. Eurhythmics for Treating Other Diagnoses 198
   Reviewing the paradigm: Teaching as treatment 199
   Eurhythmics in treating other diagnoses 203
   Eurhythmics in psychodynamic therapy 204
   A brief look at related movement theorists 212
   Final thoughts 217

   Coda: Care, Organization, Development, Achievement 218
   APPENDIX IA: INTERVENTION PROGRESS RATING SCALE 222
   APPENDIX IB: SESSION BEHAVIOR RATING SCALE 224
   APPENDIX IC: SAMPLE BRIEF REPORT OF CLINICAL WORK AND RECOMMENDATIONS FOR A CLIENT 226
   APPENDIX 2: MUSIC SOOTHES THE RAVAGED BRAIN 231
   APPENDIX 3: UNDERSTANDING THE INCLUDED SPECIAL NEEDS CHILD IN MUSIC CLASSES 237
   REFERENCES 243
   SUBJECT INDEX 253
   AUTHOR INDEX 259

Foreword

The person with a severe stutter who sings flawlessly... The student on the autism spectrum who is non-speaking yet can sing—just like anyone else—while playing the piano... The human brain that "lights up" as viewed through fMRI like the skyline of a major city when listening to music, yet becomes like a display of a fireworks finale when the individual plays a musical instrument. Whether clinicians or not, many people have used and can relate to the power of music when it comes to relating, communicating, or interacting to another person in sharing our humanity. For example, anyone who purposely left the last word or note off a phrase of music in an effort to get a response from another person has engaged in this art form to develop an interpersonal connection.

As an individual on the autism spectrum I can relate to the use of music and movement in two ways. First, as part of my parents' "intensive home-based early intervention program," initiated in refutation of professional recommendations for institutionalization. Second, in my work giving music lessons to individuals on the autism spectrum where I've seen that whatever seems to scramble the speech areas of the brain in autism leaves the musical ones intact.

My parents accepted me for who I was yet realized a lot of work lay ahead if I were to lead a fulfilling and productive life. Similarly, Dr. Berger's reframing of ASD as *Autism Spectrum Diagnosis* says it all about her equally respecting individuals with autism and other conditions as having *difference* to be worked with rather than a collection of aberrant behaviors to be modified or eliminated.

When my parents' initial attempts at getting me to imitate them failed, they, like experienced music therapists, began imitating me. As a result I became aware of them in my environment, and with much intense work on their part, speech began to return at age four. I got re-evaluated, progressing from a diagnosis of strong autistic tendencies, child psychosis, and atypical development to merely neurotic, and entered the center that initially rejected me.

Interaction with and about music was omnipresent in our house for as long as I can remember through high school and beyond. We talked and sang to music. We moved to music. Much of what my parents did with me during my younger years is strikingly similar to the activities so clearly and expertly described in the practical section of this book. Additionally, as part of "music literacy" we'd listen to compositions such as "Ein Heldenleben" by Richard Strauss, "The Quintet in C" by Schubert, and various symphonies by Mahler until every note and nuance was memorized, wearing out many an LP or cassette tape in the process. The discovery of musical scores—an entire symphony in a book—was a great boon to my studies!

My involvement with music got me through middle and high school. Commonly a time of great turmoil for the teen years, my engagement with this art form made this period of education better for me than elementary school. Why? I joined the band, giving me a structured activity to mediate interactions with my classmates. Music became such passion that I'd spend hours in the school music room learning to play as many instruments as possible. Sometimes I would assemble instruments in creative ways such as placing a bassoon reed in a trombone creating a "a tromboon which combines aspects of a trombone and a bassoon—with the disadvantages of both" as so aptly described by Peter Schikele, author of compositions and other musical buffoonery by the mythical PDQ Bach.

The requirement of knowing how to play all musical instruments for a degree in music education made that course of study a natural to me all the way through my doctoral studies in this subject before "defecting" to special education to study the teaching of students with autism and other conditions more in depth.

With the precision of a scientist, Dr. Berger has developed a groundbreaking resource expertly explaining the what, how, and why of combining music, sensory processing, and movement as an intervention. With the artistry of the consummate musician that the author is, she goes on to provide easy to implement, practical solutions for the clinician, parent, or other person to connect with and improve the lives of individuals with autism and other neurophysiologic diagnoses. This book is a must read for the layperson wishing to know more about the use of Eurhythmic techniques all the way to the seasoned professional desiring to hone their craft of musical and movement-based interventions—and perhaps most important—sharing the human experience with others.

Stephen M. Shore, Internationally renowned author,
educator and presenter on issues related to the autism spectrum
Clinical Assistant Professor of Special Education at Adelphi University
Individual on the autism spectrum

ACKNOWLEDGEMENTS

It was during my undergraduate training program at the School of Music at Carnegie Mellon University (then known as Carnegie Tech), that I first encountered the Eurhythmics of Emile Jaques-Dalcroze. It was taught by the late, internationally renowned Marta Sanchez, who had trained at the Institut Jaques-Dalcroze in Geneva, Switzerland. All music students were required to take the course. For me, this material was a revelation. The concept of embodying music rhythm, phrasing, and dynamics, seemed so logical. Furthermore, to this day, when I learn a new piece of music, I still apply many of the concepts and movement activities to aid in my understanding and embodiment of musical elements. When I began working as a music-based clinician, with a Master of Arts degree in Music Therapy from NYU, many of the activities that I had experienced in the Eurhythmics course, including various movement and improvisational activities, I discovered I was applying as treatment approaches for sensorimotor functions. I had also employed Eurhythmics interventions in my PhD research investigation. The reader will encounter many of these activities detailed throughout this book. I, therefore, would like primarily to acknowledge with gratitude the contribution of the School of Music at Carnegie Mellon University to my development as a musician, pianist, performer, and clinician, and to the ongoing pursuit of Eurhythmics training at the CMU School of Music, Marta Sanchez Dalcroze Training Center.

In addition, there are many others who deserve special gratitude and mention as well. My editors Lisa Clark, Jane Evans, and Sarah Minty at Jessica Kingsley Publishers have stood by me with great patience and kindness throughout this difficult, laborious process of book writing. I am also grateful to, and would like to acknowledge, the ongoing contributions of my colleague, former co-author, and brother, Dr. Daniel J. Schneck, Professor Emeritus of Virginia Tech, and his wife Judi, who continue to support my work, and especially Dan, who teaches me "physiology," corrects my errors, and translates many of my interventions into physiologic language. Dr. Schneck's most recent book, *Basic Anatomy and Physiology for the Music Therapist* (2015), and our previously co-authored book, *The Music Effect: Music Physiology and Clinical Applications* (2006) are supportive resources for information presented in this book. I also would like to acknowledge and thank my neuroscience friends and colleagues who directly and indirectly stimulate my music-in-science mind. Among them are Dr. Nina Kraus of Northwestern University's BrainVolts Laboratory, whose research in music, autism, musician brains, and music elements, advance the understanding of the role of music in human development; Dr. Aniruddh Patel, whose focus on music, language, and the brain continues to instigate my knowledge of music and brain function; Dr. Joseph LeDoux and Dr. Antonio Damasio, whose enormous contributions to knowledge of human emotions and brain function underlie many of my mind-body hypotheses, research, and clinical work; my professional friendship with Dr. Pamela Heaton in London, whose investigations of autism and music parallel many of my experiences and findings in music-based treatment of autism spectrum diagnoses; my friendship and interactions with Dr. Patricia Gray, UNC-Greensboro, whose research in Biomusic further informs of the capacity to stimulate and organize musical behaviors in animals and humans. I am grateful to many others not mentioned here, including many professional colleagues, friends, and students who continue to support me, and who stimulate my thinking regarding the informational needs and growth of my work, and of the music therapy profession.

A special acknowledgement and thank you to John Taylor for allowing us the use of his brain graphic. Thank you also to oncologist Dr. Mitchell Gaynor and writer Paul Collins for granting permission to use epigraph quotes from their writings. The insightful work of Dr. Gaynor inspires medically holistic approaches to cancer treatment for pre- and post-operative fear-reduction in sessions using Singing Bowls, vocalizations, and specially composed recorded music. His books, *Sounds of Healing*, and *The Healing Power of Sound: Recovery from Life-Threatening Illness Using Sound, Voice, and Music*, continue to endorse music-based treatment supporting medical interventions and patient recovery.

A very special thank you to the supportive parents who have generously given permission to publish photographs of their children taken during our music therapy sessions, however we were unable to use these in the final version of the book unfortunately. A special acknowledgement and thank you also to the indefatigable Kathryn Roberts, Founder and Executive Director of the American Institute for Neuro-Integrative Development (AIND)/Giant Steps School in Connecticut, for her ongoing support of my professional work, and for her tireless work and efforts in support of education for children with special needs, ASD, and related diagnoses.

Last, but surely not least, I thank my husband Larry, my daughters Carylin and Sabrina, my grandchildren Benjamin, Karina, and Aidan, and their father Joe, for their patience and enduring love.

Thank you all for being part of my journey.

Prelude

The great thing, then, in all education, is to make our nervous system our ally instead of our enemy.

William James, *Principles of Psychology*

Humans are, first and foremost, *emotional* beings. Before we even recognize that it was an emotion driving our impulses, our brains have already made emotional decisions ordering specific responses to any situation or circumstance. At the smell of smoke, our hearts are already palpitating, we're ready to flee. At a loud crashing bang, we immediately take cover. Cognition enters the scene *afterward*—albeit within nanoseconds after (if cognition even does become involved)—but a response has already taken place. In various public media interviews with neuroscientist Dr. Antonio Damasio, I have heard him state that "we are not thinking machines! We are feeling systems… that think." Initially, it is *emotion*, not thought, that intuitively and instinctively propels our systems toward survival. Humans respond first instinctively (automatically) based on what the brain perceives, and only afterward, cognitive awareness records and analyzes the event. Dr. Joseph LeDoux (1998, 2002) tells us that we jump at the sound of something rustling on the ground in the bushes before we recognize that it was not a boa constrictor but a twig! First there is reaction, then there is analysis. Safety and survival of the system is the brain's first and foremost concern.

Survival depends on the maintenance of physiologic variables that are critical to life. This maintenance of such physiologic variables lead, within very narrow limits, to the establishment of what are called *homeostatic* references within a human (or animal) system.

These are references that, for example, maintain blood pressure and heart rate at an average rate of 120/80 for typical human beings, body temperature at 98.6°F, various controls of physiologic circadian rhythms (sleep-wake cycles, gastrointestinal functions, flow of hormones) and the like. Homeostasis is achieved by cascading networks of sophisticated *feedback—feedforward* control systems that operate in accordance with the prescribed referential set-points such as described above (Berger and Schneck 2003; Schneck and Berger 1999, 2006). In populations with autism spectrum diagnosis (ASD), and others, these set-points tend to go awry, for various reasons that often include inaccurate sensory processing, deviating from "typical" ranges that derive optimal physiologic responses to external and internal occurrences.

Many persons with ASD, post-traumatic stress disorder (PTSD), attention deficit hyperactivity disorder (ADHD), various dementias, and other neurophysiologic diagnoses experience sensory stimuli with such variation that they can either be causing extreme discomfort, much confusion, or be so distorted or undetectable as to be totally useless. As a result, response characteristics and behaviors communicate that the system is in some state of distress, with a continual sense of danger—survival-anxiety (fear). This predominantly results from the brain's misinterpretation of the original sensory information, either improperly received in the first place, or poorly relayed and processed. When danger is perceived the system remains on high alert, over-aroused, and in a fight-or-flight conduct, which can be overwhelming, causing ongoing stress and anxiety, and at times becoming dangerous to survival.

The subject of sensory integration has been, and continues to be, investigated by many researchers in science, psychology, and various clinical professions. Pick up any book on the topic, and the bibliographic reference entries are nearly as extensive as the number of pages in any of the books. One interesting researched book I recently investigated was *The Merging of the Senses* (Stein and Meredith 1993), discussing multi-sensory interactions, both physiologically and neurologically. A statement that caught my attention and seemed to define what is actually sensory "integration," advised that:

the world is not perceived as a series of independent sensory experiences to which the integrity of each modality's "snapshot" view is preserved intact in its own location in the brain; rather, there is an interweaving of different sensory impressions through which sensory components are subtly altered by, and integrated with, one another. The product of these integrative processes is perception.

The integration of inputs from different sensory modalities not only transforms some of their individual characteristics, but does so in ways that can enhance the quality of life. (p.xi)

In other words, there is only *one way* in which we can learn to understand our environment, and our being, and that way is through sensory information processes that are whole-brain interactive functions entailing a sequence of networks to actually *multi*-process sensory information in order to derive a serviceable interpretation. In addition, *context*, the authors further explain, becomes more important in determining responses than does the specificity of the stimulus features, and it is *within context* that the brain will interweave characteristics of multiple sensory inputs. That is, the system is not dealing with just a one-at-a-time sensory input, but rather, a combination of sensory stimuli related to the context in which the dominant stimulant has been presented. The actual sequence, then, is:

sensory stimulus (what?) → *context* (from what/where?) → *perception* (it means?) → *emotion* (good/bad?) → *response* (reaction)

This sequence makes sense to the music-based clinician, since the experience of music is itself a whole-brain-whole-body activity brought about by auditory stimuli ("sound"), the context in which it is presented and perceived, influencing emotional interpretation, tagged interactively with visual, tactile, and somatosensory stimuli and references. In other words, the total experience of music is a whole-brain-whole-body event integrating the context in which the music is deployed and presented (for whatever reasons: mood alterations, entertainment, etc.), with the perception of the stimulus activating emotions and responses based on emotional determinants. The fact that music is perceived by various interactive regions throughout the brain within the context in which the music is presented, is one reason that Eurhythmics interventions that involve whole-brain-whole-body actions to music's acoustic stimuli (rhythm, tonality, etc.), serve as *holistic* treatments for sensorimotor and emotional regulation. The whole organism responds in some way to the presentation of this acoustic stimulus, instigating movement (e.g., we want to tap our feet to a march or jazz tune, since the auditory and motor cortexes are in very close proximity). Once sensorimotor and emotional regulations are in place, learning and other skills training can proceed.

About music training, and Eurhythmics as treatment

In his book, *The Eurhythmics of Jaques-Dalcroze* (1920), Jaques-Dalcroze articulates his philosophy that a mind-body approach is necessary in the education and training of musicians for deriving the consummate performer. Eurhythmics is a rhythmic, movement-based, holistic music training approach based on the philosophic belief that in order to perform music with an in-depth understanding and accuracy of music elements involved, the musician must *embody* those musical elements of rhythm, pitch (melody), phrase, harmony, timbre, dynamics, and form, to derive body sensations and responses, so that these become "instinctive," automatic, accurately sensed and aesthetically expressed. This training must take place through movement responses in which the whole body senses and responds to the music. After all, the audience experience of *hearing* music is in essence a *whole-body* sensation, as Evelyn Glennie, a profoundly deaf professional concert percussionist, informs us, in her *Hearing Essay* (Glennie 2015), and which is pointed out in *The Music Effect* (Schneck and Berger 2006, p.140, pp.174–175). Various researchers and clinical studies presented in the book *Vibrational Medicine* (Gerber 2001), continue to confirm this concept. A person not only "hears" through the auditory system, but indeed, senses and expresses music through, and throughout, entire cellular and molecular body structures (see also Findlay 1971; Jaques-Dalcroze 1920, 2009; Mead 1994; Schnebly-Black and Moore 2003, 2004; Schneck and Berger 2006). The brain enacts whole-body multi-sensory processes, thereby fully engaging the *whole* participant with the music experience (i.e., sensory stimulus + context). In some cases, hearing music becomes an actual visual, cognitive, or tactile event beyond the auditory system, as in the *cross-sensory* processing of *synesthesia*, whereby a person tastes sounds, or sees color (Cytowic 1999, 2002).

Evelyn Glennie explains that, rather than solely processing through the auditory system which is deficient, she senses the vibrations of particular higher frequencies (tones and pitches) on her forehead, lower frequencies on lower parts of her legs, and so on. This is in keeping with the above report that sensory information is processed *across* brain areas, not as a single input to just one area, but as a combination of stimulated areas, including proprioception, vestibular, tactile, visual, and of course, auditory. In short, when Jaques-Dalcroze's Eurhythmics training sought to integrate the mind, body, and inter-sensory systems, the concept was quite ahead of its time. His approach to the training of musicians involved targeting *both* the conscious and the *sub*conscious brains, not just toward hearing, but especially to the *embodiment* of music elements, holistically! Of interest to the music-based clinician is that if, in fact, this *inter*-sensory processing, and the embodiment of music elements, can so successfully impact and organize sensory information processing and response in the musically trained, might it do the same (or better) for various diagnosed persons? We can take a leap of faith to suggest that yes, perhaps the discipline of Eurhythmics music training approach to sensorimotor regulation could be a productive technique in music-based treatment for addressing and organizing multi-sensory information and inter-sensory processing, physiologic functions in many types of diagnoses, to bring about a sense of well-being. Such an approach for ASD and other diagnoses could have the capacity to reset homeostatic set-points, moving them away from continual hyper-arousal and fight-or-flight mode, to result in more functionally adaptive sensory perceptions. See, for instance, the research of Anja Kuchenbuch and colleagues (2014) who investigated the influence of musical training on audio-tactile integration, and research by Kraus *et al.* (2014) and Tierney and Kraus (2013), investigating the ability to move to a beat as linked to the consistency of neural responses to sound. Also Tierney, Kraus and colleagues investigated the role of school music classes with at-risk persons and speech, language, and reading development (Tierney *et al.* 2013). For further investigation, readers are also referred, among many others, to the Neuroscience Research Center of Northwestern University,[1] where Dr. Nina Kraus and collaborators investigate the role of various music elements (e.g., rhythm, tempo, timbre) in neuronal processing and enhancement.

The important features of Eurhythmics interventions, as will be detailed, are the driving forces of rhythm, pulse, movement, and "quick response" reactions to those elements, automatically driven by instinct. These interventions are not "choreography" nor "dance." They are in-the-moment movement actions immediately responding to the inherent music stimuli, reflecting the characteristics of the inclusive stimuli—tempo, dynamics, phrase, energy, shape (phrase and melodic contour), timbre, and form—in a quickly responding improvisatory manner. Part Two of this book articulates and exemplifies various interventions using Eurhythmics concepts for organizing and synchronizing physiologic and sensorimotor processes.

Objectives and organization of this book

Much science literature attests to sensorimotor function as being triggers to many physiological, emotional, and psychological responses (see Berger 2002; Damasio 1994, 1999, 2010; Horowitz 2012; Lathe 2006; LeDoux 1998, 2002; Schneck and Berger 2006; Stein and Meredith 1993; Wundt 1902; and others listed previously). Yet, despite the existence of ongoing empirical research in the areas of sensory coordination and brain functions in ASD, music-based treatments of autism characteristics predominantly focus on overt (observed) behaviors: social skills, communication deficits, attention, and eye contact. Sensorimotor and movement irregularities are often left to be treated by allied professionals (e.g., occupation and physical therapists), despite the possibility that by first addressing

---

1   www.brainvolts.northwestern.edu.

physiology and sensory irregularities, music-based interventions can efficaciously *prepare* the brain and body for productive function in those other areas, by organizing functional responses, altering fight-or-flight mode, and more. The theory here is that if music-based interventions were to first approach systemic causes that tend to reduce socialization skills, limit eye contact, decrease chaotic behaviors, language and motor deficiencies, and so on, then the by-product of such interventions could automatically correct these negative areas of communication, cognition, and socialization. In order to apply treatment from the sequence of sensation—context—perception—emotion—response, it is fundamental that the music clinician is trained in, and knowledgeable of, the relationship of physiology, brain, and the sensory systems, in *combination with* music elements that can alter homeostasis and derive measurable and observable results (see Berger 2009, 2012, 2013a, 2013b; Schneck and Berger 2006; Stein and Meredith 1993).

It has been my experience, as a student in and as an educator of music therapy, that there are few *systematic* approaches in our clinical practice that involve integrative music-based treatment techniques focused on sensorimotor processing. The question is, "Is it enough to just play music and hope for the best?" Also limited, in my experience, is the existence of *methodical* music treatment approaches addressing the HPA axis, and stress-driven pervasive anxiety, repetitive behaviors, and especially, movement deficits in ASD, that could be placated by discreet interventions of individual or combined music elements. Some clinicians have explored rhythmic intervention approaches, and have defined some hypotheses for physiologically tackling particular diagnoses such as gait movements in Parkinson's and stroke, or language deficiencies addressed through Melodic Intonation Therapy (see Thaut 2008[2]; see also Norton *et al.* 2009 and the Music and Neuroimaging Lab at Beth Israel Deaconese and Harvard Medical School, Dr. Gottfried Schlaug[3]). But across the profession, in general, treatment techniques

---

2   See also Neurologic Music Therapy at Center for Biomedical Research in Music of Colorado State University http://cbrm.colostate.edu/.

3   http://musicianbrain.com/#index.

are independently designed in individual sessions, predominantly based on *external* (observable) symptoms and functions (socialization, cognitions, language), without repeated, sequenced, integrated, and systematically detailed interventions. Of course the above-listed areas of observable function are important to consider in treatment, but in order to derive changes in those areas, clinicians might first intercede into *systemic* driving forces (unobservable causes) that might be responsible for propelling those externally observed behaviors. I defend the notion that interventions for such possibilities are best served by a methodical technique, because although autism has characteristics within a spectrum manner of "being ASD," the underlying features driving the characteristics tend to be very similar. By prioritizing treatment goals and objectives from this perspective the clinician can determine whether, or how, particular music elements could efficiently work to impact upon anomalies that perpetuate the observable deviations. Can music interventions assuage presenting characteristics in autism, not just from the perspective of observed symptoms, but also from unobservable *causes* driving the symptoms in order to yield homeostatic alterations? My clinical work has indicated that indeed it can. The answer is *"Yes!"*

Musicians are highly trained and disciplined individuals. Music-based clinicians are also trained musicians and performers, having undergone extensively disciplined skills training and practice, combined with studies in psychology, sciences, and clinical work. Research on music and the brain informs that the brains of persons who have had music training appear to function more optimally than of those who have not had consistent training (Kuchenbuch *et al.* 2014; Parbery-Clark *et al.* 2013; Skoe and Kraus 2013; see also music training and brain research listed on the BrainVolts Lab site of Northwestern University's Neuroscience Department).[4] If the discipline of music training can impact and organize brain, language, memory, body, and sensory coordination to such high levels, why not apply some of those techniques (i.e., ear training, rhythmic movement, etc.) to benefit atypically-functioning responses—especially movement and sensory regulation (e.g., body dynamics, auditory processing)? Through

---

4   www.soc.northwestern.edu/brainvolts/.

embodied rhythm and body dynamics, regulated quick (automatic) responses to musical sounds, and enhancement of perceptive auditory acuity, a great deal of positive changes can be, and have been gained. This is the dynamic paradigm behind the Eurhythmics-based treatment approach addressing sensorimotor integration discussed throughout this book. Thus, the paradigm underlying the goal and objectives defined throughout this book advocates that "as for the brain-body training of a musician, so for the brain-body training of a special needs person."

About this book

This book is not a physiology or neuroscience textbook. Readers are encouraged to pursue that information in references listed herein, and elsewhere. This is a book about the application of a music-based treatment technique for ASD, and other diagnoses, that *systematically* applies Eurhythmics-based concepts and interventions for addressing emotion, sensorimotor, and movement coordination. The goal in this book is to examine autism spectrum characteristics, brain and the HPA axis relative to the "survival-anxiety" flight-or-flight response, the sensory systems, the philosophy of Eurhythmics music training based on Emile Jaques-Dalcroze, and how the adaptation of his concepts and related exercises as interventions can effectively address inter-sensory inefficiencies, most likely one of the underlying causes of malfunction and behaviors of neurophysiologically diagnosed populations, particularly those on the autism spectrum. Although this book focuses on autism, many of the problems and treatment techniques discussed are adaptable in treating other diagnoses, including ADHD, Down and Rett's Syndrome, post-traumatic and other psycho-emotional disorders, dementias, and movement problems of the typical ageing population. Case studies and research are presented to demonstrate how Eurhythmics intervention techniques have been applied in ASD work, and the reader will note the value of this technique in changing behaviors and deriving positive functional adaptation.

For convenience and organization of information, the book is divided into three sections: Part One reviews five of seven "special" sensory systems, their functions and inter-relationships, an overview of information processing, the brain, the role of the HPA axis and the physiology of survival-anxiety fight-or-flight hyper-arousal, discussion of ASD and observed behavioral characteristics, including movement and sensory function, and possible sensorimotor parallels to Parkinson's, PTSD, Alzheimer's behaviors, and other neurophysiologic characteristics.

Part Two explores the philosophy of Emile Jaques-Dalcroze and Eurhythmics, the six basic musical elements as influences on rhythm internalization (embodiment), dynamics (movement energies), and overall locomotor and non-locomotor movement, and structured, methodical technique for applying Eurhythmics-based interventions to address ASD characteristics—that is, movement inefficiencies, auditory processing, sense of body, and other sensorimotor needs. Discussed are approaches to developing treatment objectives and interventions, in a hierarchical manner, for treating observed and assessed sensorimotor behaviors, in order ultimately to attain the main goal—C-O-P-IN-G. The goal of COPING presupposes the *cenesthetic* state of adaptive function that is C*alm*—O*rganized*—P*aced*—IN*tegrated*—G*rowth*. The major thrust of this Eurhythmics-based sensorimotor treatment, for any type of diagnosis, is to derive that state of *coping*, in which the person can respond fearlessly to the demands of the environment, to life in general, and from which many positive behaviors can evolve. Part Two additionally outlines and details the specific structure of sessions, including various objectives and sample interventions for sensorimotor, movement (motor-planning), and auditory regulation. Presented in Part Two are some sample cases of how Eurhythmics treatment techniques can impact, and have impacted, clients in clinical practice, in both individual and group settings and at various ages.

Part Three reviews the paradigm and related information, and discusses the potential of Eurhythmics-based sensorimotor interventions for treating other populations, such as anxiety disorders in PTSD, Alzheimer's, psychiatric anomalies, and movement rehabilitation of Parkinson's and stroke victims. Also mentioned is the application of Eurhythmics for healthy but ageing populations. Readers will note that educational techniques of Carl Orff and Zoltan Kodaly, highly respected teachers and composers who were greatly influenced by Jaques-Dalcroze Eurhythmics concepts, are not discussed herein. Information on Orff and Kodaly has been detailed in various other music therapy literature, is readily available and prominent in school music education, and has been adapted in limited ways by music clinicians through music-making on Orff instruments (i.e., xylophones, etc.). Instead, readers will obtain a brief overview of some related, *non*-music-based movement techniques of Rudolf Laban, Moshe Feldenkrais, and Frederick Matthias Alexander, with suggestions for readers to seek further investigation on those prominent personalities. Part Three concludes with a Coda, some final words of advice on assimilating the extensive information presented in the book, along with recommendations to seek further investigation and training in Dalcroze technique, with ancillary interaction with Laban, Feldenkrais, or Alexander movement for the clinician's wellness as well as that of the client.

The Appendices include two sample session-rating scales (an intervention progress rating scale and a session behavior rating scale), a brief clinical report, and two articles of related interest originally published in *TEMPO* magazine, journal of the New Jersey Music Educators Association.

A note about the terminology in this book

Because I do not consider autism (ASD), at any level, to be a *disorder*, but rather, a manner of function adapted by a person's brain in response to its assessment of planetary and physiologic elements, I replace the word "disorder" with "*diagnosis*" in defining the letters ASD (although not the accepted DSM-defined classification). *"Disorder" is in the eye of the beholder.* ASD characteristics are not life-threatening "diseases," but rather, accommodations for *that system's* survival, based on how that system's brain perceives the environment from sensory input. Although ASD characteristic behaviors do not appear to "fit the norm," those behaviors are indeed the *norm for that system*.

Also throughout this book, "music therapy" is most often referred to as "music-based treatment," and the music therapist as a "music-based clinician." These terms are used because although the term "therapy" does connote a "clinical treatment" beyond a therapeutic recreational activity, music therapy is not often thought of in terms of "treatment," nor is a music therapy session often indicated as a treatment session. The many definitions of what is music *therapy* has only recently surfaced to delineate the differences between music events and therapeutic experiences that may or may not require the presence of a music-based clinician, and music *therapy* as an *evidence-based treatment* provided by, and with, a trained, skilled music-based clinician. In differentiating music therapy as "clinical treatment" it is hoped that readers in allied health-care professions additional to music therapy, as well as parents, caregivers, teachers, administrators, and researchers, will look upon this clinical work as equal to respected scientific and medical interventions, the training for which not only includes extensive knowledge in music, but also of physiology, movement, neuroscience, psychology (talk therapy), child development, and research, for treating diverse human conditions and diagnoses.

My aim is for music-based clinicians and other members of allied health professions to enjoy the information presented and find it relevant and applicable to their own research and clinical work.

Part One

THE THEORY

Human Adaptive Function—Making Sense of the Environment

CHAPTER 1

Coming to Our Senses

Physiology is concerned with all those phenomena of life that present themselves to us in sense perception as bodily processes, and accordingly form part of that total environment which we name the external world.
Wilhelm Wundt, *Principles of Physiological Psychology*

To me, body and mind are different aspects of specific biological processes.
Antonio Damasio, neuroscientist

We are our physiology

How do we perceive the world? In essence, the only way the brain obtains information about the world and the body is through the sensory systems. Perception of things may well be considered illusions of reality, based on how brains and systems interpret information from incoming sensations. Self-awareness in relation to external and internal (physical) events is based on how each individual brain-body system assesses experience in relation to self. While initially we all arrive equipped with the similar *biological* features—brain, eyes, ears, mouth, nose, arms, fingers, legs, stomach, heart, lungs, etc.— the functions of these body parts are processed differently by each person's system. Each of us has variations of *physiologic* function that are as unique to each of our operational systems as are thumb prints. You feel cold, I am sweating; you see that color as intense red, I see it as pink and pale;

you hear that trumpet as blaring loud and brassy, I hear it as soft and mellow; you taste lemons as tart and bitter, I find lemons delightfully sweet. Regardless of these differences, all physiology operates within the same processing sequence in the brain: *sensation* (stimulus)—*context* (how, where, what)—*perception* (registration, interpretation)—*emotion* (reaction)—*response* (action).

The operational hierarchy is as follows: first, there is continuous flow of information bombarding the various senses. This occurrence is non-stop. In a bottom-up flow, the activated special sensory systems send electric signals directly into various areas of the brain in the form of action potentials. These signals that are transmitted into the brain (feedback), ultimately arrive in areas of the paleoencephalon (old brain, limbic system and related regions), that "take a look" at the information. Here the signals are interpreted to determine whether it is safe to proceed.

If the signals are *perceived* to be safe, the process continues further up the ladder to various higher lobes in the neocortex (thinking brain), followed by directives sent down through efferent networks of the CNS (downward, feedforward) in response (top-down), later resulting in such factors as cognitive awareness and *feelings*. Keep in mind that the word *"later"* refers to the second stage of the stimulus-processing sequence, *after* the lower and mid-brains have decided what to do with the raw information. This occurs within nanoseconds at such efficient lightning speeds—almost simultaneously—that we are never consciously aware of the occurrences. By the time you have completed reading this very brief description of the sequences, billions of bits of electric and chemical stimuli will have entered your system, been processed, kept, or discarded by your brain! (One hopes that pertinent information remains.)

If the brain *perceives* incoming sensory information as threatening to the body's safety—the key word is "perceived" (whether real or not)—the survival-anxiety (fear) response is immediately activated (HPA axis), preparing the body to fight or flee. In most if not all instances, we sense the world through this bottom-up/top-down sequence. No doubt scientists and physiologists will chuckle at this simplification of extremely complex processes, but for our purposes in this book we basically need to understand that our knowledge of brain and sensory processes must incorporate the reality of bottom-up (instinctive)—top-down (cognitive) sequences.[1]

Making *sense* of the environment

Recall that the only way we learn about, and understand our world and the "self" is through our senses. The only way the brain can receive information from and about the external and internal (body) environment, is through sensory receptors. Bear in mind also that physiologic function in animals, including the human animal, is initially a bottom-up process by which information stimulates sensory ceptors and is transmitted up—feedback—through afferent pathways of the central nervous system (CNS, including spinal cord and brain, or blood flow), where responses are investigated and calculated by the brain and sent back for action and reaction by the body—feedforward—through efferent pathways. This basic knowledge of some special, primary sensory system processes is vitally important for music-based clinicians when developing treatment goals and objectives, since various music elements will stimulate multi-sensory receptors simultaneously in many ways, at once obtaining instinctive physical and emotional responses (Berger 2002, 2009, 2013a; Porges 2011; Schneck 2015; Stein and Meredith 1993, and others mentioned above). The manner in which our brains process stimuli impacting emotion basically determines who we are (see Damasio 1994, 1999, 2003a, 2003b, 2003c, 2010, and others; LeDoux 2002; Llinas 2002; Schneck 2015; Schneck and Berger 2006).

The only certain reality is immediate experience, a virtual *illusion of what is real* (Blumenthal 1975; Wundt 1902). I use the word "illusion" because "reality" is determined by the manner in which each individual's sensory receptors transmit stimulus information,

---

[1] For in-depth details in neuroscience, brain, sensory, and nervous systems readers are referred to, among many others, Buzsaki 2006; Damasio 1994, 1999, 2003a, 2003b, 2003c, 2010; Fisher, Murray and Bundy 1991; LeDoux 2002; Panksepp 1998; Porges 2011; Schneck 1990, 2015; Schneck and Berger 1999, 2006; and extensive references within these references.

and the manner in which the sensory systems and brain of each individual person receives and *perceives* the information—in essence, makes "sense" of the information. This was illustrated earlier by the perceptual differences in identifying color, sound, taste, and touch. Immediate experience, then, is defined by the brain's *perception* of the information, the *context* in which it is derived, and the *emotional* response calling for reaction (Stein and Meredith 1993). It becomes "psychology" (cognition) after the input and perception of the sensory stimuli have been catalogued (coded) and submitted to memory by the hippocampus and various related regions of the brain (Schneck and Berger 2006).

When asked to list the senses, one generally cites five, known as "special" senses: hearing, seeing, smelling, touching, and tasting. In fact, these listed senses do not definitively confirm such basic functions as the body's temperature, pressure on the system, body volume (these are monitored by systems referred to as thermodynamic and biochemical corporeal senses), and position in space; where the limbs are and what they are doing; whether the body is upright, leaning, or prone in relation to gravity; how the brain knows when the body is hungry, tired, or needing to eliminate waste. Is it the Tower of Pisa that is leaning, or the body? Imagine this: you are at a party, sitting a short distance from a table on which sit two vessels, one a paper cup filled with water, and the other a delicate crystal goblet filled with wine. As a favor, you are requested to retrieve those vessels. So, you rise, walk a few paces to the table, reach for the wine goblet with one hand, and the water-filled paper cup with the other. How did you know exactly what to do to complete the requested task? Did you consciously calculate how to rise, how many steps to walk to the table, how far to stretch your arm in order to reach for the vessels, how much clasp you needed in order to grasp and lift each? Having lifted the vessels, how did you know whether you were grasping and holding each securely? Did each vessel require the same energy force and hand contractions? How much of this procedure did you *consciously* calculate so that you knew precisely how far to walk, how far to extend each arm/hand, how much muscle energy of the arm would be required, how tightly to close your fingers, and so on?

Your vision noticed the span between you and the table, and observed differences between the two vessels, but your vision could only transmit pictures (so to speak) of environment and items to the brain—size, shape, color, volume, texture, location, distance, etc. How did your brain know what message to feed forward to the body and limbs in order for you to correctly fulfill this seemingly simple task? What other information did your brain need? Your auditory and cognitive processes heard and understood the task request, but which of the sensory systems advised the brain of the position of your body, arms, hands, and fingers prior to the task, to order precisely measured extension and flexion of joints and muscles of legs, arms, hands, and fingers? And the precise grasp configuration and closure, and precise power (energy) to lift each vessel without dropping? Did each vessel require the same physical configuration and energy? In fact, how did your brain even know in what position your body was prior to undertaking the task? None of the usually listed five senses supplied this composite information. Your eyes observed the position and location of your body (visual picture), and your ears "heard" the request, but did not tell the brain about its position in order to call for the required motor plan to complete the task. This information came, in large part, from your *proprioceptive* sensory system (combined with the vestibular, explained below)! For many arts-based clinicians the words "proprioception" and "vestibular" might be new.

As we have seen, there are many sensory systems monitoring and interacting within human physiology. For the purpose of our discussions, we will limit our investigation to just those that are considered the "special" sensory systems directly related to brain regions.

Proprioception

We live inside of a container referred to as the body. While most of our sensory systems respond to the external environment, how does a person sense what is going on within this container? What provides feedback of internal events? Try this: darken a room and close your eyes tightly shut. Now hold your hand up before your eyes and move it back and forth. Can you see your hand? How do you know it is there if you cannot see it? How do you know how to move it, or even whether it is moving? Proprioception, from *proprietary*, meaning "of one's self," and *captor*, from the Latin "*capere*" meaning "to take" (Schneck and Berger 2006, p.18), is that unique sensory system that is sending to the brain most of the information the brain needs to know about the body at this moment, in order for you to execute this task. Proprioception monitors *internal* aspects of the body, referred to as *interoception*. The proprioceptive sensory system converts ("transduces") and transmits to the brain, electric signals ("action potentials") from tiny, densely packed receptors in muscles, organs, and joints, informing it about the body—its various positions and relationship to space and internal needs. Among other sensory input, it is through proprioceptive information that we humans develop our sense of our bodies—body awareness—our physical sense of *self*. Proprioception counsels the brain about whether the body is sitting, standing, lying, curled, straight, whether it is strong or weak or tired, in pain, and so forth, based on whether muscles and joints are extended or flexed (contracted), what your inner organs are doing, and much more (see Berger 2002; Damasio 2003c; Nevid 2012; Schneck 1990, 1992; Schneck and Berger 2006; Smetacek and Mechsner 2004; Smetana, Campione-Barr and Metzger 2006).

At the party earlier, you were seated a short distance from the table upon which the vessels were situated. Your brain had to know where your body was, its precise musculoskeletal position and those of your legs and arms, how much energy to call for, among other things, in order for you to rise (complying with the proprioceptive—visual—auditory—cognitive configuration of the scene), walk, move closer to the table (without falling, complying with vestibular and visual pictures), reposition your arm joints (compliance based on previous proprioceptive body maps) and signal for extension (reaching) of each arm and hand from whichever position it was in, and open each hand, spreading the fingers in preparation for grasping each vessel (confirmed by tactile information). Included in these requirements was the conjuring of proportional muscle energy (weight) for lifting, according to visual—tactile—cognitive assessment about the type of vessels, what each contained, how much lift was required (visual assessment), plus how tightly to embrace each vessel with the appropriate finger closures and strength, finally to securely grasp each item in order to lift, but not drop, it (proprioception—tactile). The complexity in just reading and comprehending these descriptive details sequencing your body's response to the task is but a small portion of the extensive complexity undergone automatically by proprioception, collaborative sensory systems, and brain, just to execute a simple task that you probably have undertaken hundreds of times in your life, without giving it any thought (practiced since infancy and now become instinctive). Surely your thinking mind was not imparting such complex calculations—you were not *consciously scheming* the many steps required for executing this activity. But your sensory systems and brain were busy. You merely stood up, walked to the table, and lifted two different liquid-filled vessels. Done! Of course this is an over-simplification of the massive physiologic processes, as you now recognize, but it demonstrates proprioception's complex function, having to collaborate with at least three other sensory systems (auditory, visual, tactile) and various brain networks, within an environmental context, in order to execute a simple one-minute task. Busy brain! Imagine the calculations involved in playing a game of tennis, baseball, or in figure-skating and hockey! The ability to perform such a seemingly simple task involved cumulative training and repetitions throughout formative developmental stages (and years of growing) at which times the brain practiced the coordination of functional responses based on proprioceptive and allied sensory information informing behavior.

In the short article, "Making sense—proprioception: is the sensory system that supports body posture and movement also the root of our understanding of physical laws?", authors Victor Smetacek and Franz Mechsner (2004) inform us that the word "proprioception" (perception of one's own, as in "proprietor") was first coined in 1906, by Charles Sherrington (1906), who searched for the sensory systems that guide a blind person's movements and sense of self. Proprioception used to be considered the "sixth sense" (Smetacek and Mechsner 2004, p.21). Indeed, devoid of vision, as you experienced when you closed your eyes and moved your hand in front of your face, and possibly coupled with some auditory impairments, how would the brain of a visually impaired person sense and know its own body, the position of its limbs, and awareness of self? In the words of the authors:

> Proprioceptors precisely measure physical properties such as muscle length, tendon tension, joint angle or deep pressure. Signals from this sensory orchestra are sent by afferent nerves through the spinal cord to the somatosensory, motor and parietal cortices of the brain, where they continuously feed and update dynamic sensory-motor maps of the body. (p.21)

The authors further submit that, in fact, the proprioceptive system also informs about the physics of the body—its dynamic masses and momentary distributions thereof, forces acting on the limbs, and the highly interactive functions of muscles, joints, and various organs. In the words of the article's authors:

> The maps derived from these complex calculations not only guide body movement, they also (together with touch) sense the size and shape of objects and measure the geometry of external space. Weight—one's own and that of objects—is measured independently by pressure sensors and muscular tension. So subjective body consciousness provided by myriad networking proprioceptors is the basis of objective knowledge of fundamental physical properties—space, time and weight—of external reality. (p.21)

Although simple actions such as lifting two different vessels is taken for granted, the myriad of calculations that proprioception and brain have to undertake to complete a simple task, as noted, requires the profound interaction between proprioceptive sense and allied sensory systems. This is how the brain of a newborn knows to sense, find, and place its thumb in its mouth and suck (proprioception—tactile—taste interaction). The infant's brain senses, helps to locate and grasp pacifiers, hold milk bottles, or mother's breast, well before any neocortical conscious planning for, and awareness of, activities have taken place. When a newborn enters the planet, its brain immediately senses that the body is no longer floating, but rather, suspended in gravity, and its proprioceptive system instantly transmits information to the brain advising it to recalculate for more muscle energies and corrective maneuvers that are now required (even though the infant is being held).

Critical for music-based clinicians is this knowledge of proprioception when administering treatment for autism characteristics, because the sense of self, and self-awareness that are so often observed as lacking in ASD, could be the result of improper proprioceptive monitoring and information processing. The human's sense of who is "me" begins with proprioception informing the brain of "me" about its body, what it is doing at any moment, where its limbs are, and so forth. Without "body awareness," without a sense of who or what is "me," without a sense of *self*, and without self-awareness, a person cannot be adequately developed, nor expected to "socialize" or communicate according to "norm." The body of a child born lacking proprioception, or harboring an ill-operating proprioceptive processing, will present with low muscle tone, lack of body awareness, uncertainty about whether limbs and fingers belong to self or someone else, what kind of energy is required to grasp a fork, pencil, or drum mallet, and much more. This would result in cognitive, language, movement, and especially social, impairments. Therefore, a music-based clinical objective addressing "self-awareness" and socialization would be defeated unless proprioceptive function is considered first, with targeted interventions applied for directly addressing the regulation of proprioceptive information processing through various music elements, particularly *rhythm and movement.*

It is interesting here to share a case described in Smetacek and Mechsner's article (2004, p.21), because in many ways it resembles various proprioceptive characteristics in Parkinson's, ASD, Amyotrophic Lateral Sclerosis (ALS), and related diagnoses. The authors describe the case of Ian Waterman who, when 19 years old, had contracted a rare disease that caused degeneration of sensory nerves relaying information from the body to the brain (bottom-up). The nerve processes were injured from the neck down, but apparently spared various top-down efferent motor nerves that could, if possible, transmit signals back to the body (feedforward), provided that the brain knew the what-and-where of the body. Ian could see, but not *feel* where his body was, or whether or not it was in motion. At his young age of 19, he was left as helpless as a "rag doll," requiring others to feed, bathe, and dress him. Any attempts on his part to willfully move elicited only uncontrolled jerks.

> However, his strong will and memory of his body enabled him to learn to gradually control and guide his movements with his eyes. But even after 30 years of intense practice, the simplest movement has not been automated, but requires concentrated visual attention so strenuous that he likens it to a daily marathon, and in the dark he will collapse like a rag doll. His case, and a few others, demonstrate that all purposeful movements, both conscious and unconscious, are controlled by Proprioception. (Smetacek and Mechsner 2004, p.21)

Although most of us are virtually unaware of the existence of proprioception in enabling movement, the system is so efficient and reliable in granting us freedom of movement that we automatically relegate our movement procedures to subconscious, *reflexive* actions. In short, we do not consciously "calculate" our movements; we undertake them instinctively. And to some extent, even *instinct* requires training and retraining.

In an experiment undertaken in the Department of Brain and Cognitive Sciences at the University of Rochester, New York, individual subjects were blindfolded and put in a dark room (see Dieter *et al.* 2014). Wiring their brains for scanning information, each subject was asked to wave his or her hand before his or her eyes, similar to what you were asked to do earlier in this chapter. Lo and behold, the task was undertaken without failure because being blindfolded and in a dark room did not prevent proprioception from transmitting the whereabouts of the eyes and body. Furthermore, the most interesting brain information was that the occipital lobe (vision) was also stimulated, despite the fact that the eyes could not see the movement of the arm. So we must consider the supreme interaction between proprioception also stimulating other sensory systems (Dieter *et al.* 2014). Indeed, most human movements are automated and driven by the basic primitive (older) parts of the brain. However, as we shall learn in Part Two, the conscious, painstaking practice of *teaching* our systems new, complex, and potentially corrective skills in order to develop many new patterns coded as movement behaviors, requires repetitive systematic practice in order to become embodied and automatic. Calibrating and screening relevant information "from the orchestra of signals supplied to the neocortex by the trinity of sensory systems [proprioception-vestibular-visual]" (Smetacek and Mechsner 2004, p.21), can develop new neural programs that can *reset homeostasis* and become relegated (embodied) into fundamental brain regions, once again to become "instinctive." Part Two of this book discusses Eurhythmics interventions, the stimuli of which can help train the senses, brain, and body to undertake new, automated responses (e.g., new muscle memory), replacing those that may be less optimal.

The vestibular sensory system

The proprioceptive system does not work alone. The "trinity of sensory systems" referred to in the above article is really a combination of five cooperative senses—proprioception, vestibular, visual, tactile, and auditory. Back to the party…you accomplished the task of lifting vessels from the table because your sensory systems cooperated, in context, enabling you to proceed without falling or dropping the vessels. You *heard* the request, *saw* the table and items, *knew* what and where about your body, stood up and moved your body without faltering (proprioception-vestibular), and *touched* and embraced the items. Now the party is over and you have been invited to go ice skating. Oops! Your brain and body are immediately put on alert about this situation. Apprehension, anxiety, and a sense of doubt (fear) arise, because you've never ice skated before. Arriving at the rink you observe, somewhat anxiously (heart palpitating, hands cold), skaters sashaying calmly and rhythmically, wearing boots with thin blades beneath, and navigating the slippery surface. Some skaters are falling, and your nervous anxieties increase (sense of danger). You are shaky, your pulse and heart are racing, and your system is in an automatic fear-fight-or-flee mode! Finally, having donned the boots, you try to walk in these unstable items. It is as if you are learning to walk all over again as you wobble to the entrance of the rink.

What's wrong? You have been walking for many years, but now your walk is slow, careful, cautious, and intense, legs spread apart more than usual. You sway from side to side trying to stay upright, knee joints tense and weak. You meander toward the open gate to the rink and step onto the ice. Whoa...by now your entire system is in the fight-or-flight fear mode—apprehensive, breathing heavily, knees shaking—and before you can do anything about it, your legs are pulling out from under you! In a flash, you personify a falling-down drunk, arms flailing about in attempts to restore balance and before you realize, you are sitting on the ice! Welcome to the vestibular system! When at the party, the brain called for you to stand up and move to the table; the brain's mission, in addition to coordinating your body parts, was to assure that gravity would not have its way with you—that you would not fall, but remain upright and correctly balanced as you moved to the table. Your brain has practiced sending corrective maneuvers for this balancing act since processing collaborative information from visual-vestibular-proprioceptive senses the day you were born through the first day you tried to stand up, at the age of four or six months old. As a toddler, through *constant repetition* of many corrective maneuvers (trial and error), you finally could remain standing unsupported, and ultimately walk to Mom and Dad. There was much anticipation (prediction) and repetition of corrective movements involved—stand up—balance—move one leg at a time (waddling)—step—oops, fall down—stand up—step—walk—fall—stand up, etc.—eventually satisfying proprioceptive-vestibular-visual requirements. By the time you were one year old, you were on your way to being an adequately walking biped.

As mentioned above, when the newborn is evacuated from the womb and the comforts and safety of the amniotic fluid, it is instantly greeted by the "G-force"—*gravity*! While quadrupeds have little difficulty balancing and walking almost from birth, biped humans require a year or more of constant practice before retaining appropriate vestibular training for walking only on two legs. The vestibular and proprioceptive collaboration is very active and busy (all your life, actually) in order for you to develop and retain appropriate motor plans for balanced independent movement. The process of learning to walk is one in which the sensory systems and brain are actually being taught how to manage vestibular-proprioceptive stimulation in order to assay motor plans for mobility. This training experienced by toddlers is similar to you now having to learn how to "walk" and slide around on the ice, eventually enabling you to remain upright, even as those boots inhibit the full movement flexibility of your ankles, feet, and toes. This vestibular training also applies to riding a bicycle, which requires the balancing of the vehicle along with your body upon it. The act of walking is, after all, a fall and rebound activity, with legs alternating balance and movement.

Balance! That is the primary function of the vestibular system. The vestibular sense relays information derived from various head positions stimulating cilia (fine hair-like follicles in the cochlea on the other side of the auditory system) and otolith sensors in the inner ear. The otolith organ has the sole job of sensing gravity to determine which way is "up." Its information derives from any of three head motions: the yes-type movement (up and down), the no-type orientation (side to side—gazing over the shoulder), and the ear-to-shoulder, side-to-side head tilts. Day and Fitzpatrick (2005) explain that the value of the vestibular sensory system and brain functions is its contribution to *perception of self*, and also of non-self motion (i.e., the motion of a boat, car, or bike, etc.), spatial orientation, navigation, voluntary movement, and oculomotor (visual) control.[2]

We humans and our four-legged friends are in constant need to know which end is up in relation to the gravitational field of the planet. Evolution of animals and humans over millennia has resolved this problem with the development of "graviceptive systems" (Day and Fitzpatrick 2005), among which is the vestibular organ. Sensing the force of gravity, and which way is up, is a constant companion of the human being as required in order to properly navigate the planet. The vestibular organs, coupled with visual validation (when vision is available), provides the brain with a very deep and special understanding of how the force of gravity impacts upon the "me"— from the possible fall of a body to lifting a leg in order to take a step, to skiing, figure ice skating, gymnastics, playing ice hockey, or simply walking in a park. The brain *predicts* the trajectory of a movement with amazing accuracy, thanks to the interaction of the vestibular-proprioceptive-visual triad (Day and Fitzpatrick 2005). The constant interaction between the vestibular, proprioception, and

---

2   For a full discussion on the vestibular system, see Baloh and Honrubia 2001; Berger 2002; Day and Fitzpatrick 2005; Fitzpatrick and Day 2004; Schneck 1990, 2015; Schneck and Berger 2006, among others.

visual systems as indicated in Figure 1.1, must be given consideration when observing, assessing, and treating movement characteristics of various diagnoses.

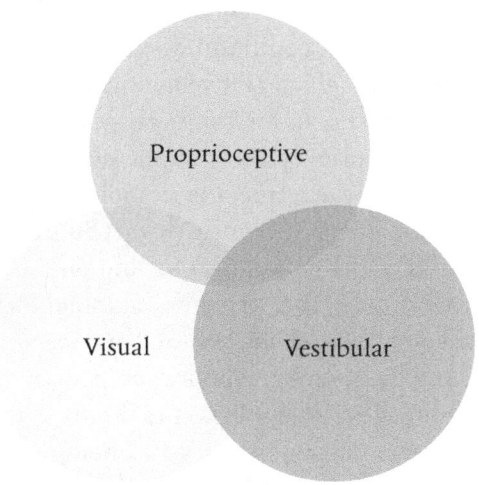

Figure 1.1 Three interactive sensory systems defining sense of self and sense-of-environment include proprioception—vestibular—visual coordination

The vestibular system's balance organs activate highly complex motor functions at predominantly sub-cortical, automatic levels, that is, the instinctive *subconscious* level, much as does the proprioceptive system. Proprioception—vestibular—visual—tactile—auditory collaboration are the major combinations providing the brain with information regarding what is happening with the body in relation to the external world, (exteroception), and the body's internal events (interoception) (see Figure 1.3). Unless the brain precisely perceives which end is up, where and in what position the body is, where the limbs are and what they are doing, and how to plan functional motor responses, there will not be adequately functional reactions (emotionally and motor-wise) to any circumstance. You can now imagine how busy the proprioceptive—vestibular—visual systems, and of course the brain, are when professional figure skaters, ice hockey players, skiers, gymnasts, and circus acrobats, go about executing their skills! Furthermore, in the case of figure skaters and gymnasts, the auditory system is also part of the team since those activities are cued with music. How lucky that all the motor-planning maneuvers are committed to *trained and automated, instinctive responses*, so that cognition does not have to take time to figure out and calculate all the movement complexities required at an instant. This is also true for the musician who has repeatedly practiced relevant proprioceptive—tactile stimulated motor plans in order to successfully execute the complexities of Beethoven's *Appassionata Sonata*; the intricacies of a Mozart flute or violin concerto; or the complexities of the ballerina's twirling on the very tips of her toes! Indeed, *we* can train for corrective, automatic motor-planning functions to become instinctive. As for your ice-skating trial, the same practice-practice-practice applies, as it does for learning to ride a bicycle—until your systems and brain get the "hang" of it, finding the center of your body's balancing point (vestibular) and body weight (proprioception), and the correct motor plan, so that you can ride the bike or sashay fluently on the ice, defying gravity. For diagnosed cases, music-based treatment will undertake similarly to "train" the client's sensory systems and brain in order to develop adequate motor plans and new (functional) responses, through practice and repetition of various interventions.

The visual, tactile, and auditory senses

By now we begin to understand the proprioceptive and vestibular senses and their interactive roles in alerting the brain to register what's up or down, whether or not the body is operating properly against gravity, in what position the various body parts are, and what's going on "in here" in response to "out there." This requires motor-planning of corrective maneuvers to retain balance and execute various tasks. Precise interaction between these two systems must be optimal for the brain to develop suitable motor plans to ensure safety and survival. Three more senses join this team: the *visual, tactile*, and *auditory*—seeing, touching, and hearing. The last two remaining systems, olfactory (smell) and taste senses, although having very important roles in survival, and also in driving the vestibular-proprioceptive systems into action, will not be detailed at this point. (In fact, the olfactory system is so crucial to survival that it even has a brain of its own.)

The *vision* system is quite complex. It typically operates in a binocular format, each eye seeing what it sees from its vantage point, according to its position in the head. The visual stimuli crisscross at the mid-line (center), where they converge information from each eye into one whole picture. Action potentials send individual bits of visual information (different in each eye) from the optic nerves to various operational systems in the brain's occipital lobe, located at the back lower part of the brain, and other related regions, where processing of visual information takes places. Central visual focus (including foveal focus, which is the extremely in-depth focus on details), and visual convergence are optimal operational norms, while peripheral vision—stimuli seen in a non-focused manner—detects ancillary, uninvolved "background" information. When you look up at a bird in the tree, the bird will be in full center focus of your view, while surrounding "landscape" is in the periphery, designated as background—vague and unfocused. It is not that the eyes do not *see* everything within their field of vision, but rather, that the mind is cognitively concentrating only upon that on which the eyes are focused at the center of vision. While looking up at the bird, you might see something whisking by you at the side. That is peripheral vision at work, seeking your attention. Now you turn to "focus" on that event to determine what it was that swept by you.

For the task of lifting two liquid filled vessels at the party, your auditory sense registered the request, and your vision sent electric pictures (action potentials) to the brain's occipital lobe for processing, passing first through the amygdala, hypothalamus, and related areas of the limbic systems that approved the stimuli as "safe to go." The occipital lobe and its vision-processing partners in the brain further processed the electric pictures of what the eyes took in—table, liquid-filled vessels, color of the wine, flowers on the table, food, utensils and plates, bottles, people, colors, and so on. Since your task was to seek two specific vessels, your vision had to locate and "focus" on those two items, their location and content, while virtually eliminating from view all other unessential visual material. The eyes actually took in all the dense visual information (lights, colors, shapes, configurations, people, clothing, furniture, etc.), but discarded most of those and only required motor plans directly involved in performing the task at hand. This process of eliminating uninvolved information from center vision is referred to, in photography terms, as "figure-ground," central focus. When a photographer focuses his lenses on you, the figure, all else is unfocused and unclear. In this case, *figure* was the table and vessels, in the *fore*ground of your eye lenses, and all else was inessential *back*ground—uninvolved peripheral visual information.

The tactile system, the sense of touch, also monitors both external and internal events (*intero-* and *extero*ception), alerting the brain and body to environmental temperatures, textures, shapes, and sizes of structures, materials that might be abrasive and injurious to the skin, toothaches, itches, pain, abrasions, and more. It is skin related, with a multitude of sensors on and under the skin that inform the brain. When, for example, the tactile system alerts the brain about the air temperature in a room, the brain instantly (automatically) calls for sweat to cool, or shivers to warm the body and keep it within its homeostatic comfort zone (i.e., normal body temperature of 98.6°F). Another simple example is an itch. Your brain is sent tactile information advising the brain about what and where that sensation resides. How does the brain prepare a motor plan resulting in appropriate scratching motion of your hand and fingers? Or that your muscle is cramped? That is a combination of tactile and proprioception stimulation. How does the brain know if a hug you receive from someone is too strong or weak? Again, tactile and proprioception. These are just simple examples demonstrating the result of interactions between the tactile and proprioceptive senses collaborating for situational motor responses.

The tactile system also experiences limited figure-ground focus. You pick up a cup of hot coffee, your tactile sense focuses on the heat of the cup, sending all other touch information (shape, size, texture of the cup) to basic background (your brain already saw that information and created a motor plan for the event). The sense of touch might have noticed that the texture of the cup was smooth and delicate, but that information was *secondary* to the fact that the liquid made the cup hot! In short, the brain tunes out information that does not require immediate response. As you dressed this morning, your tactile system and brain noted the sensations of the clothes on your skin, rough or smooth, heavy or light, short sleeves or long sleeves, wool or silk, etc., but within minutes, that information became background. Your system adapted to having certain sensation on its skin, and shortly dismissed that awareness. What's more, your sense of hunger was sending stomach-gurgling sensations up, so the sensation of clothes was on the periphery to the problem the brain more urgently had to solve—eating breakfast! The tactile system and brain adapted to the sense of clothing, and discarded the information as irrelevant at the moment.

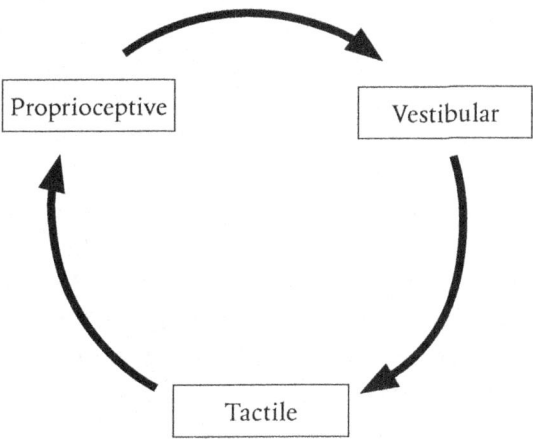

Figure 1.2 Three interactive sensory systems defining sense of self and sense-of-environment include proprioception—vestibular—tactile coordination

Do you hear what I hear? The dimension of hearing

It is said that the auditory system is the first to develop in the womb, with tactile close behind. *How* one hears, *what* one hears, *from where* sounds emanate, *how far or near* is the sound, and how the brain *discriminates* and identifies sonic information (bomb, a jet, thunder) are automatic functions immediately crucial to planning survival (motor plan) responses. Let us review some important factors regarding the sense of hearing, called *audition*. Back at the party there was a big crowd, and you had some difficulty spotting the person you were looking for. Soon, among all the visual data available, you saw and focused your eyes upon that one person, among all the others. You had located that person by visually scanning the room until your gaze stopped at the one you sought (figure), through the process of visual "figure-ground"—relegating the innumerable other faces to "background." Meanwhile, during this visual focus process, your auditory system was undergoing a great deal of sound-clutter— much loud talking, multiple conversations, music blaring, drinking vessels, plates and silverware clanging, shoes and heels shuffling, lots of laughter, cheers, and loud voices! Now, the friend you just spotted and called over began to converse with you, above all the noise. Enter *auditory figure-ground*. The auditory system and brain were working very intensely to isolate the sound of your friend's voice (foreground figure sound) from the sea of sounds in the background. Auditory focus is difficult and tiring for the brain and body. Musicians are well trained to perfect auditory figure-ground mechanisms, as research in Dr. Nina Kraus's lab at Northwestern University is discovering (see Kraus 2013; Parbery-Clark *et al.* 2013; Strait and Kraus 2014).[3] One can eliminate vision by closing the eyes to stop seeing, but the act of hearing cannot be silenced or eliminated (unless there is deafness), even with ear plugs. However, *listening*, that is, attending consciously to auditory information (auditory focus), can be dismissed. Hearing and listening are not the same things. One hears all the time, but does not always listen! The brain can dismiss and eventually tune out sounds with which it does not wish to deal (not listen)! These are two separate procedures—hearing is automatic (bottom-up); listening is a consequence of conscious commands (top-down) asking the systems and brain *to focus* on specific sonic stimuli. As with vision, the process is bottom-up/top-down.

The auditory system can present some interesting problems. To begin with, each ear is on a different side of the head, so there is

---

3   www.soc.northwestern.edu/brainvolts.

some miniscule time lapse between what is heard in one ear or the other. These are spatial considerations—does one ear pick up (hear) sound at the same rate of speed as the other? Does sound travel in similar speed to one ear as to the other? What occurs when one's head is turned away from sound, leaving one ear "closer" to the source than the other, or vice versa? In general the dichotomous (two parts—both ears at a time) hearing norm in animals (and humans) is *stereophonic*—information to each side converging to blend bits of information into a whole, while still detailing some of the individual parts. This is similar to, but perhaps somewhat more complex than, the visual process. Focusing on specific auditory information at center (figure) means listening for, and anticipating (predicting) certain specific acoustic information that unite at center, while disavowing extraneous sounds (ground) that are put into background. In trying to focus on listening to your friend speaking to you at the boisterous party, you may have moved closer to the sound source, perhaps turned your head so that the ear you thought hears better could hear, and so on. The figure-ground function in the auditory system is often trained and practiced from childhood upward, with your mom, dad, or teacher insisting that you listen and pay attention!

When one of our daughters, then eight years old, was sitting in her second grade class in a German-language school in Vienna, Austria, where we were spending a Fulbright Professorship year, we anticipated that she would enjoy the experience and learn German quickly, along with academic courses. It was, of course, classes spoken in German, which she seemed to have no problem understanding as time went on, and indeed learned to speak the language quite adequately. One day, after several months into the school year at this rather "old-fashioned" strict public school, the teacher called us in for a consultation, because apparently our daughter had appeared not to be "listening" to the teacher, since she had turned her head away from the teacher in order to peer out the window. The teacher was quite upset that our child was not looking at her nor listening appropriately! So, at the meeting, we all, child included, met with the teacher to discussed this "problem" (in German). Finally, when we asked our daughter why she had not listened to the teacher, she chimed (in English), "Mom, I was listening and heard everything the teacher was saying! I have two ears, and I heard from the one that was facing the teacher, even if my head and the other ear was turned away from the teacher's face." (From the mouth of babes!)

In music-based treatment, the clinician administers *acoustic* interventions, creating an environment of sound requiring various levels of auditory attention and perception from the listener. Important in the work is for the clinician not to make assumptions regarding the process of sound intake, as our daughter's teacher had made. Turning away or toward a sound source can indicate any number of things, good or problematic, so the clinician needs always to assess what particular responses might infer. Appearing not to be "listening" does not mean "not hearing." So often, parents, teachers, or caretakers of ASD children complain that a child seems not to hear when being called by name, despite the fact that there appear to be no hearing problems. The typical assumption is that the child is not listening, or was ignoring; or if hearing is intact, then the child simply is not "listening" (paying attention). There are many erroneous assumptions, such as these, that do not consider the other possibilities regarding auditory issues. For the music-based clinician, the function of the auditory system—hearing vs. listening —greatly influences the application of certain interventions for obtaining certain responses. We will discuss important sensory problems in later chapters.

One of my dear colleagues, a composer and music teacher of special needs children, was born blind and with severe auditory deficiencies, rendering him beyond profound visual and auditory impairments. He processes auditory information through various audio-phonic implements in his ears. He would often come to my clinic-studio to play and improvise music with me, and explore other available instruments such as xylophones and drums. Once, as we embarked on various improvisational activities on the piano, he made a point of stating, "Dori—don't assume that what *you* hear as being a piano, is what I hear. I don't hear the piano, or any music, the same way that you do." Of course, he could not clarify or elaborate on what those differences between our hearing abilities might be, since he could not hear what I heard, nor could I hear what, or how, he heard—*perceived*—in sound. But I was suddenly daunted in realizing that possibly I had been making vast errors of assumptions when playing piano with and for him—and perhaps was erroneously assuming as well in my other clinical work. My assumption was that what I was putting forth musically, was being received and *perceived* in the same manner in which it was being presented by me. In other words, the old "do you hear what I hear?" Christmas song lyric came to mind!

In two of our previous books, several chapters discuss the mechanics of the auditory system and erroneous assumptions that I, and music therapy clinicians, may be making about the function of hearing vs. listening (see Berger 2002 and Schneck and Berger 2006). I may also have incorrectly assumed that particular music interventions I was administering to my autism clients would have positive impact on some of the auditory deficiencies. No. Music-based treatment will not cure a profoundly deaf person. But, suppose the person hears *something*, somehow, but the auditory system perceives and responds to the information by having heard it differently, incorrectly, or adversely? How can this be determined? A person with auditory implants does not hear timbre and overtones in the same manner (if at all) that a typically functioning auditory system can discriminate. Frank Musiek (1983), Musiek, Guenette and Fitzgerald (2013), Musiek, Shinn and Hare (2002), Douglas L. Beck and Teri James Bellis (2007) are just a few of the many audiologists working with central auditory processing issues, and advise errors in assumptions often made in diagnosing, assessing, and treating Central Auditory Processing that are important for language learning. Dichotomy Hearing Tests and Trials, especially with ASD or other non-verbal populations, present many variables that could impede the accuracy of the indicators involving the auditory brain stem and various related brain regions. In addition, Beck and Bellis (2007) inform that "(C)APD may affect up to 75% of the elderly population and can compromise success with hearing aids" (p.47). In addition to ASD, clinicians treating various geriatric populations take this into account.

In determining what or how a client is processing music and other sounds, central auditory processing and related aspects of auditory processing *must* be taken into consideration by the music-based clinician. As therapists who themselves have accomplished ear training, auditory focus, and listening for music information, the music-based clinicians have well-trained listening/hearing skills. Ear training for musicians includes what I refer to as "dimensional hearing" (see discussions in Berger 2002; Schneck and Berger

2006). This involves being trained to listen for and within specific information, such as listening for and tracking dense harmonic and polyphonic structures, voice leadings, melodic contours, polyrhythmic patterns, tempo and pulse, timbre discrimination, tracking of leading voices against harmonic densities and variations, distinguishing between top, inner, and lower voices within harmonic structures, hearing key centers and tonal relationships (major, minor, modulations, etc.), and so much other music information. In addition, music education trains for listening and identifying differences in musical forms (e.g., rondo, theme and variations), period styles (e.g., Baroque, Classical, Romantic). In effect, all of musical training, outside of instrumental skills, is based on training the auditory system to "focus" its listening, hear and understand what is being heard, and *perceive* in a defined (cognitive) manner, that which is presented in a music work. This is why the consideration of applying some music-training approaches to assist with acoustic clinical work involving auditory processes, is feasible.

Dimensional hearing is an auditory listening and hearing skill of great importance in music-based treatments of sensory function. This includes: *sound discrimination*—identifying source and context of sound; *figure-ground focus*—separating essential from background sounds, an aspect of auditory focus; *linear sound tracking*—following and linking sound relationships between one another (as is done when tracking a melodic line, or language sentence). This ability is vital in language processing. *Auditory sound location and depth perception*—where is the sound, how near or far; *auditory memory*—is what is heard now the same or different from what was heard before; *auditory/visual integration*—does what is heard confirm what is seen, and vice versa (e.g., I hear a drum but I see a pot); *auditory/motor coordination*—physically rendering, on a drum, the exact rhythmic pulse or pattern being heard, are all inherent factors in the hearing/listening process that may be problematic in various diagnoses.

These are just a few of the areas in which assumptions are made. Music-based clinicians must investigate, assess, and understand these possibilities of deficits precisely because music involves acoustics, physics of sound and vibrations, and because so many ASD and other behaviors revolve around inefficient auditory processing. There has been quite a bit of research in the role of the auditory system in relation to visual processes that contribute to visual discrimination. In a recent study (Feng *et al.* 2014), it was shown that noticeable sounds (non-task-relevant sounds) activate neurons in the visual cortex. This cross-modal activation of visual cortex by certain sounds seem to facilitate the discriminative processes of a visual target at the location of the sound. In other words, since sound location and visual confirmation are important survival mechanisms, the interaction between the auditory and visual is an important factor in discriminating an object and a location of an object. Important to music-based clinical work is this factor of sound (especially music—complex sounds) for visual acuity and discrimination.

Summary

We do not merely perceive objects and hold thoughts in our minds: all our perceptions and thought processes are felt. All have a distinctive component that announces an unequivocal link between images and the existence of life in our organism.

Antonio Damasio, neuroscientist

We are our physiology. That is a given! The only way in which we can understand our world is through the senses. Sensory information is the only way the brain can obtain information about the body, and the planet. The sequence of this process is first bottom-up (feedback) followed by top-down (feedforward), in a sequence flowing from *sensation* to *context* to *perception* to *emotion* to *response*, in a nanosecond! For the most part, awareness comes after the response has happened, though at times this could occur almost simultaneously.

Humans have seven "special" sensory systems, adding proprioception and vestibular to the list that includes vision, auditory, tactile, olfactory, and taste. These seven are not the only sensory systems existing in the body, but for the purpose of our discussion and concerns within this book, we will omit systems such as thermodynamic and biochemical monitoring, and mainly discuss senses that appear to be relevant in most behavioral concerns observed in ASD, systems that impact problems of motor-planning, sensory coordination, auditory and visual concerns, and such. Therefore, let us keep in mind that proprioceptive—vestibular—tactile triad (see Figure 1.2) are fully interactive, verifying and validating each other's information. This is further confirmed by the visual and auditory systems (Figure 1.1; Figure 1.3), and on occasion, also taste and smell (olfactory). In persons who have both auditory and visual deficiencies, where vision and hearing cannot undertake cooperative exteroceptive (external) monitoring of events, nor validate the information of other systems, the trio of proprioceptive—vestibular—tactile systems can act alone. These three can adapt and continue to monitor, sometimes even more intensely, the bodily and environmental events, and can influence the rendering of efficient motor plans to protect the individual's safety and survival. In brief, these three systems will function well, regardless of visual and auditory references. The olfactory (smell) and taste senses can influence proprioception for safety responses as well: i.e., you smell smoke, you have to be prepared to flee; you taste something awful, your stomach is prepared to discard it. However, for the purpose of this book, these two important players will also not be discussed in depth, except to encourage readers to seek information on taste, smell, and thermodynamic and biochemical systems in various other publications, and especially Schneck (2015). Investigating in-depth physiologic information beyond those provided within this book, can be quite beneficial for clinical development of Eurhythmics-based treatment interventions.

In sum, sensory leaders are the proprioception (internal monitoring of muscles, joints, and organs) and vestibular systems (balance—monitoring gravity), informing the brain about the body's relationship to space, and how to navigate Earth's gravitational pull, along with the auditory, visual and tactile. Sense of self, self-awareness, and sense of one's body are direct results of proprioceptive information enabling the brain to map its body and body parts. Balance is a direct result of vestibular-proprioceptive information based on head movements and body positions. These two primitive and special sensory systems interact very tightly with each other, and with visual and tactile (touch) senses, creating a continuous four-way integration, each influencing the other at any given time, on an ongoing basis. Add to these the sense of hearing (auditory system), the information accuracy from which is crucial to safety and survival, and we have a continuous five-way interaction securing survival: proprioception—vestibular—tactile—visual—auditory, although the first three operating together can, if necessary, be operational.

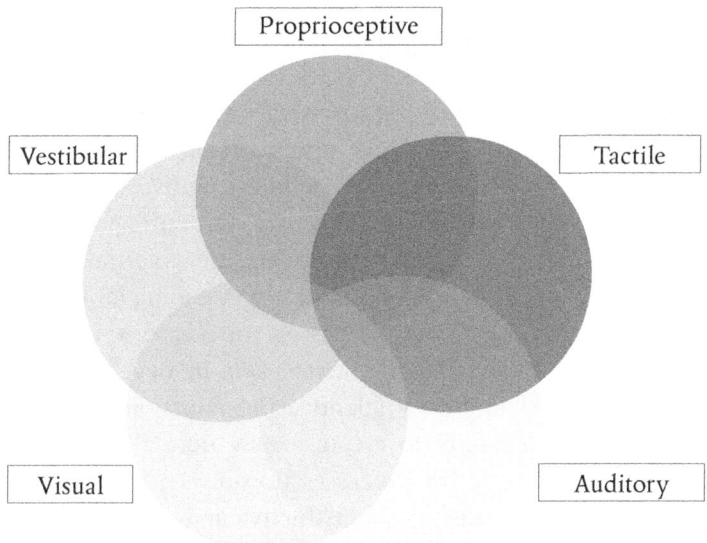

Figure 1.3 Five of the seven important sensory systems interact continually to inform the brain (feedback) of internal (body) and external conditions

The music-based clinician is fully aware that the astute function of the auditory system is of prime importance, because the various ASD treatments available, the complexities of musical interventions, and the acoustic environment created, best address auditory/cognitive processes. Central auditory processing impacts upon language and cognitive development, so it is vital for music-based clinicians to be well informed about dichotomous hearing, auditory perception, and figure-ground acuity—not necessarily from the intricacies of neurological function, but especially from the perspective of sonic information perception. This is where ear-training approaches typically undergone by musicians could be extremely beneficial, because this involves much repetition to teach the brain how to *listen*, hear, and discriminate.

With the olfactory (smell) and taste systems, the seven senses transmit their electric signals to the brain, presenting multi-dimensional pictures of internal and external events. The brain codes and ultimately decides the type of motor plan required in response to incoming sensory information, returning signals down to the body through efferent pathways of the CNS.

For the *"me"* animal there is absolutely no separation between brain and body! If there were, we might all be "rag dolls." Brain and body must function as one complete, indissoluble entity—*holistically*. In conclusion, keep in mind that the brain's main concern is *survival*—yours, and of the species. We are emotional systems that think, but operate predominantly on automatic pilot. The brain receives, perceives, and processes the sensory information in context, automatically reacting *emotionally* in developing motor plans that become functionally adaptive behaviors, automated, and homeostatically set or reset to create a new normal! However, let us not discard the cognitive processes (top-down) because despite the fact that sensory processing is instinctive and automatic, there is also a constant interaction between the sub-cognitive and cognitive regions of the brain. The physiology of perception and responses for sensory information depends on the psychology of cognition and recall of previously experienced events. The thoughts and work of Wilhelm Wundt, presented in the quote opening this chapter, along with the various quotes of Dr. Antonio Damasio, amalgamate the concept of *sensed* (intuitive) and *learned* (trained) responses, referred to as "physiologic psychology," because even psychology is physiology. Although the immediate process begins bottom-up, within nanoseconds or less, cognition, the prefrontal cortex, and many related regions in the neocortex (upper, newer thinking brain), immediately become involved.

In the next chapter, we take a look at some brain mechanisms involved in sensory perceptions that impact emotion, feelings, and the physiology of stress, survival-anxiety, and fight-or-flight responses.

CHAPTER 2

This is Your Brain on Sensations!

> *Science is the attempt to make the chaotic diversity of our sense experience correspond to a logically uniform system of thought.*
>
> Albert Einstein (1879–1956)

To understand ourselves is to understand ourselves as *emotional animals*, beyond just thinking machines, as acknowledged in the Prelude to this book (Damasio 1999, 2003a, 2003b, 2010; Gazzaniga 1998; Kandel 2007, 2012; LeDoux 2002; Llinas 2002; Schneck and Berger 2006). Furthermore, as outlined in Chapter 1, understanding ourselves as *emotional* animals requires the understanding of how we receive and process information as one complete physiologic unit—holistically—involving simultaneous interaction of *all* the systems of the brain and body toward one common goal—survival! Science is an attempt to turn uncoordinated sensations into some form of logically uniform thought. In fact, science is an attempt to help us understand our planet, our human physiology, and our own behaviors! This infers that human function is first an instinctive and intuitive, bottom-up process followed immediately and almost simultaneously by top-down "logic" processes, as discussed in the previous chapter. Still, there is so much to be learned about emotion, perception, feeling, conscious thought, and human behavior.

Long before the neocortex (new, upper brain) became enlarged for enabling complex cognitive (conscious) processing of information, humans automatically (instinctively) responded to sensory stimuli in order to survive—survival of both the individual and the species. Long before cognition and psychology became buzz words for defining and analyzing human experience and thought, human systems responded (and continue to respond) instinctively as a result of spontaneous emotional appraisal of perceived events. It is this *emotional instinct*—the instinct for survival in the face of *perceived* danger (real or imagined)—that continues to drive human physiology. Thought is a luxury that one controls *after* the fact, so thought could be more aptly termed *after*-thought, a process that turns on or off *after* the reaction has already taken place automatically. Thought, or awareness, of internal and external occurrences happens after an emotional event has taken place, sometimes almost simultaneously and sometimes a bit later, as mentioned earlier. *Instinct* is an immediate tool for survival, a requirement for perpetuation of the species. It cannot be turned on and off. It is an integral part of physiologic function, hard-wired into our being, passed on genetically and automatically from generation to generation.

In the book *Synaptic Self: How Our Brains Become Who We Are*, Joseph LeDoux (2002) reminds us that:

> What a person is, and what he or she thinks, feels, and does, is by no stretch of the imagination influenced only by consciousness. Many of our thoughts, feelings, and actions take place automatically, with consciousness only coming to know them as they happen, if at all.

Furthermore, quite often, "many things that the brain does…are not available to consciousness." He continues that, "Most of the time, consciousness is informed after the fact" (pp.10–11). Recall that this was discussed in Chapter 1 where the sequence of physiologic experience and response was outlined as:

sensory stimulation—context—perception—emotion—response

Sensation happens within a context influencing both perception and emotion (sometimes sequentially interchangeable) that calls for responses. Knowing, that is, awareness, is not the precursor to behavior. *Emotion* is.

What about *emotion*?

Neuroscientist Antonio Damasio (1994, 1999, 2003a, 2003b, 2003c) suggests that there are distinct differences in classification and connotation when referring to emotions vs. feelings. In *Looking for Spinoza: Joy, Sorrow, and the Feeling Brain* (2003a), Dr. Damasio differentiates between the two expressions in the most succinct manner, when saying that: "Emotions play out in the theater of the body. Feelings play out in the theater of the mind" (p.28). This concept also implicates referential differences between brain and mind, emotion and feelings, subconscious actions (instinct) and conscious awareness (thought). Dr. Damasio continues to inform us that, "Emotions...are part the basic mechanisms of life regulation; feelings also...contribute to life regulation but at a higher level." Moreover, "Emotions and related phenomena are the foundation for feelings" (p.28). In brief, emotions *precede* feelings, in a sense, and the awareness of "feeling." Therefore, one becomes aware of emotion by way of bodily sensations that become translated, recognized, and defined as feelings. It is validating to hear from the world of neuroscience that psychology is physiologically driven—again, that we are our physiology, and that even psychology is physiology. For the purpose of this book I forgo an in-depth discussion of *emotion* vs. *feeling*, except to point out that the emotional responses obtained from sensory stimuli (bottom-up) confirm the sequence of bottom-up/top-down human functionality as presented earlier. Nevertheless, the words "emotion" and "feeling" continue to be interchanged. However, as in the differences between *hearing* vs. *listening*, or *seeing* vs. *looking* (focusing), by differentiating the individual meanings we can understand the differences and integration between physiology and psychology—separate but equal interactive systems. This is relevant knowledge when addressing autism spectrum or other diagnosed characteristics, because behavioral responses that are driven first by perception and emotion, as in ASD, Alzheimer's, post-traumatic stress disorders, and other diagnoses, might not be recognized by the person experiencing an emotion or feeling, in the later "feeling of what was sensed" (awareness) stage of what is happening, or has happened to one's self, both in the body and mind. The "feeling" sensations (psychological awareness of emotional states) often are not available or consciously recognized by a person diagnosed with neurophysiological deficiencies, even as the emotional system is actively responding to sensory stimuli. What's more, if the emotional interpretation of sensory information is incorrect, due to inaccurate reception, perception, or understanding of a stimulus or context within which the stimulus occurs, then uncharacteristic responses will result. On an ongoing recurrence of such misinterpretations, responses will ultimately become the *recurrent behaviors* of that system—its own "normal." Remember that physiologic function is *individual* to each person, according to the manner in which each one's own system has received, perceived, and processed stimuli, within various contextual references to which corresponding survival-based responses were established. In subsequent chapters we will investigate various ASD and related characteristic behaviors possibly resulting from precisely such misinterpretations of sensory information, whereby "emotions" are active while "feeling of knowing" (awareness) may be absent.

As for identifying "feelings" following sensations and emotional processing, for the most part, in many diagnoses, such higher-level conscious *feeling awareness* of what a sensation might have indicated is often imprecise, confusing, or totally absent. Sometimes, when I inquire of a young ASD client about how or what he or she is generally feeling on the given day, I receive either no reply, a blank stare, or a reply in one-word statements such as "fine!", "good," "perfect," often uncharacteristic or unrelated to the actual event or sensation. Although the client may be able to identify a graphic picture, in a book, of a feeling or mood pose, or on a face in the picture, such as a sad, angry, or happy face, there is little connection between the label of the feeling depicted and being observed, and the feeling as *actually sensed* or replicated within the client's own body—within the self. In other words, seeing and labeling a picture that is intended to depict a "feeling" often does not become more than just that—a picture of a face defined as being "sad" or "happy." The personal sensation of, or empathy with, the depicted feeling is often not generalized or translated as a personally sensed "feeling" awareness. (For an interesting explanation of emotion and the "seeking" and reward systems of the brain, it is recommended that readers investigate Panksepp and Biven 2012, Chapters 2 and 3.)

Emotion and survival-anxiety (fear)

Joseph LeDoux (1998) and colleagues tell us that fear, what I consider to be survival-anxiety, could well be the single most underlying emotional thrust driving human behavior. It is irrelevant to the brain whether someone cognitively (consciously) recognizes (is aware of the presence of) one's survival-anxiety. For, by the time the information comes to the level of awareness (feeling sensation) through processing in the cognitive centers of the neocortex, the sub-cortical paleoencephalon (paleo—old; encephalon—Greek: within the head—brain) has already assessed and elicited responses to what it *perceived* as a threat to survival (fear factor). Furthermore, most often one is not cognizant that, in fact, it was survival-anxiety (fear) that caused the response. Here I take a moment to explain that by the word "fear," I refer to what will furthermore be addressed as "survival-anxiety." This is anxiety that is *instinctive*, uninduced by thought, but rather, is an automatic response resultant from the brain's impression that the system is in some sort of danger. Animals undergo survival-anxiety continually, though not necessarily continuously. Anxiety in dogs result in barks and growls; in cats much meowing and fleeing; in humans, heart palpitations, heavy breathing, sweating, indigestion, and more.

By the way, many seemingly positive feelings can be translated as forms of survival-anxiety responses (fear-driven emotion). Love, for instance, could be a kind of survival response…a primal "emotional seeking" that must be satisfied for "fear" of self-destruction and extinction of the species. In many ways, one could also argue that religious beliefs derive from survival-anxiety; laughter is often a release of anxiety-driven energy (Schneck and Berger 2006). The music-based clinician's self-understanding of his or her own survival-anxiety (inner fears) and anxiety-driven responses is worthy of self-investigation that could provide further insight and recognition of possible anxiety-related causes of emotional outbursts and behaviors of a client. Observed behaviors in persons with dementia or Alzheimer's demonstrate survival-anxiety reactions. Most observed behaviors in ASD imply various states of survival-anxiety distress.

Survival-anxiety, stress, and sensory processing

In *The Music Effect: Music Physiology and Clinical Applications* (Schneck and Berger 2006, Chapter 5, pp.90–116), information is presented on how survival-anxiety (the "fear spiral") evolves, both physiologically and psychologically. It is explained that when sensory processing goes awry, the brain may be receiving and perceiving uncoordinated, inaccurately transmitted, *out-of-context*, or erroneously interpreted information, resulting in the brain's inability to determine socially acceptable ("normal") responses. Instead, the brain calls for reactions that are "appropriate" in relation to what it has perceived. For the most part, the information that is actually quite safe, is *perceived* and acted upon as if it is dangerous. I put the word appropriate in quotation marks because what is "appropriate" varies according to subject, sensory assessment, and contextual events. I also use quotation marks to remind the reader that each brain and physiologic system determines "appropriate" for itself, on an individual basis; what is appropriate for one system may not be appropriate (norm) for another, or for society.

The theory throughout this book, as presented here, is that inaccurate sensory processing will cause the emotional reaction of the system to implement a survival-anxiety modus operandi, proceeding to prepare the system for fight-or-flight. As mentioned earlier, many of the behaviors observed in autism spectrum, Alzheimer's, PTSD, and other diagnoses revolve around the possibly inaccurate transmission and perception of sensory information that is predominantly perceived as dangerous, as will be discussed in following chapters and clinical work approaches.

Information processing and the brain

In order to understand instinct, it is helpful to have a brief overview of the various routes that sensory information travels before it finally lands in the areas of cortical awareness and thought. Information processing is a very complex matter, involving many simultaneous areas of the brain and body. Although many readers will have encountered the information on the sensory system and brain function, it is worth taking a quick look. The human brain consists of a highly complex system of interactive and interdependent regions, the functions of which depend on the type of information entering from the senses. There are several different brain regions. For example:

- The brain stem: moving anatomically upward (head-ward) from the upper part of the spinal column, this area includes the medulla oblongata (literally, "oblong-shaped marrow"), the pons ("bridge"), and the reticular ("netlike") formation that is the mesencephalon ("mid-brain").

- The tri-lobed, bilateral cerebellum ("small brain") which is attached to the upper rear of the brain stem.

- The globus pallidus, or paleostriatum: an ancient mass of gray matter containing the earliest basal nerve cells; and, since primitive reptiles roamed planet Earth relying for survival primarily on their sense of smell, the olfactory bulb (for sense of smell) has its own location in the brain.

- Rhinencephalon ("smell brain"), or bilateral olfactory bulbs.

This Reptilian—(or R)—complex of tissues is concerned purely with survival functions, which include: musculoskeletal balance and equilibrium (proprioceptive/vestibular processes, posture, locomotion, and coordination of muscular activity), autonomic functions such as breathing and heart rate, levels of alertness (an early-warning system for possible threatening sensory inputs), and primitive types of survival behavior (often aggressive, mean, and self-serving, which persist even today, unfortunately (Schneck and Berger 2006, pp.72–73).

Several hundred million years later, for reasons still not definitively understood, the extensive areas often connoted as the limbic system, intensified. This area of the brain is so-called because it is comprised of a group of interconnected neural structures arranged in border-like fashion (limbus—Latin for "border") surrounding the mid-line surfaces of the cerebral hemispheres, at the top of the brain stem. Also known as the paleomammalian (ancient mammalian) brain, or the paleopallium, or the limbic cortex, connecting with already existing regions, it forms the paleocortex and connects directly with the brain stem.

The limbic area, the second-oldest brain region, begins its anatomical journey around the brain stem at the front (stomach-side) surface of the cerebral frontal lobe, under the septum pellucidum (literally, the "translucent partition"). It continues rearward, up and over the corpus callosum—a bundle of 300 million nerve fibers that connect the left and right sides of the brain. Along this path, it is known as the cingulate gyrus (cerebral convolution), which ends as the parahippocampal gyrus at the medial (toward the mid-line of the body) surface of the temporal lobe. The limbic "system" includes the:

- *hippocampus* ("sea horse," because of its appearance)
- *thalamus* ("inner room") which, as its name implies, receives incoming sensory information
- *amygdala* ("almond," because the amygdaloid body is shaped like one)
- *parolfactory area* associated with the sense of smell
- *mammillary body* ("breast-shaped" structure at the rear of the hypothalamus)
- *fornix* (Latin for "arch")
- *hypothalamus* (literally, "beneath the thalamus"), which, together with the thalamus and sub-thalamus, form the *diencephalon* (the "through-brain," or *thalamencephalon*).

(Schneck and Berger 2006, p.73)

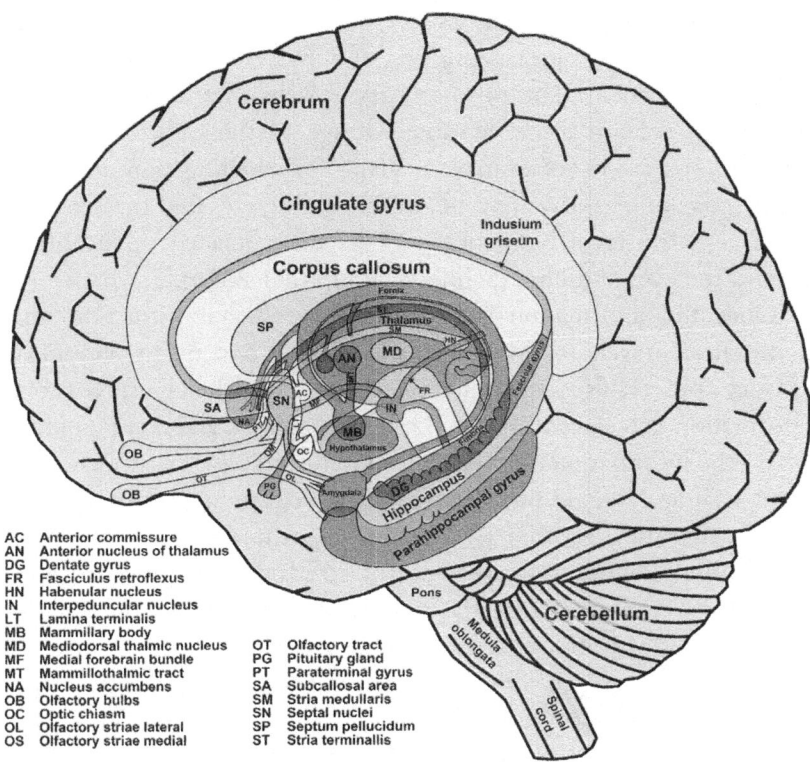

Figure 2.1 Limbic system major organs and related areas
Courtesy of John Taylor

All sensory information, *except smell*, arrives and is sifted through the reticular activating system (RAS), known as the "reticular formation," at the very top of the column, as shown in Figure 2.1. The sense of smell takes on a more direct route connecting immediately to its own "cortex"—its own brain. The RAS (the size of one's little finger) includes the medulla oblongata and the pons varolii (pons meaning bridge). Here a very densely packed bundle of nerve cells, resembling Brillo-wool, sift through the incoming information to determine whether it will be sent further along to the limbic areas and beyond, or whether it will be discarded! Researchers have not yet determined precisely why some information is included and others discarded but it is thought that approximately 75 percent of the *billions* of bits of information stimulating sensory nerve cells per second is discarded without any further processing or one's awareness that it has ever entered the system. The only sensory system that does not travel this spinal column route, as noted above, is the olfactory (smell), which is so critical for animal survival, for smelling prey for food, dangerous animals, dwelling possibilities, fire, etc. that the sense of smell actually has a brain organ of its own, located in the brain, behind the eyes and nose (Schneck and Berger 2006).

Once the information has passed the reticular formation, the information travels to the limbic area, to the two major players of sensory processing—the amygdala and hypothalamus. Sensory information is received first by the hypothalamus and the amygdala, where the information is assessed for safety or dangerous threat. The amygdala and the hypothalamus are in constant communication with each other, continually determining the status of incoming information. Limbic areas are concerned with the more sophisticated physiologic processes directly associated with *homeostasis*—status quo of body operations. These include the more refined control of body temperature (e.g., 98.6°F), heart rate, respiration rate, blood pressure, blood sugar levels, acid-base balance, sleep/wake cycles, digestion, instinctive emotions, and fight-or-flight predictions. The limbic region also moderates behavior related to survival of the individual and the species, such as thirst/hunger reflexes, the drive for sexual fulfillment, and even competitive behaviors. Closely allied with the above considerations are emotional instincts, reactions, and memories, which is why the limbic area is also referred to as the "emotional brain," and why music, reflecting emotional energies, connects so immediately and intimately with this second-oldest cerebral structure.

This area of the brain is where sensory information can run into problems. If the limbic organs deem the information to be safe, the information then proceeds onward to the hippocampus (memory organ) for registration (coding), followed by dispersal to relevant processing lobes of the neocortex (cognitive brain). The prefrontal cortex, also in constant contact with the amygdala, is a major player up there, at the frontal lobe of the cerebrum (neocortex), and it is referred to as the "executive brain"—the CEO of human behavior.

The prefrontal lobe is part of the top-down (cognition) process: thinking, making decisions, organizing thought and decisions for actions, and so forth. Also in the cerebrum are found the various lobes—top-down players—that handle motor, auditory, visual, language, and sensorimotor processes. Recall that these areas are interactive and often simultaneous processes rather than individual, one-at-a-time occurrences. Right and Left cortical areas are assumed to play certain roles. The assumption has been that the Right hemisphere is the "intuitive" lobe, while the Left is the analytical, calculating lobe. The Right lobe controls the Left side of the body, and the Left lobe controls the Right side of the body.

What happens if information is deemed unsafe?

So far, so good. We see and hear well, we touch, we sniff, we taste, we walk without falling, we wave our arms in joy, the hypothalamus and amygdala approve of the information, and it's all been coded by the hippocampus into memory for use some other time. But what if things were not approved? Aye, there's the rub. If this area of the brain thinks that some information is threatening to the body's safety and survival—regardless of whether this is true or not—most other brain activities immediately shut down for the moment, while the brain prepares the body for the fight-or-flight response. Everything else stops. Cognition, memory, learning, even digestion, are suspended in order for the brain to prepare the body to flee!

Remember your reaction at the ice skating rink? What were *your* sensations? Probably you felt anxious, heart palpitating, blood flowing more quickly than usual through your veins, your knees were unstable, shaky (anxious about moving). Your eyes were scanning the entire scene, focusing on everyone, everywhere; you sensed your adrenaline flowing. You did not plan or organize these responses. Your survival-anxiety instinct took charge. These reactions were happening, because at this moment, your sensory systems and brain perceived potential danger and were flooding the body with flee potions. This instinctive survival-anxiety response involves the immediate activation of a unique triad of limbic and body systems—the instant intervention of the **H**ypothalamus-**P**ituitary-**A**drenal system—referred to as the HPA axis! All potentially dangerous *perceptions* by the brain's amygdala (which, as noted above, is in constant communication with the sensory-assessing hypothalamus) will call for the urgent activation of the survival-anxiety response—the HPA axis preparing the body to escape!

Survival-anxiety and the HPA axis[1]

Let us consider, briefly, what happens in the body if or when the brain assesses that the system needs salvation, or regulation of the homeostatic set-points because "error signals" are received by the brain indicating that things are not functioning according to the "norm," such as receiving sensory information indicating threat to survival. In Chapter 7 of Dr. Daniel Schneck's book, *Basic Physiology for the Music Therapist* (2015), readers can find an extensive description of the endocrine and hormonal systems called upon by the brain to regulate and control the system for sustaining ongoing physiologic "consonance," that is, to minimize "error signals" and regulate homeostatic set-points. The reader is encouraged to investigate that book for further, in-depth understanding. For our purposes, I summarize some of the information in order to ensure a comprehension of the HPA axis, because much of the music-based clinical work applying Eurhythmics sensorimotor treatment technique for autism interventions (i.e., *neurophysiologic* sensorimotor-based music therapy) seeks to address the HPA axis and sensory regulation in order to quell survival-anxiety, stress, and fight-or-flight behaviors that might be triggered by sensory misinformation.

Consider that survival requires that physiologic systems work in coordination with the sensory flow of information, and that this flow of information be equally coordinated. As stated earlier, sensory

---

1   *Note*: The description of the HPA axis, hormones and interactions in the survival-anxiety demeanor has been drawn from Schneck 2015, *Basic Physiology For the Music Therapist*, Chapter 7. London: Jessica Kingsley Publishers. Brain graphic in this chapter courtesy of John Taylor.

information processes are *interactive* one with another, within the *context* of the information and how the brain receives and *perceives* neurologic impulses. Remember that the brain does not "see," or "hear," and so on, but rather, it receives electric (action potentials) or chemical signals and must instantly determine the value and interpretation of those signals. When *regulation* and a kind of "normalcy" exists, survival-anxieties are minimal, hormonal flows act according to homeostatic set-points, and all is well with the body/mind continuum. However, in a great many diagnosed conditions, especially in ASD, as we will later discuss, survival-anxiety reactions are pervasive, with the HPA axis overreacting. As indicated previously, HPA refers to the hypothalamic-pituitary-adrenal axis secreting an extensive flow of hormones that ultimately alter homeostasis toward a continuous survival-anxiety mode, with fight-or-flight responses as the "norm" for that system. (For example, it could be that a Type A hyper-reactive personality is a continual survival-anxiety demeanor with a hyperactive HPA axis.)

Hypothalamus: As mentioned before, this limbic system organ is the primary processor for sensory information. The hypothalamus actually manufactures and secretes some of a myriad of hormones, including, among others: oxytocin, corticotrophin-releasing factor (CRF), thyrotrophin-releasing hormone (TRH), growth-hormone-release inhibiting hormone (GHRIH), antidiuretic hormone (ADH) including vasopressin and pitressin, to name just a few. The hypothalamus makes these hormones and sends them to be stored in the master gland—the pituitary gland.

Pituitary (hypophysis): As stated, the "H" of HPA (hypothalamus) sends its manufactured hormones for storage and eventual secretion by the "P" of HPA—pituitary gland—referred to as the "master gland." These hormones include (among others): oxytocin/pitocin (stored/release), thyroid-stimulating hormone (TSH, thyrotrophin, TTH), adreno-cortico-trophic hormone (ACTH—adronotrophin), growth hormone (ADH, vasopressin, pitressin), and follicle-stimulating hormone (FSH). By releasing ACTH, the master gland calls upon the "A" of HPA—adrenal gland—to then do its secretions, ultimately preparing the energies and hormones required for the fight-or-flee response.

Adrenal (suprarenal): The "A" finalizing the function of the HPA axis for preparing the body to fight, or to flee in the face of danger, is the adrenal gland, sitting atop of each kidney in the body. We have all become familiar with some of the secretions we experience (though not actually sense consciously) when in fight-or-flight readiness—racing heart, shut-down of systems, fast breathing, and more. Hormones excreted by the adrenal glands include cortisone, cortison, corticosterone-A, corticosterone-B, deoxy cortisol, deoxy-corticosterone, aldosterone, dehydro-epiandro-sterone, androgens, estrogen, progesterone, epinephrine (adrenaline), norepinephrine (noradrenaline), dopamine (the "feel good" hormone to regulate anxiety).

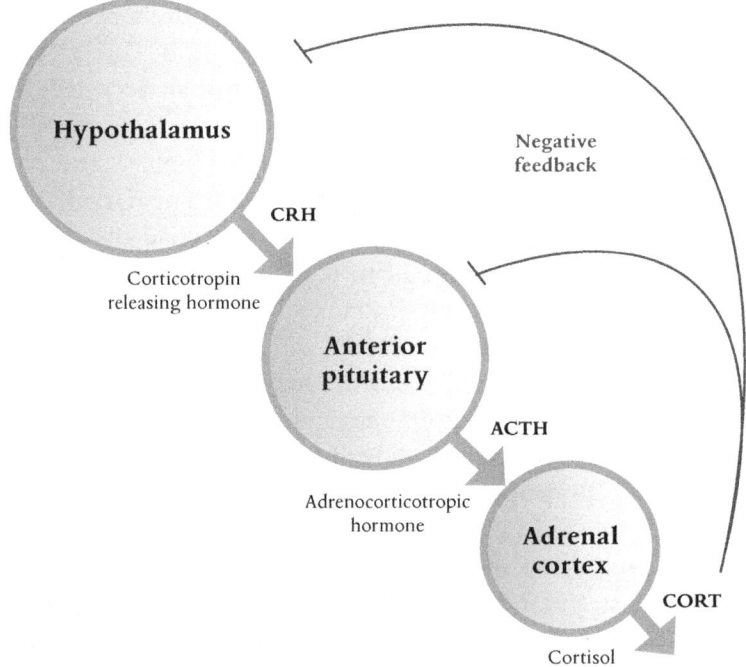

Figure 2.2 The HPA axis

Of course there are several allied organs contributing to survival-anxiety reactions and behaviors (such as thyroid, kidneys, etc.), but the major triad of the HPA axis that secrete hormones is headed by the "H"—Hypothalamus. Although this brain organ, part of the limbic region, is technically not part of the endocrine system, it is often listed among endocrine organs because it actually does *manufacture* hormones and transmits them for secretion by its partners. The hypothalamus controls the pituitary and the kidneys through its use of "releasing hormones and factors" and their opposites, "release-inhibiting hormones and factors" (simply put, it tells the pituitary to release, or *not* to release, depending on context of information). Furthermore, by way of the many hormones that the hypothalamus manufactures and sends to be stored by other vital systems, the "H" can assist in controlling and regulating homeostatic set-points such as body temperature, circadian cycles, cardiovascular activity, sugar and fat metabolism, hunger, activity of the endocrine and the autonomic nervous systems, emotional feelings of anger, rage, and as mentioned, the fight-or-flight survival-anxiety responses.

Now, the "P" of the triad—the pituitary gland—although second in importance to the hypothalamus in the function of the HPA axis, is first and foremost in importance as the master gland of the endocrine system. Through this gland's secretion of "tropic" hormones (tropic hormones are endocrines that a gland itself has not produced but has been sent by another for storage and excretion), this tiny gland, situated just below the hypothalamus at the base of the brain, virtually controls *all* of the functions of the other major endocrine glands of the system, including their morphological development! The posterior side of the pituitary is the *neural* portion of the gland (neurohypophysis) where it shares neural pathways with the hypothalamus. Two hormones: ADH (antidiuretic) and OT (lactogenic oxytocin) are stored and released from this portion of the gland, in response to direct nervous stimulation—anxiety—from the hypothalamus (which also synthesizes ADH and OT secretions from this gland). The anterior part of the "P" stores and secretes hormones as called upon to either release, or inhibit release of hormones, depending on physiologic states, but not especially related to anxiety and stress.

Finally, the "A"—adrenal gland—comes into the act to complete the survival-response axis. Two adrenal glands are situated, one each, atop a kidney. Referred to as suprarenal glands, this glandular structure contains two sections: the glandular adrenal cortex and the neural adrenal medulla. Important to note is that these organs' blood supply receives adrenocorticotrophic hormone (ACTH) from the pituitary, and manufactures and secretes at least 11 or more adrenocortical hormones—corticoids—which are steroids, derived from cholesterol precursors. In other words, the pituitary emits ACTH through the blood to the adrenal glands, which then are called upon to secrete glucocorticoids—in effect, steroids! Adrenal steroids impact upon proper metabolism of electrolytes, carbohydrates, and proteins, and are very important to understand because *any and all types of stress promptly activate the adrenal cortex to respond!* In response to receiving impulses from the nerve fibers of the sympathetic portion of the autonomic nervous system (ANS), the neuronal adrenal medulla manufactures and secretes three major adrenomedullary hormones: dopamine (precursor of adrenaline, derived equally from the adrenal medulla and the hypothalamus); norepinephrine (noradrenalin), and epinephrine (actual adrenaline, the principal adreno-medullary secretion). These hormones are called catecholamines manufactured principally from amino acid precursors. Their major physiologic impact is upon metabolic regulation and cardiovascular function—particularly in response to emotional and anticipatory (anxiety) states. These catecholamines prepare for the fight-or-flight response when threat to survival is perceived, whether real or imagined. Furthermore, responses of the body to these hormone secretions are elaborated upon by the thyroid gland secretions and others.

What does this all mean?

So why do we music-based clinicians need to know the information of sensory processing routes and the HPA axis? Because if theories and treatments can be developed to address observed behaviors in various diagnosed populations, we need to understand the possibilities, within physiologic function, that could be contributing to various reactions and responses—that is, possible *causes* (chemistries) from which are derived particular behaviors. With knowledge of the impact of anxiety and stress—the survival-anxiety state of mind—we can better determine how to apply various music elements to, for instance, quiet an HPA axis and reduce the flow of dangerous catecholamines.

Catecholamines (steroids) are needed in moderation, as stated above, for various physiologic regulations such as cardiovascular and metabolic function. In and of themselves, catecholamines are not dangerous when traveling the blood stream for a specific purpose, *temporarily*. However, when a body is in continuous stress, in a state of survival-anxiety, and the body is infused with steroids, cortisone, and other catecholamines on a continuous basis due to ongoing anxiety, these hormones become lethal, endangering organs and muscles, and more! Many of us have knowledge and/or experience with cortisone. In general, cortisone levels are higher in the mornings, and lessen throughout the day. That is the basic "norm." But some research is now in process to investigate levels of cortisone in, for instance, ASD youngsters, and the jury is out on connecting various levels with states of anxiety and depression so pervasive in ASD. It remains to be seen with further research. Nevertheless, continuous flow of catecholamines, steroids, and cortisone, is surely something that music clinicians can (or should) address in treatment.

In sum, the HPA axis response to threats, emergencies, and the survival instinct is a major player in many observed behaviors of ASD, as well as diagnosed neurophysiologic characteristics and responses of other special needs populations. If sensory information is inaccurate, or perceived as threatening, the system will undertake a survival-anxiety manner—fight-or-flight behaviors. This is observed often in PTSD, in which perpetual and pervasive anxiety distorts sensory information, putting the information within the *context* of "danger" or fear, calling upon HPA hormones—steroids and chatecholamines—for various lengths of duration. Catecholamines and steroids work wonders in the immediate moment of danger, of course, and we are glad to have these hormones. But on an ongoing continuous basis, these are lethal chemicals. The same is true when observing an Alzheimer's patient suddenly scream or attempt to flee, or appear in desperate distress. These behaviors do not happen without autonomic nervous system and hormonal operations responding to sensory input of one kind or another—imagined, mostly. These acts are not called upon by *cognitive* decision to behave in certain ways. They are survival instincts—yes, perhaps invalid in the context of real time, but valid within the imagination and perception of the brain. Thus, reality is only what the brain/mind-body deems it to be—and may not be what the observer to such behaviors experiences at that moment.

Music, as we know, alters moods, can organize behaviors, and can reduce stress. Vibrations can soothe muscles and impact upon cellular and molecular systems. Ultimately, as we know, certain music can quiet the amygdala and the HPA axis to obtain a sense of calm and quiet, or even positive animation. Once we learn a bit about sensory processing, and the role of the HPA axis in response to survival-anxiety, we are better able to formulate new objectives and approaches relevant to treating the *cause* of responses, along with the resulting *symptoms* (i.e., behaviors, reactions, etc.).

Let us proceed to investigate behaviors observed in ASD in Chapter 3, and how this information interacts with ASD characteristics.

CHAPTER 3

Interpreting Autism and Sensory Characteristics

> *Autists are the ultimate square pegs, and the problem with pounding a square peg into a round hole is not that the hammering is hard work. It's that you're destroying the peg.*
>
> Paul Collins, *Not Even Wrong: Adventures in Autism*

The past several decades have produced a myriad of literature on autism, a diagnosis alleged to be increasing considerably. Five shelves in my own bookcase are filled with books and stories about autism spectrum "diagnosis." With all that, the actual causes of ASD are speculative at best, including everything from hereditary DNA to neurologic distortions to childhood inoculations. Much is still exploratory, unknown, or not well understood. In reviewing the many theories, research findings, and treatment approaches for this diagnosis, the main concerns are with language and communication, socialization skills, and cognition, as defined in various diagnostic and assessment manuals. Deliberations emanating largely from the neuropsychological community seek answers in concepts about "Theory of mind," "mirror neuron," "polyvagal theory," and others, the functions of which are assumed to be causing deficient socialization and emotional skills (see, for instance, Baron-Cohen 1995; Baron-Cohen, Tager-Flushberg and Cohen 1994; Baron-Cohen, Tager-Flushberg and Lombardo 2013; Frith 1991; 2008; Frith and Hill 2003; Porges 2011; Wan and Schlaug 2010; also Wan *et al.* 2011). Although many theories are quite valid in explaining certain characteristics of this diagnosis, an important point is often overlooked—that is, ASD is *a way of being*. Despite all the existing literature on autism this notion is rather poorly defined.

Autism is not a "disease." Rather, it is a *dis*-ease in navigating planetary and societal demands in tandem with personal physiologic fundamentals, and fitting into a culturally established norm. As Paul Collins (2004) reminds us in the above quote, perhaps ASD characteristics, and other *a*typically functioning populations, are pegs of different shapes, and trying to fit those into "typically shaped" slots is actually to destroy the peg. Recall that "adaptation," as stated in Chapter 1, is relevant *per individual*; each one's physiology having its person's physiologic fingerprint. Therefore, responses are appropriate on an individual basis, according to how that individual brain processes information and determines adequate responses (feedforward) based on *that brain's* perception of sensory feedback. In short, each one's mind-body responds to its own "normal." What we clinicians would like to attain is the gentle *reshaping of the peg* through treatment that addresses physiologic function, without "pounding the peg," in order to provide the brain with new, better options for "fitting into" the appropriate peg-hole—a new normal. The question is, whose desire is it to fit an atypical peg into the "typical" hole? My clinical experience has indicated that it is usually not the autist, but those who fit into the "typical" niche (parents, teachers, clinicians, and society), and want atypical pegs to fit in as well, even if superficially, at best. So there are programs devised that appear to be enabling the "peg" to fit in (e.g., ABA, TEACCH, Floor-Time, RDI, SCERTS). Of course, each approach has its merits, and one can only hope that some physiologic betterment of function can result from such processes.

The music-based clinical approach outlined and discussed in this book upholds the theory that autism (and other diagnoses such as Down, Williams, ADHD, OCD, etc.) is not a disease to be "cured," but rather, features characteristic adaptations in atypical ways of functioning, each having its own, individual normal. Indeed these characteristics may often appear unpleasant to both the person and especially to society, and interventions can be helpful. The goal in music-based treatment is not to "cure," but to safely reshape the peg, as stated above, to develop functional ways of managing behaviors, and COPING: Calm—Organized—Paced—INtegrated—Growing. The adaptation and application of Eurhythmics in interventions for sensorimotor regulation and general COPING is based on the following hypotheses:

Hypothesis 1: Focused Eurhythmics-based music treatment can reduce pervasive survival-anxiety (HPA-driven fear factor) driven by sensory misinterpretation to yield functional coping skills

Theory: Observed behaviors in ASD and other neurophysiologic diagnoses indicate fight-or-flight reactions driven by sensory stimuli that are transmitted, processed, or perceived incorrectly. Eurhythmics-based music interventions that can directly address the cause of characteristic behaviors will help organize sensory interactions, reducing ongoing anxiety, and resetting homeostatic set-points away from operating in perpetual survival mode, to yield better COPING skills.

Indeed, this sensorimotor hypothesis is a lot to ask of the music-based clinician, but it is an area of treatment that remains most often unaddressed. Let us consider that observed characteristics of autism behaviors, anywhere along the spectrum, reflect responses that are often operating in survival mode, that is, fight-or-flight (over-stimulated, hyper-aroused and hyperactive). These reactions could result from a brain's continuous incapacity to predict safety or danger accurately, and make functional (or appropriate) sense of the planet, in large part due to deficient (or insufficient) transmission, coordination, reception, and perception of incoming sensory information (feedback), in misinterpreted context. It is hypothesized that homeostatic set-points of such systems are set for predicting danger requiring ongoing survival-anxiety reactions in circumstances that a "typically functioning" person would find safe. Combined with, and derived from, a possible mis-reception and mis-perception of cross-modal sensory information, these deviant set-points act to maintain the body in a persistent fight-or-flight response that this system's brain has decided is appropriate for moving away from danger (even if none exists), based on the information it received that appeared to imply danger (i.e., misperceived sensory information).

Several neuroscientists (Amaral and Corbett 2003; LeDoux 1998, 2002) delineate between anxiety and fear, attributing to the latter an inherent sense of *predictability*. Unfortunately, this predictability factor within the interpretation of sensory information in ASD is typically inaccurate. If the brain in ASD could predict accurately, there would be less frequent "melt-down" fight-or-flight behaviors! Rather, many (if not most) sensory information experienced and processed by an ASD brain is, indeed, *un*predictable and often incoherently assessed regarding safety or danger. Therefore, the instinctive, pervasive, ongoing state of survival-anxiety, stress and mistrust is fed forward for corresponding response—usually scream and run! The result of this apprehensive, restless state of being, and an inability to distinguish (emotionally, intuitively, contextually, cognitively) between safety or danger can be, and most likely is, responsible for much of observed ASD behaviors. This includes a limited sense of self and other, a limited body- and self-awareness, and a general inability to cope with changes. This survival-anxiety hypothesis suggesting that behaviors and reactions observed in ASD are most probably due to inefficient sensory processing and interaction and can be addressed by targeted Eurhythmics-based interventions.

Although some physicians and researchers may argue the existence of the survival-anxiety factor, or tend to dismiss the possibility that ongoing state of survival-anxiety could be a trigger of ASD behaviors, a literature review, and my own clinical work and observations, case studies, and research, uphold the feasibility of this theory (see Berger 2009, 2012; Schneck 2015; Schneck and Berger 2006). Of course there may be a small percentage of individuals with ASD who do not outwardly display survival-anxiety or "fear," or in whom such emotional reactivity may not be totally operable or detectable. However, in the great majority, across all age groups, and I believe even in those who appear not to display such, many anxiety-driven behaviors and fight-or-flight reactions are apparent and quite noticeable.

The hypothesis of pervasive survival-anxiety is consistent with several research studies investigating emotion, amygdala volume, and HPA hormonal release in ASD. One study postulates that the brain's "fear hub" (the amygdala being the brain's "fear center," as discussed in Chapter 2) sometimes *shrinks* in autism's most severely socially impaired (Nacewicz *et al.* 2006). In this research lab, such individuals displayed a slowness in differentiating between emotional and neutral facial expressions, and showed extremely minimal eye-gaze. Researchers concluded that these findings supported a model of amygdala hyperactivity (i.e., highly active) that could explain most volumetric findings in autism. Another interpretation could be that with the inability to even sense "danger," and the lifelong isolation and social apathy, the amygdala is almost not needed, and therefore shrinks, in contrast to hyperactive amygdala and hyperactive behaviors.

Several other studies have found enlarged amygdalae in ASD populations in early developmental states through the teen years, beginning as young as two years of age (see Mosconi *et al.* 2009; Munson *et al.* 2006; Nordahl *et al.* 2012), again suggesting inconsistent (or inaccurate) function of a hyperactive amygdala in accurately assessing safety, probably more often deeming information as dangerous, and triggering HPA axis for fight-flight preparations. This cycle sustains continuous survival-anxiety demeanor and behaviors.

Remember the catecholamine, cortisol?

In Chapter 2 we learned that the adrenal gland excretes cortisol, (produced and sent from the hypothalamus (ACTH) to the pituitary for further release by the adrenal glands), along with other catecholamines (adrenaline, noradrenaline, etc.), in response to threat and danger, preparing the system to fight or flee! Indeed catecholamines have important roles to play in the momentary face of danger, but on an ongoing basis, cortisol is lethal (poison) and destructive to organs and muscles of the body. This is why your doctor will prescribe cortisone only for a limited time, with gradual withdrawal so that the system can effectively acclimate without destruction. Perhaps cortisone had once been prescribed to you for an injury or ailment, because your brain may not have recognized the injury information as particularly "dangerous," so your adrenal gland was not excreting sufficient curative amounts. On the other hand, perhaps the HPA activated, and your blood stream did receive abundant cortisone at the very start of the injury, but subsided (thankfully), so that more was required from external sources. In any case, in relation to Hypothesis 1 and ASD survival-anxiety function, there is abundant research on excessive cortisol in ASD.

A research paper by Heather C. Abercrombie and colleagues, in the journal *Emotion*, of the American Psychological Association (Abercrombie, Kalin and Davidson 2005), studied effects of cortisol on affective experience. Investigation yielded that acute cortisol elevations caused heightened arousal in subjects who were presented with objectively *non*-arousing stimuli. Participants who were given 40mg of cortisol (showing extreme cortisol elevation within the physiologic range) rated neutral stimuli as more highly arousing than did participants in the placebo and others in the 20mg group. Although the research was conducted with "typical pegs" as subjects, the inference is that a system, diagnosed or not, that operates on heightened cortisol excretion (fear-cycle HPA), would likely misinterpret stimuli and respond with heightened arousal. In other words, excessive cortisol causes distortion to prediction of safety or danger. Hypothesis 1 above suggests that this occurrence is evident in rousing ASD behaviors. Furthermore, in a state of fight-flight, cognition and memory shut down and the hippocampus shrinks (LeDoux 1998, 2002; Schneck 2015; Schneck and Berger 2006). Any attempt to "learn" or "remember," when in this state of response, will be futile.

Additional research papers and book chapters discuss the HPA axis as being either over-active, or malfunctional in ASD subjects who display increased or untypical cortisol levels in the blood stream. This state of being causes irregular circadian rhythms and responses to stress (Corbett *et al.* 2006). A study by Spratt and colleagues (2012) indicated enhanced cortisol response due to stress in ASD. Analysis of data in that study found significantly higher-peak cortisol levels, and prolonged duration and recovery of cortisol elevation, following research-administered stressors in children with autism. These researchers determined that the evidence suggested increased reactivity of the HPA axis to stress and novel stimuli in this population. Fear and anxiety, in any population, whether diagnosed or not, can affect young children's learning, behavior, and health (see Fox 2011). In general, and across many diagnoses and psychologically-physiologically driven behaviors, the factor of chronic stress and a dysfunctional HPA axis alters pathophysiology (Guilliams and Edwards 2010). While the jury is still out on the efficacy of the HPA and cortisol in ASD behavior, this is an area of function that music-based clinicians can positively treat, given the ability of music to reduce stress and anxiety. (For further information see Graeff and Zangrossi 2010; Schneck 2015; Tan, Zhong and Yan 2004; Yang, Huang and Hsu 2004.)

Remember oxytocin?

Chapter 2 informed us that the HPA axis is led by the brain's hypothalamus that produces oxytocin (OXT), along with many other hormones, and transmits it for storage and future excretion into the blood stream. Thankfully, OXT is *not* a catecholamine, and its role is the *antithesis* to the fight-or-flight response. The flow of OXT *calms* the amygdala and HPA, yielding a sense of empathy and better social cognition! Research by Heinrichs, Chen and Domes (2013) reports that OXT increases social approach by *reducing* social stress reactivity, given the evidence of lower cortisol during OXT administration. The result is the boosting of social motivation. They advise that the amygdala is the target of OXT, and that OXT dampens amygdala response. The investigators even explore the potential of OXT as therapy for social anxiety, and for deficits in social cognition (Heinrichs, Chen and Domes 2012; Heinrichs *et al.* 2013). Music therapy interventions intended for developing socialization skills could well consider that before socialization skills can be developed or strengthened, attention to altering hormonal function needs to be addressed—that is, the calming of the system first, before other treatment objectives can be realized. Or, vice-versa—that a system appearing to be slow, lethargic, and reclusive (see Nacewicz *et al.* 2006), might be operating on an overdose of OXT and related hormones. Therefore, interventions that animate (actually excite the

HPA and flow of catecholamines), could ultimately bring about a better hormonal balance. Withdrawal and the "freeze" response in "fear" is, after all, the other side of survival-anxiety behavior. There is a great need for music-based research in these areas of ASD function.

Thus, Hypothesis 1 suggests that if and when the music therapist's "clinical eye" assesses observed behaviors as indicating some level of ongoing survival-anxiety responses (fight-or-flight), then the *first* treatment objective would be to calm the amygdala and HPA axis survival-anxiety with interventions that can thwart the flow of dangerous catecholamines (except for the inhibiting hormone dopamine), and stimulate excretion of OXT, or, vice-versa, that can animate a lethargic under-responsive HPA axis by inducing more adrenaline flow simulating survival mode to attain levels of enthusiasm and energy. The clinical objectives would be to either quiet or animate the amygdala and HPA axis, and attain balance and functional physiological adaptation (regulation).

Hypothesis 2: Movement, and motor planning timing deficits, often unaddressed in music-based treatment, can be improved with Eurhythmics-based music and movement interventions

Theory: Flexibility of movement and motor-planning deficits are inherent and pervasive in ASD and other diagnoses, but often overlooked as being a cause for erratic survival-anxiety behaviors. Movement and gait deficits impact upon learning and language delays, muscle tone and body dynamics, and social and emotional coping discomforts. Movement dynamics and motor planning deficits indicate some malfunction of proprioceptive-vestibular-visual sensory coordination, contributing to ongoing anxiety and stress. Eurhythmics-based interventions places this deficit within treatment priorities to further reduce stress, and to increase appropriate quick motor-planning responses, movement dynamics, and self- and functional kinesthetic awareness through focused auditory training and responses to music directives.

Contributing to survival-anxiety, stress, and erratic behaviors is an array of uncoordinated and under-regulated physical motor activity—body movement. This kinesthetic characteristic of ASD also contributes to survival-anxiety and social anxiety, lack of sense-of-body and self, and to deficits, the second survival-anxiety responses. Undiagnosed or overlooked motor/movement function, and ineffective motor-planning, translate as the general inability to plan movements instantly and accurately, with appropriate body dynamics and movement fluidity, in any given circumstance. Although every now and then music and movement autism research and treatment papers do appear (see for instance, Amos 2013; Atigh *et al.* 2013), Hypothesis 2 suggests that for the most part, the movement factor driving survival-anxiety and stress is often omitted in music-based treatment and research, and left to other therapies such as occupational or physical therapy. However, it is proposed that rhythmic movement with music elements and "ear-training" interventions can achieve much growth and correction of motoric responses, and that Eurhythmics movement interventions can coordinate movement and motor-planning in ASD.

Recall the vestibular, proprioceptive, visual sensory triad

We know how the vestibular system falters and the brain is very busy when we've had too much to drink, have difficulty navigating terrain, or are dizzy and require immediate corrective maneuvers in order not to fall. Keeping humans upright, balanced, and appropriately able to move arms, legs, head, and body often can make the difference between safety and danger. As discussed previously, the vestibular system coordinates with the proprioceptive and visual systems on a non-stop basis, providing information to the brain about the position and conditions of the body. Interactions between these systems must be *optimal* in order for the brain to develop motor plans promptly and suitably for any given circumstance. In Chapter 1, the example of two liquid filled vessels that you were asked to retrieve required *accurate sequential processing* between the proprioceptive, vestibular, and visual systems in order to originate the precise motor plan enabling you to see, rise, balance, move to the table, lift the vessels, and so on, without either you or the vessels dropping to the floor You did not *consciously* (i.e., cognitively) plan these maneuvers, but rather, these were *instinctive* (bottom-up) sequences of sensory-physiologic events that the brain practiced for many years. Although this is quite an elementary description excluding the many CNS processes, it serves to reiterate that many human actions are automatic and bottom-up, most of which are developed throughout stages of growth, or taught to become automatic, as in walking, swimming, skating, bike riding, playing musical instruments, and so forth. Unfortunately, not everyone's sensory system processing is able to form functional automatic and efficient motor-planning. Autism Spectrum Diagnoses, among others, present innate movement inefficiencies and great difficulty in motor responses, gait, and also oral-motor requirements.

Movement malfunctions in ASD have been researched quite extensively, with implications to the function (or malfunction) of the basal ganglia, cerebellum, and frontalstriatal-gait processing in the brain, where multi-modal sensory processing is thought to take place. Frontostriatal circuits are neural pathways that connect frontal lobe regions with the basal ganglia (striatum) that mediate motor, cognitive, and behavioral functions within the brain (Alexander, DeLong and Strick 1986). These circuits are part of executive functions that include selection and perception of important information, manipulation of information in working memory, planning and organization, behavioral control, adaptation to changes, and decision making. These circuits are involved in neurodegenerative disorders such as Alzheimer's disease, and Parkinson's as well as neuropsychiatric disorders such as schizophrenia, depression, OCD, and disorders such as ASD and ADHD. Damasio and Maurer (1978, 1979) propose that abnormalities in posture and balance, similar to those described in autism as well as in Parkinson's, are well related to basal ganglia and related frontostriatal-gait structures dysfunction mentioned above, including an absence of position-related nystagmus (an involuntary rhythmic side-to-side movement of the eyes). This implicates the visual system's accuracy or inaccuracy in its interaction with the vestibular and proprioceptive systems. This deficiency is not limited to ASD, but, as mentioned, also includes schizophrenia, Parkinson's, and various dementias. Damasio and Maurer propose that

> the "vestibular" disturbances in childhood autism seem to be neither primary nor specific. It is possible that along with defects in attention, affect and motility, such disturbances signify the presence of some form of dysfunction in basal ganglia and related structures, which may be present in a variety of psychiatric disorders, such as autism or schizophrenia. (Damasio and Maurer 1979, p.658)

The past decades have seen research investigations of movement malfunctions prevalent in ASD, including such characteristics as hypotonia (low muscle tone), motor apraxia, reduced ankle mobility, history of gross motor (motor-planning) and toe-walking (implicating visual misinterpretation), fine-motor deficits, and other movement-related issues and motor deficits as being a major basis for ASD behavior characteristics, as well as cognitive, language, and social ineptitude (see Esposito and Pasca 2013; Freeman, Sultanifar and Baer 2010; McCleery *et al.* 2013; Ming, Brimacombe and Wagner 2007; Nayate, Bradshaw and Rinehart 2005; Torres, Yanovich and Metaxas 2013; Trevarthen and Daniel 2005; Trevarthen and Delafield-Butt 2013). Several authors suggest that stereotypic movement disorders are often missed in a variety of diagnoses, not only in ASD, and sub-characterize these deficits as stereotypic movement disorders (SMDs) (Freeman *et al.* 2010). Clinicians have observed a variety of such "disorders" in ASD (self-stimulating ticks and arms flicks, wobbling gait, toe-walking, stiffness and side-to-side motility, etc.), but also in other syndromes such as Down and ADHD. Noteworthy to us is that many such SMDs apparently are overlooked in many diagnoses and treatment applications.

As for ASD and Hypothesis 2, Trevarthen and Delafield-Butt (2013) are quite zealous in suggesting "that autistic spectrum disorders have their origin in early prenatal failure of development in systems that program timing, serial coordination and prospective control of movements, and that regulate affective evaluations of experiences" (2013, Abstract, p.1). Given the findings of these researchers of disturbances in posture, locomotion, and prospective motor control in children with autism, as well as of their facial expression related to interest and affect, and of attention to expressions of *other* persons, these authors propose that an examination of the psycho*biology* of motor affective disorders, rather than later-developing cognitive or linguistic ones, may facilitate early diagnosis. Furthermore, they believe that imitation activities and "expressive art" therapies, which respond intimately with motor activities, can be most effective at later stages of childhood development! This train of thought directly relates to Hypothesis 2—suggesting that the inefficiency in kinesthetic locomotor behaviors will impact upon survival-anxiety and language—and especially to socialization anxiety, as well as psycho-emotional and cognitive regulation. Therefore, it is important that music-based clinicians undertake interventions for movement irregularities, placing such treatment high in the hierarchy of objectives. More on this in Part Two.

Additional research in movement deficiencies can be found in a recent articulation by McCleery and colleagues (2013), who discuss issues in motor development and motor *resonance*—that is, mirroring/imitation—that present difficulties in ASD, as others have also suggested. Authors here recommend the relevance of providing early intervention for language and communication skills. Their paper continues to discuss oral-motor therapy, along with other interventions, and supports the importance of employing mouth instruments, such as the recorder, harmonica, or kazoo, in clinical music-based practice that can address head, visual, oral-motor movement and breath-control difficulties. Hypothesis 2-based treatment approaches assess and determine ASD interventions for whole-body and extremities oral- and locomotor needs, and breath control that can be addressed through various rhythmic elements and wind instruments. For example, in language development, many music-based clinicians are familiar with the work of melodic intonation therapy (MIT), the melodic intoning of words while simultaneously using arms to tap syllabic rhythms. Interventions developed along those line are those of auditory-motor mapping training (AMMT), that instructs for the association between sounds and articulated actions by using vocal intonation and bimanual motor activities (Wan *et al.* 2011). AMMT is related to MIT. This concept is already inherent and expanded upon in the application of Eurhythmics that helps embody the rhythm of words for later recall. It is akin to the singing of words that employs regions on both sides of the brain.

The subject of movement and rhythmic-movement deficiencies is worthy of further investigation and the reader is encouraged to seek further information in this area that can benefit clinical physiological evaluation of targeted objectives for developing music-based treatment interventions. The more implicit the factors contributing to defined ASD behaviors are, the more clinicians are able to address those from the perspective of *cause* and effect. (For further reading, see Dowd *et al.* 2012; Green *et al.* 2009; Rinehart *et al.* 2006.)

A look at typical autism behaviors

Before listing some ASD characteristics observed in many settings, let us recall the concept of *functional adaptation*. Functional adaptation is how the brain has determined to resolve an issue. Functional adaptation is individual—unique to each person's system—the fingerprint for behavioral reactions. The adaptation manner to sensory information eventually becomes homeostatically set so that circumstance X yields response Y, 99.9 percent of the time. It becomes *that* system's "normal." Remember that adaptations set as one body's normal are not necessarily the same as another's normal, and in general, usually do not conform to socially acceptable norms. Strangely the majority of ASD behaviors in persons on the spectrum, regardless of age or gender, are similar to one another. So for the ASD population, there must be similar sensory processing that yields similar responses to environmental factors, especially anxiety. Functional adaptation in this diagnosis manifests as the fight-or-flight response. And fight-or-flight responses are amygdala and HPA axis-driven survival-anxiety that is uncontrollable. In some ways, one considers ASD as a form of PTSD, except without the post-traumatic experiences and hallucinations (dreams, recall of events); rather it is an ongoing "traumatic experience" of misinterpreted sensory and social cues. For that brain. In many ways, ASD does resemble a "traumatic stress disorder," perhaps rather than "Post" it is a "Pervasive Traumatic Stress Disorder."

When observing behaviors that are typical in ASD populations, there are some typical characteristics:

- persistent survival-anxiety (fear-like) responses (fight-flight meltdowns)
- repetitive or disorganized movements
- satelliting around a room, and/or evasive actions
- seemingly confusing or undefined sensory sensations
- hyper- or hypo-arousal states; emotionally labile
- inability to focus or remain on task (ADHD-like restlessness)
- auditory and visual distress; limited eye contact; peripheral vision; ambient hearing and auditory integration issues
- modulation and attention difficulties
- language and communication insufficiencies
- cognitive and emotional setbacks
- social ineptitudes and uneasiness
- movement inflexibility; motor-planning deficits
- …and many other observed stereotypic characteristics.

Unless sensory information is properly received and perceived, many of the above responses will become the "norm." In addition to a pervasive state of anxiety, the auditory system's many deficiencies, especially in relation to language development, requires special consideration, since music-based treatments are acoustic interventions addressing auditory functions, and could uncover possible central auditory processing deficits. This deficit often manifests in an inability to sequentially track and then blend (link) sound elements of words (letter sounds, etc.), evaluate high vs. low frequencies and prosody accurately, and many other problems. In addition, when in survival mode, the auditory system resorts to ambient hearing rather than focused and unified stereophonic sounds in the environment (auditory focus). For the most part, auditory processing in ASD amounts to the brain receiving an unfocused tsunami of sounds rather than processing information in a figure-ground manner. Remember your cocktail party in Chapter 1? Fortunately you were able to distinguish your friend speaking to you in the midst of external noise (clanging, other voices, etc.). This is most often unavailable in ASD.

The visual system in ASD most often operates in survival mode as well, with vision being peripheral more than central. Consider that when the brain senses danger and the HPA axis begins its work, one's vision becomes peripheral, since survival requires that one sees everything out of the sides of the eyes, rather than just at the center! And, surely "eye contact" with another being is dismissed since peripheral vision is busy, limiting central visual focus. The system in survival distress is too busy to consider details. The general intake of the environment is crucial in order to know where and how to escape danger. What's more, if the proprioceptive-vestibular-visual systems are not accurate or cooperating, the brain becomes hyperactive in attempting to solve the problem. In addition, tactile sensations become heightened for assessing danger! This is just more HPA involvement accounting for either hyper- or hypo-arousal, a kind of freeze effect of under-arousal (hypo-). All these areas require keen assessment and treatment objectives.

Summary

In bringing these Part One—theory—chapters to conclusion, and to proceed to the clinical work employing Eurhythmics in music-based sensorimotor treatment, a brief summary of salient points rendered in the three chapters may be helpful. Ultimately the reader will amalgamate and absorb the information that at first may be new and somewhat overwhelming, in order to successfully follow the treatments presented in this book, that refer back to many of the factors discussed so far, and the hypotheses upon which this treatment approach is based.

The important things to review and keep in mind are as follows:

- Humans are first, *emotional animals* functioning on instinct—bottom-up.
- The only way the world and the body are perceived is through interweaving sensory information as transmitted and perceived by the brain.

- The sequence of sensory information processing is: sensory stimulus—context—perception—emotion—response, with the possibility that perception/emotion can reverse, depending on events.

- Functional adaptation refers to the manner in which the brain resolves an issue, and is programmed in the body as homeostatic set-points (status quo). Functional adaptation settings are unique to each individual system, based on each system's information processing and response. Observed behaviors in ASD are functional adaptations of those systems. ASD functional adaptations appear to be somewhat universal, supporting the possibility that pervasive survival-anxiety and sensory processes are similarly evident, setting homeostasis for similar responses, within individual variations, across the spectrum.

- In the face of *perceived* danger and fear arousal, the HPA axis is activated, releasing catecholamines (cortisol, adrenaline, etc.) to prepare the body for fight-or-flight response.

- Hypothesis 1 maintains that ASD and other diagnoses are in constant states of survival-anxiety (fear), presenting behaviors indicative of fight-or-flight responses possibly resultant from inadequate sensory processing. Therefore, treatment in this area needs to be high on the priority list of objectives in music-based treatment, in order first to calm the amygdala (fear hub), and HPA axis in order to derive additional objective results successfully.

- Hypothesis 2 proposes that the evidence of movement deficits in ASD supports the idea that movement deficiencies contribute to lack of self-awareness, awareness of others, and language delays, impacting upon social skills. This area of function appears often to be misunderstood or underserviced in music-based treatment goals, and ought to be second on the priority list of treatment objectives.

- The ultimate goal for Eurhythmics interventions in sensorimotor music-based treatment is to develop and provide new options for functional adaptation leading to improved levels of coping in ASD and other diagnosed persons.

We have now reached the conclusion of Part One—the theory section of this book. Some additional readings listed below may further illuminate information presented in this first part of the book. Let us now move on toward investigating how the clinical work applying Eurhythmics interventions can become a formalized treatment technique to music-based sensorimotor interventions for ASD and other neurophysiologic characteristics.

Further Reading

Cytowic, R. E. (2002) *Synesthesia: A Union of the Senses.* Cambridge, MA: The MIT Press.

Lemley, B. (1999) "Do you see what they see?" *Discover 20*, 12 December.

Otto, T. U., Dassy B. and Mamassian, P. (2013) "Principles of multisensory behaviour." *The Journal of Neuroscience 33*, 17, 7463–7474.

Ramachandran, V. S. and Hubbard, E. M. (2003) "Hearing colors, tasting shapes." *Scientific American 288*, 5 May, 52–59.

Schoen, S. A., Miller, L. J., Brett-Green, B. A. and Nielsen, D. M. (2009) "Physiologic and behavioral differences in sensory processing: a comparison of children with Autism Spectrum Disorder and Sensory Modulation Disorder." *Frontiers in Integrative Neuroscience 3*, 29, Available at www.frontiersin.org, accessed on 5 June 2015.

Skipper, J. I., van Wassenhove, V., Nusbaum, H. C. and Small, S. I. (2007) "Hearing lips and seeing voices: how cortical areas supporting speech production mediate audiovisual speech perception." *Cerebral Cortex 17*, 2387–2399. Available at http://cercor.oxfordjournals.org/, accessed on 5 June 2015.

Part Two

THE PRACTICE
COPING

Calming—Organizing—Pacing—
INtegrating—Growing
Reaching for Functional
Adaptation

CHAPTER 4

What is This Thing Called Eurhythmics?

Music creates order out of chaos: for rhythm imposes unanimity upon the divergent, melody imposes continuity upon the disjointed, and harmony imposes compatibility upon the incongruous.

Yehudi Menuhin, violinist, educator

Many have romanticized about music—what it is, what it does, how it works, how it changes moods, emotions, general health, and more. But "music" is not one thing. It is a synthesis of multifarious elements, the acoustic energies of which serve to communicate the fundamental nature of its creator—the composer—and the physical, emotional, and mental energies of the performer. Furthermore, each physiologic system and brain processes music differently, according to whether the listener's body rhythms and energies resonate with the incoming intricacies of this aesthetic form of expression, without which human beings seem unable to live. Music is everywhere. Not a day goes by that one does not encounter it in some form or other—whether in commercials, films, TV shows, iPods, iPads, and so on. Given this reality, if music is "healing," then it would follow that everyone exposed to music on a daily basis is healthy and smart. Additionally, musicians should be the healthiest individuals, since they are exposed to music in depth, well beyond just hearing it. Alas, this is not the case, so there must be more to music than meets the ear.

What is music?

In order to understand the potential of music for treating physiologic and sensory concerns, it is helpful initially to consider that regardless of how "music" is identified in its various aesthetic structures, music, first, is acoustic *energy*. Energy is kinetic. Energy vibrates. When activated, energy moves across space from one source to another. Energy vibrations oscillate, converting from *potential* energy to "*kinetic* energy" (see Schneck and Berger 2006, pp.38–60). This is the cyclical process that evolves within periods of vibrations: potential—kinetic—potential—kinetic, and so on. Energy cycles are referred to as "frequency of vibrations." These frequencies are calculated in hertz (Hz), the number of times that conversion from potential to kinetic takes place. In order for this to occur, the "status quo" of energy must be *disturbed*. This disturbance does not signify something negative, but rather, is more of an "activation" that changes a state of existence or situation from one state to another. The disturbance is referred to as the "forcing function" of an "adequate stimulus" (that which prods a status quo) to which designated animal sensory receptors respond. Hertz is the number of energy cycles per second that determines how energy oscillations are *perceived*. For example, as you read this somewhat perplexing information, your visual system is perceiving light, among other things (unless you are reading in the dark). Light is energy. Your visual sensory system perceives this energy as light and color when the frequency of vibrations of this energy is within the range of 400–750 terahertz—that's a million-million (i.e., trillion) Hz! Reducing and slowing the frequency of vibrations (Hz) down to 1–400 terahertz stimulates your tactile system to perceive the energy as "heat." At an even slower range of 20 Hz–20,000 Hz per second (i.e., 20 kilohertz), your auditory sensory system is "disturbed" to perceive the energy as *sound*. In short, sensory system receptors are designed to receive adequate stimuli in the form of energy oscillations that are forcing functions instigating various sensory receptors and responses.

Now, music is energy (as is expressive language) that vibrates and is perceived when acoustic vibrations are within the 20 Hz–20 kilohertz (20,000) range, as stated above. Actually, what we call "music" is an assemblage of various frequency vibrations (i.e., timbre, tone ranges, volume, etc.) that is *perceived* by the brain in various dissected segments, reunited back later in an amalgamation of sound frequencies. Recall that the brain does not hear *music*. Music's acoustic energy "disturbs" auditory receptors (in the auditory canal), then becomes converted into electric signals (action potentials) that are transmitted to the brain. That is the way the brain receives "music"—sonic energy translated into electric signals. After first passing through the reticular formation, amygdala, hypothalamus, and so on, as previously discussed in Part 1, these acoustic energy signals are dispersed to various collaborative areas of the cortexes for further processing, in locations that dissect pitch frequencies, timbre, rhythm-pattern and pulsation, volume, language areas if required, and so on. Ultimately, these electric signals are reconstituted, hopefully in the order in which they were originally transmitted and coded, so that cognitive areas of the brain can ultimately recognize the "all" as being *music*. Verbal language is in the category of acoustic sounds, the frequency vibrations of which include vocal timbre, tonal register and inflection, rhythmic syllabic articulation, volume, and so forth (Schneck and Berger 2006, pp.27–90).

So, music is an adequate stimulus serving as a forcing function emitting acoustic energy, "disturbing" the status quo of sensory systems being stimulated by the vibrations, and calling for response. This forcing function activates human sensory systems to respond, thereby influencing homeostatic settings, both in the moment, and for many in its ongoing presence (e.g., trained musicians), over the long run. As a result of continuous disturbance in the trained musician, the brain and body have been sufficiently stimulated to adopt new, automatic (homeostatically set) manners of response to the acoustic and visual (notation) stimuli. Muscular/physical, cognitive, and emotional reactions have become automatic, prompted by black dots and scribbles (notations) on a number of lines, and by the constant repetition of listening and instrumental practice. Years of instrumental and/or vocal training and practice—repetition…repetition…repetition—force changes in the musician's brain and physiology, deriving new homeostatic settings required in functionally adaptive cause and effect response to the stimulus. In most cases, music behaviors resultant from training become generalized in daily life skills—ability to focus, stay on task, develop keen auditory and visual skills, coordinate limbs, body and muscular movement, improve cognition and memory, enhance proprioceptive—vestibular—tactile—visual—auditory processing, and much more. It is not required that music training results in performance. Just the ongoing discipline suffices to generate positive functional adaptations to external and internal events. Of course this is a vast generality, but research, as presented in previous chapters, supports this impression. The obtainment of similar results may be quite possible when music-based clinicians approach sensorimotor interventions from a "music training" viewpoint. After all, music therapy is a form of training, using music interventions to teach the brain and body new options for responding and behaving.

Music is temporal aesthetic energy moving across time and space, the organization and compilation of which is a *human invention*. What's more, humans created music using fundamentals that the brain and body understand:

- periodicity: cycles; rhythm; movement
- complex frequencies: pitch (melody); timbre; harmony
- energy: amplitude of dynamics—volume
- structure: form and systems.

These, and variations of these characteristics, comply with human physiologic function, and parallel planetary and cosmic behaviors. We live within cycles, energy, and rhythmic movement. We are continuously confronted by innumerable cacophonic sounds, lights, pitches, timbres, shrieks, sirens, loud and soft sounds, and environmental systems (weather, day/night, seasons, etc.) within which we formulate our lives. The human brain can only replicate that which it inherently knows; the brain cannot go beyond its own knowledge. Thus, music contains and represents that which the brain already knows how to process, knows about its self, its body and function, the environment, its sensory and nervous systems, and the planet. The magic of music is that it is a mirror reflecting human and planetary behavior. Music acts like we do—displays anger and joy, runs, walks, slides, jumps high, grovels low, is loud, is soft, it is complex or simple—all expressed as a result of emotion. Emotion is energy. That energy is duplicated as expressed within music. If music is a mirror reflecting the composer, the performer, and life on the planet, then the music-based clinician can reflect and transform the client by changing the music, creating new energy vibrations and sensory stimuli, as it were, with interventions that reflect new, modified behavioral alternatives. The answer to the question about why humanity is not healthy resulting from extensive exposure to music, is that the *treatment potential* within music—each of the six elements—whether individually or combined, must be *clinically administered* by the trained clinician, in order to have music specifically address ongoing ailments, not just to be available as entertainment. This means that rhythm, timbre, melody, harmony, dynamics, and form, the six basic rudiments of music, each can have a specific role to play in treatment, while in addition, these essentials combine to provide an enjoyable sensory and emotional succor along with revised responses. Therefore, it is with *targeted intent*, that music can reach beyond "aesthetic entertainment" to achieve health and well-being. And of course, this implies that the clinician understands human function and how the intervention of various music features can address specific behavioral treatment goals and objectives.

What is Eurhythmics?

> *"Eurhythmics" is defined as: early 20th century English: from eu—"well" + rhythm + -ics.*
>
> Collins English Dictionary 2012

There are many origins of this word, flowing from Greek to Latin to English. Recall back to the Prelude of this book that it was Emile Jaques-Dalcroze (1865–1950) to whom this word is attributed. Jaques-Dalcroze used the term as a way of defining his approach to music education and rhythmic training with the incorporation of body movements internalizing music fundamentals. Jaques-Dalcroze opined that performers were deficient in delivering appropriate rhythmic accuracy and interpretive understanding. He observed that the training of musicians was greatly lacking in the teaching of music's profound fundamentals and delivery system thereof, especially of rhythm, but also phrase, dynamics, and the emotional sagacity of various harmonies and form structures. His philosophy introduced the idea that there was a distinct relationship between rhythm and body movement. He also believed that body blockages were indicators of physical rhythmic blockages. He was of the opinion that relaxation was the ultimate requirement in support of the body and movement, and that breathing, the fundamental rhythmic body activity (in addition to the heart) was fundamental in obtaining relaxation! These views resulted from his studies of human function, whereby, through some experimentation, he began to realize that the source of all rhythm, including music, is found *within* the body—heart beats, breathing, circadian rhythms such as sleep/wake/hormonal cycles, walking, running, swaying, bouncing, and so on. He surmised that the body, itself, is the best vehicle for instilling rhythmic sensibility since the energies of many body rhythms are simulated within the energies of music rhythm, and because playing or singing music involves rhythmic physical movement and breathing.

Jaques-Dalcroze (2010a) also ascertained that the full understanding and incorporation of the essence of music's various essentials in performance must first be sensed and experienced in physical movement. Thus, he was convinced that the most effective way to achieve this is through the *embodiment* (internalization) of rhythmic relationships through kinesthetic activities reflecting the language of music, in order for these to become *intuitive*. He upheld that such embodiment, produced and perpetuated through movement and breathing exercises, will not only be effective in duplicating facets within musical content through instinctive, internalized awareness and response, but will also derive bodily self-awareness, intuition and naturally spontaneous reactions when performing the music's intent. In essence, Eurhythmics is the coordination of ultimate "entrainment with," and "embodiment of" music rudiments, attaining the highest perception of self and music for achieving the peak performance level of musical expression. Ultimately, Jaques-Dalcroze ascertained that, since music moves in time and space, this kinesthetic component to music education presents the definitive unification of mind and body—the integration of the physical with the emotional sensitivity required in the aesthetic (music) expression of and within music. In short, the training of musicians must be *holistic*!

The time of Emile Jaques-Dalcroze (1920, 2012a) was also a time when the approach to general education of children was being brought into scrutiny. An important influence in Jaques-Dalcroze's thinking was his friendship with Edouard Claparede (1873–1940, Geneva; see Hameline 1993), a renowned psychologist with eclectic and controversial ideas on the education of children. Claparede insisted that educational systems should understand the science of human function, in order to approach the education of children on a much higher level of physiologic understanding of learning styles. Claparede was in critical and active opposition to accepted educational practices of the time, and, as stated, called for recourse to science and scientific objectivity as a basis for a new approach to the education of children. Claparede and Jaques-Dalcroze were close colleagues and collaborators, the timing of which resulted in Dalcroze Eurhythmics exercises often adopting and employing psychological games of *change and quick reaction*, in order to develop better focused attention and self-knowledge, and to increase learning and internalization (entrainment) of musical concepts.

Eurhythmics ("good rhythm") activities in accordance with Dalcroze philosophy (1920, 2012a), involve movement responses predominantly to rhythm and *improvised* music provided by a Dalcroze-trained instructor who improvises music at a keyboard or piano. The music is geared toward instilling various rhythmic and musical concepts to which participants respond in movement. In terms of music education, the Jaques-Dalcroze approach does not lay down a specific system or curriculum sequence, as do the educational systems of Carl Orff, Zoltan Kodaly, and others. Rather, there are recommended approaches and exercises based on the overall philosophy of rhythm embodiment and the value of unity of mind-body. Three distinct areas of training for skills attainment comprise the basis of the Dalcroze Eurhythmics music training approach:

1. *Eurhythmics—rhythmic movement*—rhythmic training through body movement simulating the physicality and *embodiment* of pulse, tempo, pattern, phrase, etc. by automatic *quick and intuitive responses*; movement actions immediately reflect the musical content; the replication of rhythms and elemental structure in kinetic motion (e.g., strong/weak dynamics;

high/low frequencies; fast-slow momentum; rhythmic patterns, use of spatial dimensions; limbs and head, etc.).

2. *Improvisation*—in body movement, voice, instrument, developing the ability to depart from the printed page, to improvise *spontaneously*, in the moment, in accordance with emotional, cognitive, aesthetic needs of a given musical thought or theme, concept, or tonalities represented in music; developing the ability to improvise body flow and movements commensurate with the auditory stimulus, or in silence.

3. *Ear training—solfeggio*—quick and accurate responses and vocal replication of pitch, intervals, sight-reading, tonal and harmonic identification; standard ear-training exercises; movement and included vocalizations employed for bodily sensing of acoustic content and tones.

Fundamental to the success of this training is the overall objective of "quick response" reactions to the acoustic stimulus. Jaques-Dalcroze judged that purposeful and appropriate quick response indicated that profound embodiment and knowledge of rhythm and music expressions were indeed taking hold, becoming intuitive. If a quick response appropriately parallels the stimulus characteristics, then it would follow that something must be changing, increasing, developing physiologically, to yield "instinctive reaction"—that rhythm and music elements are being *physically* and mentally automated, sensory systems accommodating, and motor-planning becoming functionally forthcoming. The primary elements of music having been *embodied*, the musician is properly prepared to understand and deliver the music. Emotion is already inherent in music's vocabulary, so once the embodiment of musical language becomes infused, the performer will profoundly understand self and music, and be able to deliver the emotional content of a composition intuitively and flawlessly. This approach to music education is admirable and ideal, though not often utilized in schools of music. Although Eurhythmics was never intended to be dance, or dance training, the basic Dalcroze philosophy of understanding music through movement greatly influenced the development of new dance training approaches at the time, and gave way to Modern Dance, developed by dancers of that era who studied Eurhythmics at Dalcoze schools.

While the goals of Eurhythmics training are to produce excellent musicians, many of the concepts are functionally adaptive as music-based interventions. Music therapy professes to be *holistic* treatment addressing the whole being, both body and mind. Therefore, the Eurhythmics approach to music education—"holistic" mind-body integration, embodiment of stimuli, improvisation, ear training, dynamic movement activities and "quick response" reactions, and motor-planning requisites—parallels many of the goals of the music-based clinician on behalf of rehabilitation and health. For the music-based clinician, many of the recommended activities in Eurhythmics training are transferrable to interventions for specific *sensorimotor* and kinesthetic goals of music-based treatment: ability to instinctively and quickly respond (motor plan) to environmental stimuli; auditory and visual regulation, ability to attend, to ear-train for figure-ground improvement; to increase body dynamics, instigate vocalization and breath control for language development, attain sensory and physical coordination, self-awareness, and self-expression, among the many other skills sought when addressing ASD sensory systems and movement characteristics. In as much as music therapy does not often provide such direct or systemized approaches to treatment addressing many ASD and similar characteristics, it is of benefit to consider the results of music training on the brain, body, and mind, and how those results also might be obtainable for rehabilitative health purposes. Before discussing the specific therapy approach and interventions based on Eurhythmics, let us briefly discuss what is meant by "sensorimotor," followed by a quick overview of the elements of music fundamentals.

What does sensorimotor mean?

> *Sensorimotor is defined as a biological term: of or relating to both the sensory and motor functions of an organism and/or to the nerves controlling them.*
>
> Collins English Dictionary 2012

This definition upholds the intent of Eurhythmic-based interventions for sensorimotor concerns, as we shall soon discover. "Sensorimotor," or sensory-motor, refers to *sensation* and *movement*. Inaccurate or inefficient multi-sensory interaction can lead to mistaken perception of information, leading to stress and survival-anxiety, as proposed in the previous chapters. Motor deficits are attributed to inefficient sensory processing of proprioception and vestibular information, mid-line orientation, poor body dynamics (e.g., low muscle tone), visual incongruities, and most of all, motor-planning inefficiencies. Treatment for sensorimotor deficits is not new to the work of the occupation therapist. Occupational therapy involves treating sensory deficits through various movement activities addressing aforementioned concerns. Most if not all of the interventions in OT involve *movement*—swinging and swaying, sensory "brushing" and joint contractions, trampoline jumping, fine-motor movement, and much more. Most movement activities automatically are rhythmic articulation of muscles and joints, mostly unbeknownst to the therapist or the client. These are movements based on *instinctive* rhythms that are executed within a rhythmic sequence. It is interesting to note that the vocabulary of music, especially rhythm, for sensorimotor interventions and active music making, and movement improvisation, can address similar treatment goals but reach beyond OT, physical therapy, or other therapies that address sensory processing. In addition, areas undertreated by OT are auditory/visual deficits, an area that acoustic intervention best addresses. Based on information and research presented in Chapter 3 on sensory, kinetic (movement), and motor-planning deficits in ASD, the treatment of sensorimotor concerns through systematic use of Eurhythmics concepts, and interventions stimulated by music, seems a natural progression moving from the "training-of-musician" goals to the mind-body sensorimotor healing goals of music therapy.

A quick overview of music energies in clinical work

Here is a very brief review of information that music-based clinicians already know, but is worth revisiting in the context of

Eurhythmics-based treatment that will follow. Music, acoustic energy, basically consists of six denoted energies: *rhythm* (pulsed, patterned energy); *timbre* (complex tonal energies); *melody* (sequentially linked tonal energies); *harmony* (contrapuntal multiply superimposed energies; also tonal energies flowing within systems of modes and key structures); *dynamics* (volume; exertion of energies); and *form* (unification of energies). These parenthetic descriptions are not intended to define the physics of sound per se, but rather, to help the reader envision the elements of music within the framework of acoustic energies that are the adequate stimuli acting as forcing functions for sensory and systemic responsiveness and homeostatic change. Parenthetic descriptions of these elements also aim to describe each of their roles in treatment, stimulating commensurate movements and behaviors through some Eurhythmics interventions we will be investigating further. Keep in mind that music requires *no semantic definition*, explanation, or understanding, but rather is an energy that penetrates directly into the brain's many cortical and neocortical areas and the physical body. Humans, being emotional animals first, instinctively respond to music, requiring no further knowledge or preparation for processing its acoustic energy. The six fundamental elements of music are as follows.

1. Rhythm

Rhythm is the energy that serves to organize and stabilize events within a temporal time-frame of occurrences (moving across time). Rhythm is kinetic, the movements of which consist of: *pulse* (beat); *pace* (tempo); *pattern* (sequential event relationships); and *continuity* (continuous repetition of pulse, pattern, and pace). Rhythm's role in music-based treatment is to develop organized motor-planning, physical coordination, and body movements. Rhythm contributes to the sustainability of attention and task performance, functional motor plans, paced movements and spatial navigation, expressive language acquisition through rhythmic syllabic patterns, and various other roles as deemed essential in the assessment for treatment. The important factor in rhythm, at times under-considered in clinical work, is the potential role of *tempo* in addressing anxiety behaviors and emotional and physical energies. In addition, *rhythmic patterning* serves the role as indicator of levels of cognition, inventiveness, abstraction, and task development abilities of the client. Since rhythmic patterns keep the brain interested, it helps the client sustain prolonged task attention.

2. Timbre

This is the acoustic texture of energy emissions based on overtone series housed within instrumental, vocal, and most natural sound-emitting sources other than electronic-rendered tones that often are not inclusive of "overtones," but rather, are referred to as "pure tones." The role of timbre in music-based treatment addresses the survival requirement of auditory perception, acuity, and discrimination, also of importance in receptive and expressive language development, identification of environmental sounds for safety or danger, differentiating among sounds and voices, and more. All sounds contain some kind of timbre, which allows for separating danger from well-being, recognizing flute from bird, and so on. Timbre is akin to "texture" of a sound. Survival depends on accurate assessment of timbre, so its use as a clinical music-based resource is quite important, especially in attaining calm, diverting ongoing survival-anxiety, and aiding in the development of acute auditory discrimination.

3. Melody

Melody is the prosodic kinetic expression of emotional energy. Like expressive language and speech inflection, melody is the linear relationship of sounds combining one tone to another, in sequential temporal flow and contour. Melody characteristics consist of *pitch* (tones); *relationship* (the manner in which one note connects to another); *pattern* (the rhythms in which one note flows to another); and *profile* (the contour of melodic flow from highs to lows). Melody flows across time and space. As a music-based treatment resource, melody is first cousin of language prosody, containing similar patterns of highs and lows in inflective contours, rhythmic relationships between tones, and emotional renderings within linear tonal variations, all of which can be applied in training for emotion recognition and expressive language acquisition. Melody in clinical work is also an essential intervention for reducing stress, engaging the brain's interest, and simulating emotional interactions. The ability to sequence and link tonalities (as in the ability to recognize or sing a tune) is an important feature for expressive language development.

4. Harmony

Harmony is the superimposed multi-tonal energies often flowing within harmonic structures of modes and keys; multi-tonality energies that can be perceived as pleasantly consonant, or unpleasantly dissonant, depending on cultural exposure and listening experience of the listener. Harmony is energy that supports the emotional expression and melodic content of a musical composition. Moods and emotions can be manipulated through harmonic structures (chords), movement between modes and key signatures, and consonant or dissonant accompaniment to melody. Counterpoint, that is, multi-melodies moving simultaneously, develops harmonic chordal structures in a vertical manner, while flowing in a termporal horizontal manner. In music-based clinical work, harmony, counterpoint, and key structures are used in interventions seeking emotional recognition and responses. Pleasant harmonies will reduce anxiety, while dissonant structures will cause animation and often some levels of distress and irritability. Depending on clinician assessment of emotional needs, harmony is a resource unlike any other in immediately addressing cause and effect of feeling sensations. Experience with listening to harmony also aids in figure-ground and dimensional hearing.

5. Dynamics

The music volume of loud and quiet, strong and weak, is the direct emission of acoustic energy. Dynamics replicate emotional energy sensed in stress and anxiety, calmness, joy, sadness, anger, and moodiness, and support and immediately reflect the emotional intent and movement of melodic and harmonic energies. Dynamics in music-based clinical work are often underutilized. In many interventions, the clinician will sing or play an instrument in one dynamic, with little movement between and within dynamic ranges. Yet music dynamics are the precise simulation of human energies of self-expressed emotions. When we whisper, or speak low, we are transmitting one kind of emotion. When we shout or speak loudly, another emotional sensation is rendered and obtained. Therefore, it is essential that music-based clinicians consider how, why, and when an intervention inclusive of a particular *dynamics* level can serve a discrete clinical objective.

6. Form

Form is the ultimate unification of musical contents within a structured container flowing from beginning to middle to conclusion. Form enjoins all the musical energies of a composition to form a sequential relationship within an overall whole, the puzzle pieces coming together to form a complete picture. Form can be one of the most important factors in music-based interventions. Thematic repetition such as rondo form, theme and variation, and several movements, contribute to anticipation, which is a state of attention.

For ASD, ADHD, and other diagnoses, the development of the ability to "attend" is crucial for cognitive development. Providing music-based interventions containing a specific form can increase the ability to "wait until done," or to anticipate the "next," or to recall the theme, and much more.

Thus, each of the six elements of music has a role to play in treatment, at times in collective unity with other elements, and at times individually, depending on the clinician's assessment of need, and determined goals and objectives.

Summary

With the understanding of the terms Eurhythmics and sensorimotor comes the recognition that music, as an acoustic amalgam of sonic energies, provides features that serve as independent and combined resources to address physiologic functions under treatment.

Acknowledging the role that each individual element can undertake for rehabilitative purposes enables the clinician to apply the resources more directly to the goals and objectives of treatment. In combined varieties, such as rhythm and form, or harmony-rhythm-dynamics, and so on, more treatment objectives can be addressed. When music fundamentals are detailed as treatment, and are experienced and embodied through movement, the body and brain are urged to respond in new ways, influenced by the insistence of the forcing function of adequate stimuli and continuous stimulation.

Thus, the individual fundamentals have been revisited here in order that we might consider them as *individual*, as well as combined, treatment resources in music-based sensorimotor interventions. In drawing this chapter to a close let us keep this thought in mind: if Eurhythmics training can bring out the best coordination and new instinctive responses in musicians, then despite diagnoses, this approach to treatment might also impart favorable results for clients with ASD and others. My own research and case studies have indicated positive results. Let us investigate treatment designs and sample interventions.

CHAPTER 5

Eurhythmics in Music-Based Clinical Work

> *You can look at disease as a form of disharmony. And there's no organ system in the body that's not affected by sound and music and vibration.*
>
> Mitchell Gaynor, M.D., *Sounds of Healing*

In my years providing music-based clinical work to a variety of populations, I have observed that music and vibrations impact the entire human system, in any of its states of being. Recall that humans are *emotional* animals receiving any and all information about the planet and environment (internal and external) from sensory systems, and first responding instinctively (i.e., automatically). Instinct precedes calculated response (thought). Sensory systems are activated by *adequate stimuli*, vibration frequencies that are in motion moving from potential to kinetic, measured in hertz, functioning as *forcing functions* that excite sensory receptors. Recall also that the predominant concern of the brain is *survival*! Sensory information must be approved by the amygdala (emotion organ), thalamus, hypothalamus, and related brain regions, before it is deemed safe for transmission to upper-brain regions for further processing and storage. Remember that when information is *suspected* to be threatening, whether real or imagined, the hypothalamus-pituitary-adrenal (HPA) axis is called upon immediately to release an array of hormones (catecholamines) to prepare the body for fight-or-flight. Keep in mind also that predominant behaviors observed in ASD seem to indicate just that—the fight-or-flight mode predicated upon a state of continuous survival-anxiety and distress (i.e., ongoing fear), most probably due, in part, to misinterpreted sensory information. In addition to continual anxiety, many movement and motor-planning discrepancies appear pervasive in ASD, as well as in many other neurophysiologic diagnoses. Treating these factors with a methodical Eurhythmics approach that addresses emotional (fear-related) and movement deficits, lack of eye contact, social ineptitude, cognitive and language development, sensory deregulation, and more, can be quite productive, as suggested in previous chapters.

As you continue further, bear in mind that music is processed by the *whole body*, as Evelyn Glennie reminds us, and that the brain does not actually "hear" music, but rather, it receives electric signals (action potentials) from the sensory system that has been activated by incoming adequate stimuli, forcing nerves, cells, and molecules to act in response. Given these considerations, the music-based clinician is now aware that the auditory stimuli presented in treatment may not be adequately received or transmitted to the brain, perceived or coded in the same way in which the stimulus was transmitted by the clinician! (In other words, "Do you hear what I hear?") Therefore, the therapist's keen clinical eye will determine the impact of an intervention, how often to present the stimulus, when to stop it, and so forth, as responses are assessed, and causes of behaviors or reactions determined. The bottom line here is to consider that "adaptation," being unique to each individual physiology, depends on the function of sensory systems (among other systems), and the *perception* of each individual brain-body to a stimulus. A great many behaviors observed in ASD are adaptive for that system, often suggesting ongoing survival-anxiety and environmental stressors. With this in mind, let us begin to explore the sequence of Eurhythmics-based sensorimotor treatment sessions, the overall goal of which is to help retrain the brain and body for the ability to cope in a more comfortably functional adaptive demeanor.

When developing an overall plan for Eurhythmics-based approach addressing survival-anxiety, movement deficiencies, and physiological subsets of related issues, the predominant goal is to adjust responses, move the brain away from ongoing distress, help organize brain-body, in order ultimately to derive a dexterous level of COPING: Calm—Organized—Paced—INtegrated—Growth.

We learned earlier that, music (sonic energy) is the clinical adequate stimulus, the forcing function that incites into action sensorimotor receptors. Whether listening to, or making music, the experience is more than a whole-brain event, it is a *whole-brain-whole-body* experience. As Dr. Gaynor advises in the quote at the start of this chapter, there are no organ systems in the body that are not affected by sound and music and vibration. Furthermore, all cells and molecules vibrate with the pulsations of this acoustic energy (entrainment). The act of making music is an intrinsically *physical* act. One cannot play an instrument or use the voice without moving many parts of the body! In the abstract of "Cortical plasticity induced by short-term multimodal musical rhythm training" researchers Lappe *et al.* (2011) eloquently remind us that "Performing music is a multimodal experience involving the visual, auditory, and somatosensory modalities at well as the motor system." Playing an instrument, regardless of size and weight, automatically involves sensorimotor activation of proprioception, tactile, vestibular, visual, and auditory interactions. A person cannot lift a drum mallet suitably unless the brain knows where those arms are located, how much energy is required to lift the limbs and items, where or how far the drum is located, and therefore how far to extend the arms, how to apply muscular intensities for striking the drum, and how to sustain movement repetition, among other things (e.g., mid-line orientation). Using the voice requires muscular and breath control, and speaking requires complex oral-motor movements. All this takes motor-planning! It is our job, as clinicians, to *teach* the brain how to perform these actions, if it does not already know, or is limited in planning for these actions. The motor plan involved in a seemingly uncomplicated task of lifting a mallet to play a drum is extremely complex, as we learned in Chapter 1, when you were asked to fetch two liquid-filled receptacles. Motor-planning must be quick and instinctive in order to be successful. Thus the Eurhythmics concept of "quick response," explored by Jaques-Dalcroze, as explained earlier, immediately serves this clinical objective encouraging instinctive motor-planning. And instinctive motor-planning is absolutely essential for undertaking *any* type of physical action, especially in music making that requires precise rhythmic continuity.

Body movement is a very complex, multi-sensory interaction among at least five of the seven sensory systems: vestibular, proprioceptive, visual, tactile, and auditory. Where the body is, what it is doing, where the legs and arms are in relation to the head, torso, and gravity, how much body energy is required to balance against gravitational pull and adequately transport the body elsewhere, all require sensory expression. Body movement also involves instant, continuously shifting body parts within defined sequential rhythmic timing. The ability to balance (proprioception-vestibular-visual) must be geared up for navigating spatial relationships (visual and cognitive component—distance calculations). Energy, particularly in the form of body dynamics (i.e., strong or weak muscle tone and flexibility, etc.) requires knowledge of self and body, and quick and accurate motor-planning in order to execute functional partial- or full-body movements. Many deficiencies in limb movements implicating sensorimotor concerns are inherent in ASD, dementias, strokes, Parkinson's, and others. Eurhythmics-based treatment for sensorimotor deficits is not simple, and does require the clinician's full knowledge of physiologic function in order to assess with a sharp clinical eye what an observation means, and how to modify interventions for the benefit of successful progress. It also requires a well-organized, structured treatment approach that can be repeated over many sessions, until positive "learning" and change can be observed and logged. Success depends on a systematic and repetitive approach undertaken to address treatment objectives. Keywords: systematic approach; recurrent interventions.

Treatment structure—Goal: COPING

The structured approach to Eurhythmics-based music therapy treatment sessions, for any length of time, whether one-on-one or group, flows in an arch-like manner in five discrete modules entailing objectives and interventions addressing the goal, and progressing from seated slower activities, to upper-body work, to full-body energies and movements, winding down again to seated activities, as follows:

MODULE 1: BEGINNING THE SESSION, SEATED
Objective (a): breath control for reduction of anxiety

Water break

MODULE 2: SEATED
Objective (b): rhythmic upper-body organization
Objective (c): eye contact, memory, task focus, rhythmic embodiment

Water break

MODULE 3: FULL-BODY MOVEMENT GROSS-MOTOR MOVEMENTS IN AND ACROSS SPACE: UPPER-/LOWER-BODY ORGANIZATION
Objective (d): "quick response" upper-/lower-body motor-planning and coordination; rhythmic multi-tasking and movement
Objective (e): body dynamics: develop control of movement energies and flexibility
Objective (f): auditory focus and figure-ground training; continued breath control

Water break

MODULE 4: INSTRUMENTAL AND RHYTHM IMPROVISATIONS, SEATED OR MOVING. DRUMMING AND/OR VARIOUS RHYTHMIC INSTRUMENTAL AND MOVEMENT INTERACTIONS TO ADDRESS:
Objective (g): sense of self, rhythmic internalization, mirroring (imitative responses), creative self-expression (also expressive language), and task development

Water break

MODULE 5: CLOSING THE SESSION, SEATED
Objective (h): reducing energies of session; winding down of activities and return to calm; some singing, instrumental improvisations, creative invention

Water breaks are important for centering and replenishing energy while refocusing the brain. The opening and concluding modules of the structure are always in the same sequence. The interim modules can be combined in various ways, depending on the clinician's assessment priority, session objectives for that day, and allowing for age, mood, and demeanor of client(s), session length, and other considerations. The interim modules can also be shortened to one objective, to be addressed over several consecutive sessions. This, again, is determined by the clinician, and depends on the age of participant(s), presenting problems, length of time of each session, and factors that may be impeding in-the-moment-of-session participation (i.e., feeling ill, lethargic, unwilling to cooperate, etc). Other interventions, in addition to those listed within the above modules outlined below, can be designed by the clinician, based on the interests and objectives of both the clinician and the client or group, and presented according to assessment for objectives and treatment priorities. However, regardless of the type of intervention created, treatment priorities are *always* related and relevant to *emotional* and *sensorimotor* coping skills, teaching the brain-body new options for regulating and coordinating the system, the senses, and movement. Subsumed within these predominantly physiologic areas of treatment are communication (language), cognition, various behavioral response characteristics (e.g., repetitive movements, ticks), and social skills. Objectives listed focus on ultimate attainment of a comfortable level of functional adaptation enabling also the development of ancillary abilities. The organization of the auditory system is important for attaining calming of brain and body, developing task focus and continuity with an ability to tolerate otherwise upsetting sounds, learning to apply figure-ground auditory attention, and more (Berger 2002). This treatment technique is equally effective either in group treatment or one-on-one.

Important note: The success of Eurhythmics in music-based treatment modality is predicated upon in-the-moment piano improvisation skills of the music-based clinician. Many movement interventions in this treatment protocol entail the clinician's ability to comfortably use the keyboard, preferably acoustic piano, but also an electric keyboard housing many timbral opportunities. Although the clinician's primary instrument—guitar, violin, harp, saxophone, flute, or any other—certainly can be employed throughout a session, the multi-timbres, impactful dynamics, expanded register ranges, and vibrations that an acoustic piano and electric keyboard can provide (i.e., a keyboard able to regulate dynamics and timbres) offer the best natural sonic resource to yield physiological and emotional reactions, auditory discrimination skills, and body dynamics. What's more, clinicians are encouraged to participate in some Dalcroze Eurhythmics training classes themselves, in order to gain first-hand insight into the philosophy and activities of Eurhythmics that can be further adapted into one's own clinical work.

We now look at the clinical approach in detail beginning with Module 1.

Module 1—Beginning the session, seated

Objective (a): breath control for reduction of anxiety

In Chapter 4, we read about Jaques-Dalcroze's belief that *relaxation* was the ultimate requirement in support of the body and of movement, and that *breathing*—one of the body's major natural rhythmic activities—was fundamental in obtaining relaxation! As we know, yoga and like relaxation techniques begin with breathing exercises to relax the mind-body and attain inner focus. Since the primary goal of Eurhythmics in treatment is to derive a comfort zone for COPING, the opening interventions first seek to calm the amygdala, the HPA axis and nervous system, and to move the system away from recurrent survival-anxiety fight-or-flight demeanor. Intervening with breathing exercises, in various rhythmic patterns, can induce deeper breathing, breath control, inner focus, some self-awareness, and calmness. So, Eurhythmics-based sessions begin with breathing exercises appropriate for all ages, including adults. The recorder instrument is used for this purpose. This is more practical than asking a client to simply inhale/exhale, especially a very young client, since that task is often not fully comprehended, or may not be readily available. Therefore, breathing in certain ways into an instrument that produces sound and provides the brain with sensory information (the sense of taste often enters the picture here), is prescribed for this intervention. Each participant owns his or her recorder, which also can serve as a psychological "transitional object" (each client entering and leaving a session carries his or her recorder—a personal possession providing a sense of safety and comfort in anticipation of the upcoming session). The clinician supports the task by blowing his or her own recorder, jointly with the client, or by accompanying on a keyboard or other instruments. Playing recorder with the client provides the opportunity for the client to observe how to blow, and to imitate rhythm-patterns, while sustaining the metronomic pulse of 60 beats per minutes (bpm). Resting heart rate is between 60 and 80 bpm, (sometimes a bit higher in younger children), so the 60 beats per minute (bpm) pace serves well to attain calming or slowing down of a fast-paced, hyperactive system. Reasons for opening the session with the blowing of a recorder are multi-faceted:

- Many clients either cannot, or do not like, to emit vocal sounds in breathing exercises, so the recorder assumes that role.

- The recorder provides acoustic and sensory feedback—feed-forward—aiding the participant's brain and body to focus while "hearing" the breathing, along with sensing the breath and sound physiologically within the body.

- The continual inhale-exhale while hearing/sensing the results tends to distract and redirect anxious energies toward a calmer state.

- A mouth instrument, such as recorder, harmonica, flute, or whistle, brings both arms to center; the tongue is also centered, mouth and lips pursed surrounding the mouthpiece, and the eyes tend to focus front. (OT uses whistles and other blown items, for similar reasons.)

- Blowing a recorder in designated rhythmic patterns addresses cognition, memory, and organized breath articulation (a language requirement, since we speak on the exhale).

- Opening recorder instrumental activity provides a positive music-making interaction between clinician and client who duet, either both on recorder or with the clinician's instrumental accompaniment paralleling and supporting the activity.

Furthermore, the use of the recorder at the opening of a session brings eyes forward, helps instill a sense of task focus and purpose, and provides the first success-oriented duet participation, placing both client and clinician on a somewhat equal level in music-making. (In other words, it's not "you do this" but "let's both do this together.") What's more, the client will "synchronize" his or her behavior with that of the clinician, both in movement (e.g., head-bobbing the pulse) and manner of blowing. This opening intervention serves as the "Hello" module music-based clinicians are used to undertaking, although a song is not sung, for several reasons. Often, in my practice, it was observed that clients with absolute pitch or other auditory function would become immediately agitated by the sounds of the voice and singing—at least at the very beginning of sessions! Reasons for this are not always forthcoming. Perhaps the client is unable to tolerate a particular vocal timbre or sung pitches, or the clinician may have been singing too loud, or in "the wrong key," depending on what the client's ears were accustomed to hearing. Maybe the client simply did not like the particular voice! Whatever the reasons, client(s) can become instantly hyper-stimulated, defeating the purpose of the intervention. Thus, the use of the recorder is preferable as a welcoming multi-purpose activity. The recorder register recommended is the soprano, although in some cases, an alto recorder may be better, depending on the clinician's assessment of a client's auditory processing of higher or lower registers. Moreover, an alto recorder could be used in order to provide a deeper vibrational massage for the participant, since lower pitches have broader frequency spectrums, and at times are sensed better by persons with sensory issues. In a younger or smaller client, the alto is less practical because it is too large or heavy, so the soprano is preferable. The choice is up to the clinician and client.

INTERVENTION 1: BLOWING LONG TONES (60 BPM METRONOME)

In this first exercise, the client holds the recorder by encircling the upper part of the instrument with the left hand, and the lower part with the right. This supports the instrument at vertical mid-line, in front of the body. No fingering is involved, although if the client has experience fingering pitches, it can be included. (Several of my cases enjoyed fingering some tones while undertaking this exercise.) The blowing begins with *a deep inhalation,* followed by a *slow exhalation,* lips pursed around the mouthpiece to render a lo-o-o-o-o-o-o-ng sustained tone from the recorder. Musically it is equivalent to holding the tone the length of two-tied whole notes, for a total eight counts in one breath. The pulse is set to the tempo of 60 beats per minute (bpm), and the clinician audibly counts the numbers aloud if he or she is not joining in the playing. The counts can be done by the clinician's fingers indicating the counts, or by nodding or tapping the counts in tempo. If a keyboard with pre-programmed rhythm-patterns is available, it is strongly recommended that a simple *patterned* rhythm be selected, such as three quarter-notes followed by two 8th-notes (♩♩♩♫) in order to keep the brain focused on the pulse, rather than hearing just a tick-tock of a metronome that the brain will tune out. A simple rhythmic pattern will drive the pulse and sustain the brain's interest. The intervention of four 8-count slow exhales is as follows: Take a deep breath, then slowly exhale into the recorder—**one** (2–3–4–5–6–7–8) inhale-slow exhale **two** (2–3–4–5–6–7–8) inhale-slow exhale **three** (2–3–4–5–6–7–8) inhale-slow exhale **four** (2–3–4–5–6–7–8)—rest—sip water—repeat, three more times. That is the requirement of this endeavor, although I have had some cases that could sustain for as long as ten or more counts, while others could barely blow one short blurt, and could only execute interventions once. In some instances, depending on the age and capacity of the client, the exhalation will be short and clipped, perhaps sustained for only three to five counts, but through repetition over several sessions, this does get better. Clinicians will also encounter some clients who simply cannot, or do not, "blow." Nonetheless, the activity is continued to be presented, regardless of ability and success.

After four (4) consecutive 8-counts long tones have been rendered, a one-minute rest and sip of water ensues, as indicated above, and the exercise begins again for *up to* three repetitions (maximum). Progress in this activity can easily be followed with a rating scale tracking the number of counts for which a tone was held, at each of the repeated exercises of four long-tone exhales (see Appendix 1a for a sample tracking log). The successful sustaining of an 8-count slow exhalation can indicate that there is a level of self-awareness and breathing controllability taking place (motor-planning for pacing inhale/exhale). Task difficulties can signal deficits that may require further intervention.

CASE EXAMPLE 1

Arnold, a spectrum-diagnosed high functioning, verbal 26-year-old with whom I've worked since he was an 11-year-old school boy, has progressed from standard "treatment" to piano study as treatment. With perfect pitch and acute sense of musical logic, he now plays Bach, Schubert, various Sonatinas, and show tunes. However, Arnold continues to be riddled with survival-anxiety—outright "fear" behaviors. His parents were concerned and have him on a relaxant medication. In order to help Arnold reduce his anxieties prior to the piano lesson, I directed him to bring his recorder to lessons from then on, and that before sitting at the piano, he sits on a comfortable chair in the studio, and proceeds to blow ten very slow, long tones on the recorder, each tone to be held for as long as his slow exhale could handle. I leave the room and allow him the privacy to execute this task. When done, he calls me back, drinks about four ounces of water, and we begin the lesson. This sequence has made a huge difference in his ability then to attend to the music, focus visually, understand corrections and directives, and enjoy the encounter. In effect, he experiences a stress-free lesson, even when corrections might agitate him. He COPES! As a result of this successful opening intervention, Arnold was asked to do this breathing activity three times a day, at home: once in the morning after breakfast, once prior to beginning his piano practice, and once again in the evening sometime between the completion of dinner and bedtime. Although "self-report" and anecdotal information are not considered "science," the validity of parental observations of the "before and after" relative to this prescription of breathing exercises is compelling. According to his parents, Arnold's stress levels seemed to be lessened and longer lasting as a result of this breathing exercise. The sound of his recorder intrigues Arnold, and with the breathing and sipping of water, his anxiety demeanor subsides. He has been able to practice for two to three hours non-stop! And, it seems that the psychotropic medication was reduced.

Whether or not this sample case is "scientific proof" of the impact of the breathing task is incidental to the fact that this person was, indeed, *calmer* as a direct result of the exercise, as observed in the piano lesson that followed.

In all clients who were required to undertake this particular breathing activity in treatment, and in my own empirical research that included measuring heart rate along with successful task performance (see Berger 2012), similar results of increased breath control and calm were indicated. Furthermore, interventions for other issues were able to be undertaken more easily and with focus, after this opening activity. Of course some clients could barely blow one short tone, let alone four consecutive long tones, break, repeat. Others could blow many more and longer tones, break, repeat. My research project (Berger 2012), indicated, anecdotally, that the research subjects with the least expressive language ability also presented with the least ability to blow the recorder. Although this information was not sought after in the designated empirical study, it was rather an interesting side note, and does beg for further future investigation.

Clinicians will encounter clients of any age who have never been able to blow. Parents and aides of many participants I encountered would inform me that the client "does not blow," meaning, does not know how to purse the lips, inhale, and exhale to blow out a candle or understand the idea, have never blown, and would probably not blow the recorder. In any case, I continued to present this stimulus, and would prompt by closing the client's hands around the recorder, or myself holding it, or asking the parent or aide to hold the recorder to the mouth of the client, while I blew into mine, intermittently singing or saying "blow—blow—blow for me" (to the "Row Your Boat" tune). The parent or aide also had a recorder, and undertook the activity along with us. The natural instinct to move the tongue, to taste the object and suck, and so on becomes activated in this task, and because the recorder is near the natural breathing movement of the client, suddenly a tone comes out! We shriek with excitement, applaud the client, and encourage another try. In the excitement, the brain, being a curious organ, seeks repetition. More "accidental" tones are sounded. After many sessions, and homework requiring the presentation of the recorder several times throughout a day, eventually the brain is "taught" the action of blowing. One parent once came to a session screaming that their child could, for the first time, blow out her birthday candles when the parent began to sing the intervention song (Blow-blow, etc.)! This occurred again with a 42-year-old woman with ASD who never, in her life, could blow, and the mother came to her session excited that Vanna suddenly could blow!

As for clients for whom "blowing" is not especially an issue, the clinician's observations of results can determine the length and number of repetitions of this activity, how many times to do and break for rest and water, and so on. This is individual, depending on the case. In most instances, or after the opening long-tones exercise is either omitted altogether, or has concluded, the next objectives are undertaken, proceeding to *patterned* breathing.

INTERVENTION 2: RHYTHMIC BREATH CONTROL (60 BPM METRONOME)

Expressive language is about rhythmically patterned syllables and oral-motor-planning. Laughter, for instance, is a patterned exhalation "ha—ha—ha." Asking "why?" is often a longer exhalation, or saying "I don't know" in one breath. Blowing rhythmic patterns on the recorder can involve oral-motor activity, such as the tongue depressing against the mouthpiece to produce "toot—toot—toot," interrupting exhalations. This can also assist in language development later. Thus, while calming the system through breath control it is advantageous to continue blowing with a rhythmic pattern task:

4/4 ♩ ♩ ♩ ♩ ♩ ♩ ♩ ♩ (continue to half-notes)
   1 2 3 4 5 6 7 8

Two consecutive lines played four times through non-stop. Rest, water break, begin again

This pattern entails eight (8) shorter tones, each the length of a quarter-note, one count each, followed by four (4) longer tones, each the length of a half-note, two counts each. This two-line, four-measure rhythmic phrase (in 4/4 time) is played four times through, non-stop, totaling a 16-measure phrase, occupying one minute four seconds of session time (64 seconds at 60 bpm). The short quarter-notes are best blown as if saying "toot—toot" or "too—too," pulsing the tongue against the mouthpiece along with the exhale (as if spitting into the mouthpiece). Not all clients will understand to do this, but when possible, it is preferable in order to obtain clipped (staccato) short notes.

After the 16-measure phrase is completed, participant breaks for one minute, sips water, and begins again. The full exercise of 16 measures is repeated another three times, for a total of four 16-measure repetitions, totaling approximately eight or more minutes of session time. Depending on the ability of the client to execute this exercise, the clinician will role model the task with the client, playing exactly the same thing, offering the client the opportunity to observe and "imitate" (mirror) the task by seeing-hearing the other's face, demeanor, and recorder blowing. The clinician can accompany on piano or another tonal instrument, playing the same rhythmic blowing pattern. Sometimes a familiar tune can support this pattern. A tune like "Frere Jacques," which reaches a semi-cadence in the eighth measure, can reinforce the task creating a sense of "anticipation," as long as the clinician can replicate the actual blowing rhythm-pattern in some manner, perhaps with left-hand chords, so that the client's auditory system will hear the pattern supporting and imitating the blowing. This pattern can also be performed as a round, one person beginning and the other entering eight counts later, further inducing and supporting imitation, attention, and focus. In some instances, as a developmental activity, this pattern can change to eight (8) short toots followed by two long whole notes (four counts each), reinforcing the long-tone exhale of the previous exercise. Some clients may exhale more quickly (less controlled); others may be able to sustain tones longer than required; still others may not be able to undertake this activity at all. Clinical observation and interest in moving the client further along will determine the scope of this exercise.

The important thing is to continue presenting this intervention in order to continue training for breath control. The alternation between short and long tones provides an opportunity for body sensing, awareness, and controlled breathing. If a session is only 30 minutes long, the number of repetitions can be reduced to last less than eight minutes. If treatment is a group activity, repetitions can be undertaken individually (solo), in dyads, or as a full group, as a round, enabling clinicians to work within the group. Many variations for this intervention can be created, as long as the scope remains the same: patterned short-short tones alternating with looong—looong tones. At the conclusion of this variation, there is also a longer rest break and sipping of water to replenish brain and body energies while the clinician logs the results.

CASE EXAMPLE 2

Ronald came to me when he was nine years old, diagnosed ASD, with many sensory issues, limited to no expressive language, quiet, anxious though silent, with low muscle tone, but very compliant. He enjoyed listening to music preferring that I "entertain" him rather than he join in making music with me. We began each session, as per my usual protocol, with breath control, especially to assist with language development as well as COPING. From the start of the session it soon became clear that Ronald could either not understand, or undertake (motor plan) the blowing of long tones! For the first time, his mother noted this inability, much to her surprise, since no other clinician (in his private school for special needs students) ever detected this problem, not even his speech pathologist. We began the exercise by having Ronald just blow into the recorder, so that I could assess what he *was* able to do, but shortly after he began, I took my recorder and began to blow in a rhythmic manner—tone—tone—tone—just quarter-note tones in a gasping manner, for an unmeasured amount of times—perhaps six or seven tones, break, sip water, repeat. Meanwhile, since I was also playing almost right to his face, he looked at me as he blew, and soon was "mirroring" (copying) my playing, which was blow—stop—blow—stop—blow-blow-blow—stop. This rather unstructured manner kept Ronald focused, aware, and wanting to imitate. Since Ronald could not sustain long tones, I omitted that opening module and continued toward the patterned quarter-notes to half-notes as indicated above. Well, Ronald tried his best, but his motor plan for long notes was not available. He would inhale deeply, but exhale quickly, so there was a beep on the recorder. Rhythmically, he seemed to understand what I was asking for, so he blew the eight quarter-notes correctly, in pulse, but for the half-notes he blew, followed with a rest (for the quarter beat), blew again followed by a rest, the required four notes, but instead of half-notes, they were quarter-rest-quarter-rest, and so on. But there was a bonus in this event, because Ronald began to hum a tone as he blew the recorder. This occurrence led to many future repetitions of this pattern, both blowing the recorder, and adding the variation of singing the tones in quarter- and half-note rhythm. Once we began to add the vocal portion, it resulted not only in Ronald's brain recognizing what it had to do regarding inhale/exhale for the task, but also for talking! Now his verbal responses were not just short "yes," "no," but began to include longer words ("maybe," "I don't want this," etc.) requiring slower controlled exhalations. Progress has taken several years of repeating this breathing task, and many variations that included movement. This exercise was also included as homework with the recorder, to begin to obtain longer tones (some dotted quarter, rest), and only recently has Ronald been able to produce the full half-note exhale, as well as a half-note vocal tone. Meanwhile, his expressive language has increased, and his speech pathologist begins her sessions with him also with the recorder, for breath regulation.

In subsequent weeks of interventions, Ronald's treatment sessions included movement alternating with blowing tasks, vocalizations, and other Eurhythmic interventions that assisted in the development of his breath control and language articulation.

INTERVENTION 3: BREATHING AND THE KAZOO (NON-METERED, FREELY IMPROVISED)

The breath control calming portion of the session concludes with the kazoo. Expressive language happens on the exhale. In speaking, we inhale and exhale vocal sounds in various oral-motor and inflective ways that give semantic meaning to the sound. In clients with expressive language deficiencies, it is useful to practice various ways of exhaling *vocal* sounds. But, many clients either do not understand how to do this, are shy, have lost the ability through various traumas, or simply require some motivation to practice vocalization. The kazoo is fun and provides motivation! Placing a kazoo between the lips provides much vibration to the mouth, often stimulating lips, tongue, and oral-motor action. The kazoo also allows a bit of visual distance between self and other (as did the recorder), so vocal improvisations are safe and easy, even when one is shy. A kazoo is not blown! One must *hum* into the instrument, using one's voice and obtaining timbral vibrations of the vocalized sounds. The kazoo is used in many Mountain Music orchestrations, since it can be easily hand made, can cover any voice quality, and requires no previous training! In the treatment session, the module segment of humming into a kazoo immediately follows the above recorder intervention segment. The clinician hums nonsense and silly sounds, highs and lows, repeated sounds, funny sound contours, animal sounds—whatever inspires the moment—and the client attempts to imitate, or create, his or her own silly sounds. This experience accomplishes several things: it secures the relaxed demeanor and further focus, creates fun, joy, and laughter, and the session is comfortably ready to continue. It encourages vocalization that might not otherwise be undertaken, at times helping to lengthen vocal cords in many diagnosed populations (such as Down Syndrome that has short or limited vocal cord flexibility, and persons with Parkinson's who also have vocal limitations). The kazoo portion involves just a few minutes of improvisatory howling and vocalizing. Only vocal expressions are applied, without instrumental accompaniment, so that the brain only hears vocal, albeit somewhat distorted, acoustic information. Sometimes, the kazoo activity serves as the "language" in a two-way kazoo-based conversation, with inflections being hummed into the kazoo as a way of "speaking" to the other in a communicative manner. In all, humming is vocal exhalation!

My clients consider this portion of the breathing exercises to be the most fun, so the kazoo becomes a sort of reward following the recorder, because of the joyful improvisatory nature of the activity. But with each client, the *objective of breath control* still prevails, and at times, the humming into a kazoo would be patterned similarly to the recorder task, or just humming long hums in various vocal registers, to further practice controlled inhale/exhale for reduction of anxiety and increase of language development.

Summary

Breath-control interventions serve any and all diagnoses and age groups, from toddlers to geriatric adults, regardless of diagnoses or medical issues. For ASD in particular, by now the reader is fully aware that the major goal in the application of Eurhythmics-based sensorimotor treatment, beginning with breath control, is to develop coping skills by focusing on major issues that appear to impede the development of such functional abilities. This means focusing treatment for regulation of emotion, physiology, and sensory components contributing to anxiety and stress. Training the brain and body to *breathe* in various controlled (rhythmic) ways not only can result in a calmer amygdala and HPA axis and muscular relaxation, it can also address expressive language issues, focus, upper-body and oral-motor-planning and movement, and more. Opening of the treatment sessions presents three inhale/exhale and vocalizing exercises, employing the soprano recorder and kazoo, two instruments that provide safe, unselfconscious, fun ways of addressing this need to calm the system through structured breathing. The work relies on the clinician's improvisatory-supportive piano skills and knowledge of sensory systems, Eurhythmics, and music-based clinical approaches to treating emotional, physiologic, sensory, and movement concerns. After the first eight to ten minutes of these interventions, the client is re-paced to a calmer status, and the clinician can begin movement interventions addressing motor-planning, vestibular and proprioceptive "quick response" exercises, and auditory focus.

Movement stimuli will commence with upper-body activities using arms, head, and legs in seated position, progressing to full-body movement activities within the room.

A word of advice: Client *inability* to execute an intervention *should not be a deterrent in this clinical work*. The less the ability, the more these stimuli are needed. The objective is precisely to *enhance* ability, not defer to *in*ability, even if the client is wheelchair bound with very limited mobility. The music-based clinician is willing and able to present an intervention with the understanding that in some manner physical hands-on prompting of the client may be required, and is appropriate, of course with the client's consent. When available, an aide or caregiver can be asked to assist with prompting or role modeling, which could also carry over as homework when at home or in school.

Another note of caution is that "progress" is not immediate. It may take many, many sessions before progress can be observed and documented. This also should not be a deterrent to continued presentation of this intervention. For the most part, the repetition of this breath-control module can be an anticipated and expected part of the clinical routine, after which the client is relaxed and better settled into the session.

Final note: Recorders should be authentic "instruments," not toys, because accurate pitch is important for auditory development (ear training), and especially to avoid distress in participants with absolute pitch. Toy recorders are rarely correctly pitched. I have had success with the Yamaha plastic recorders, but I do not suggest any particular brand, other than that it be a real instrument. In addition, a plastic instrument serves best because it can retain correct pitch, and is easier to keep clean than a wooden instrument. Keeping this in mind, we move forward to the movement modules of the treatment session.

CHAPTER 6

Sensory Organization Through Quick Response Movement

The human body is a machine which winds its own springs.

Julien Offroy de la Mettrie, *L'Homme Machin*

To Julien Offroy de la Mettrie (1709–1751), a French philosopher and medical man of the eighteenth century, quoted above, man was a machine that worked as the result of mental thoughts depending on bodily actions. He believed that mental processes were caused by the body, and expressed these thoughts in his work, *Man a Machine*, in which he upholds that humans worked like machines (Wellman 1992). This theory somewhat reflects Descartes and the philosophy that the mind and body were separate entities, with the human body working as a machine (Brett King, Viney and Woody, 2009). La Mettrie believed that humans and animals were different only in regards to the complexity by which matter is organized. The idea that essentially no real difference exists between humans and animals was based on his findings that sensory feelings were present in animals and plants (Brennan 2003). While La Mettrie's ideas may possibly be accurate, we know that human emotions find greater forms of expression beyond those of animals and plants. Humans not only "bark," humans create and communicate with "barking" music and arts!

I begin this chapter with Julien Offroy de la Mettrie to underline two thoughts as we continue to investigate music-based treatment and body expression. First, at the risk of sounding reductionist, I concur that indeed, humans and animals share physiologic functions based on sensory input, and that the human being is, in a sense, a physiologic "machine" capable of "winding its own springs," in a most efficient, "engineering" sense. Second, those *wound springs* of humans result from *intuitive emotions* (bottom-up) and ensuing recognition of those emotions, referred to as "feelings" (top-down), as discussed in earlier chapters. We keep those ideas in the forefront of our thoughts as we work with rhythm and acoustic stimuli to reorder sensory collaboration, emotion, and body movement's driving "quick response" (motor-planning), wherein reside instinct, emotions, and subsequent feeling sensations, in the sequence suggested in the Prelude of this book:

sensory stimulus—context—perception—emotion—response

When addressing sensory issues and body movement in ASD and other populations, we recognize that body movement reflects instinctive sensations, coupled with earlier movements logged through observation, imitation, and continual rehearsal (e.g., as in learning to walk). Body sensations are derived from sensory feedback to the brain, that then sends feedforward response requirements to the body. The human machine is equipped to "wind its own springs" in order to survive, but if the winding components and springs function improperly, those mechanisms require interventions to accomplish adequate functionality. When the person feels comfortable in his or her body, and learns better to assess safety from danger, survival-anxiety can subside, allowing the opening of the door to cognition and socialization (see Chapters 1 and 2). Music-movement-based treatment influences the feedback-feedforward loop. The philosophy of music-based treatment is to trust the body's machinery to automatically do its job, once suitable interventions have tried to "fix the springs." As La Mettrie suggests, the body can dictate to the mind (while the brain dictates to the body), so music-based clinicians devise interventions that address brain, body, and mind through movement regulation that will influence the "repair" of body mechanisms, including cognition and thought. Chapter 3 provided information on research related to observed movement inadequacies in ASD: rigidity and imitation "mirroring" difficulties, among other issues (see Baron-Cohen 1995; Trevarthen and Delafield-Butt 2013, among others listed).

Having completed the initial breath-control interventions for calming the system, the treatment session now proceeds to movement and improvisational interventions for further rhythmic embodiment and regulation of brain-body, limbs and head, mind and memory. As we are aware, moving the body enhances blood flow and assists with breath control, visual and auditory acuity, cognitive attention, and general centering. Movement also prepares the brain to receive information and to learn. With the motor cortex and the auditory cortex in close proximity in the neocortex, rhythmic music tends to initiate instinctive movement (e.g., foot-tapping, clapping). Essentially everything in the brain-body systems are entraining (synchronizing) with the pulsations of the music beat. Here clinicians also consider the four aspects of rhythm: pulse, pattern, pace, and persistence (repetition), and how these drive attention to the beat and the movement.

That is to say, in addition to pulse, the body detects and can understand polyrhythmic patterns within music, the pace with which the rhythms function (fast, slow, etc.), and the repetitiveness of the pulse. Eurhythmics interventions use precisely these aspects of rhythm to address and improve proprioceptive and vestibular motor-planning. Careful selection of tempos for various interventions is a key consideration. In my research, a pilot project investigating the role of *tempo-specific* rhythmic interventions for pacing and reorganizing erratic autism behaviors, results indicated a clear and definitive positive direction toward focused and controlled body responses, as long as the speed of the music intervention was at a pace with which the brain and body could comfortably entrain (see Berger 2012).

Along with extensive attention to proprioceptive and vestibular rehabilitation, accurate *auditory function* must be addressed. Because of the acoustic environment music creates, Eurhythmics-based interventions play a major role in the treatment of auditory issues, in approaches similar to "ear training." The objective of acoustic music-movement interventions is to train the auditory system to listen for specific sounds, to discriminate one sound or timbre from another, and to train for auditory depth perception and auditory figure-ground, so that the auditory system is not simply assaulted by a tsunami of sound that the brain cannot process (Berger 2002, 2013a, 2013b). This is a major reason why people on the autism or dementia spectrums display fear responses: auditory information that the brain receives is often translated as dangerous to the system. It is not about whether the sound is too loud or too soft, but rather too filled with undecipherable or unpredictable sonic information that cannot be accurately processed by the brain and rendered as *safe*. This is why, for instance, many listeners to very dissonant, seemingly uncoordinated music find the need to squirm, grimace, cover the ears, and want to leave the concert hall. The brain of those with ASD has no clue what all that "noise" is, and sets the system in motion for fight-flight! (This is also why shopping malls are so frightening to those with ASD.)

Before describing the ensuing rhythmic interventions that, in addition to sensory concerns, also seek to teach the brain how to "imitate" movement, a word about "segmentation" to shed light on the process involved in "mirroring," or imitating, an action. In ASD, theories maintain that mirror neurons are few or ineffective in the ASD brain, thus the instinct to imitate an action is basically non-existent. This is also felt to be a contributor to lack of social skills (see Baron-Cohen *et al.* 2013). In my clinical work, I have not found this to be quite the case. Rather, the inability to imitate seemed more to be due to a basic lack of *strategic planning* (memory motor plan) for copying an action, thus inhibiting the ability or desirability to imitate. Imitation is a somewhat instinctively learned process. We see and copy facial and body expressions (such as shrugs), a gait, arm movements during language expressions, and so forth, without really being "conscious" of doing so. But even as an instinct there is strategy involved in this kind of learning. Recent research into theories of "event segmentation" and "movement segmentation" tell us that the instinctive strategic process of imitating (learning) an action or movement lies within a person's ability, *intuitively*, to recall portions of observed movement from within his or her list of previously learned actions that have been coded into memory; that is, movements that have been filed in memory's *movement library* (Blasing 2015; Meier, Theodorou and Schaal 2012). The strategy of movement learning entails dividing an action into small segments, piece by piece, so that the brain instinctively recognizes familiar aspects of a movement, and adds additional new ones to that "library." After all the new pieces have been learned and combined with what was already there, it all comes together as a new "whole." It is like knitting a sweater loop by loop until the whole garment emerges. Imitation, mirroring a behavior or action, whether facial expressions, torso and limb movements, or sounds, undergoes such a segmentation learning process, adding new to the already learned and familiar. Therefore, a clinical intervention is able to "teach" a client to "imitate" an action, song, sound, movement, by providing this erudite strategy through role modeling and reducing the whole into segmented parts that can be learned, imitated, retained, and looped together once the segments are embodied. This breeds familiarity with an action or motion, and can be replicated in a "quick response" manner whenever it is called upon. In music-based clinical work this segmentation means presenting the intervention in sections, perhaps with many role modeled repetitions, or through hand-over-hand prompting, addressing the "imitation" segmentation strategy for later recall.

Module 2: Seated

Objective (b): rhythmic upper-body organization
Objective (c): eye contact, memory, task focus, rhythmic embodiment

The following interventions are effective for any age group and any diagnosis. Some factors may require a bit of modification, but in essence, all of the exercises have been applied in various ways to clients from toddlers with ASD to adults with Alzheimer's and also in psychodynamic treatment for persons with various psycho-emotional concerns (e.g., PTSD). Treatment interventions focus on addressing upper- and lower-body movements, motor learning, and auditory attention factors, through breaking down movements and sound into manageable segments requiring imitation, or prompting, in order to learn the actions that are driven by sound cues. Further along, in "quick response" actions to auditory cues and multi-tasking rhythmic movement addressing the vestibular system, proprioception, visual and auditory focus and figure-ground, and some tactile stimulation, segmentation (a breakdown) of actions may also be required in order to teach client to "mirror" (imitate) a required and acquired response.

We now continue with the second treatment stage involving arm movement sequences, in *seated* position, that help to pace arm movements, reinforce motor-planning, and retain eye contact, concentration, task focus, memory, and rhythmic embodiment. Important to note is that most of the upcoming interventions are administered predominantly *non-verbally*. Music cues and instrumental improvisations provide the directives and impetus to guide the client's responses. The body senses the energies transmitted by the music, and, with very limited verbal guidance, the client learns instinctively to respond in-kind, quickly reflecting the outgoing music energy.

The sequence of hand claps outlined below, in a repeating rondo form, is undertaken in a seated position in order to alleviate the brain's vestibular concerns of balance, for the moment. It is an intervention led non-verbally, addressing motor-planning and proprioception in arms and legs, and requires initial clinician role modeling with the client who simultaneously copies and performs the task. The clinician sits directly in front of the client, asking the client to undertake this task in tandem with clinician (imitate). In addition to assisting in developing proper motor-plan and mirroring skills, this intervention tends to yield excellent eye contact, since the client is looking directly at, and visually following, clinician movements that secure the accuracy and memory retention of sequence. The clinician does not ask for eye contact. This is inferred and is automatic, regardless of the age of the client. Motor-planning segments required in this intervention include, among many, knowing where the arms are (proprioception), how and how high to lift, how far to open and close for arms to meet at center and sustain pulse, whether hands should be open or clenched, where the thighs are, lifting legs alternately, and much more. Once again the tempo is set to 60 bpm, with a recurrent simple rhythmic pattern sounding from a pre-programmed keyboard or other rhythm device (other than a metronome!), to keep the brain interested. Claps are quarter-note pulsations throughout, without pattern. Attaining entrainment is an important purpose of this intervention, to help pace the system physiologically and cognitively, in preparation for later rhythmic movement activities.

The clinician might wish to count the 8-counts aloud, when initially modeling the task. In situations with expressive language needs, the client can be asked to speak the numbered counts aloud as well. This 32-measure sequence of continuous pulsing is a mesmerizing event, of sorts, that helps to sustain the calm, focused demeanor and concentration previously attained in the breath-control interventions. The rondo-form sequence is as follows:

4/4   1   2   3   4   5   6   7   8   (60 bpm)

♩ ♩ ♩ ♩ ♩ ♩ ♩ ♩   (quarter-note beats)

1. Eight hand claps, one clap per quarter-note beat
2. Eight thigh claps with parallel arms/hands
3. Repeat 1 (hand claps)
4. Eight thigh claps alternating arms (right hand/right thigh, left hand/left thigh), for 8 counts.
5. Repeat 1 (hand claps)
6. Eight alternating foot stomps
7. Repeat 1 (hand claps)
8. Eight thigh claps crossing mid-line: right hand over left thigh; left hand over right thigh.

Total intervention: 32 measures

Rest, water, repeat

Sequence time consumes 64 seconds total (one minute, four seconds), at the 60 bpm pace. Several repetitions of this sequence are recommended, perhaps three or four times, depending on the ability of the client and other factors determined by the clinician. If a client presents with the inability to undertake this physical task, the clinician must prompt hand-over-hand to "teach" for the motor plan and pattern of the sequence. Prompting can be done in several non-threatening ways: from the front, with the clinician gently pushing along the side of the arms or hands of the client so that the hands meet at center; or from behind, with the clinician standing behind the seated client, lightly embracing around the upper arms (as if hugging from behind), and enveloping the arms and hands to assist throughout the entire sequence. When undertaking this intervention, the clinician might "sing" lyrics describing the actions, reinforcing the segmentation process for sequence recall and continuity. When a client's recall of the sequence becomes secure, the clinician can forgo role modeling or prompting, and instead play a percussion instrument to provide stimulating *counter-rhythmic* patterns accompanying the client's pulsing. This maintains the client's attention and interest while also helping to further sustain the pace and pulse.

CASE EXAMPLE 3

In my research study, one of the subjects, a young girl with many physical inabilities, limp arms, low muscle tone, and erratic and uncontrolled arm and hand movements, was presented with this task. Her aide immediately informed me that the girl would be totally incapable of performing this activity, and urged me to suspend it and move on. Instead, I insisted we try, if only once through. I selected a pre-recorded, ongoing simple rhythmic pattern on the electric keyboard, in 4/4 meter, 60 bpm, in which each measure concluded with the sound of a hand clap (i.e., three quarter-notes ending with a quarter-beat clap). The young girl became immediately attentive to the "music" and I proceeded to prompt her clapping while her aide sat directly in front of her role modeling the exercise. Within the fifth hand clap of the first eight claps the girl withdrew her hands from my prompting, and began trying to clap by herself! But one hand kept missing the other, so instead of connecting in a clap, the hands crossed each other. However, the pulse of the movement was exactly on time! She continued trying to clap, maintaining the open-and-close motion of her arms in time with the pulse. The next part, clapping thighs, was simpler, since it did not involve arriving at mid-line. The mid-line and visual deficit, along with the motor-planning problem, were clearly evident. I asked her aide to continue prompting while I undertook the role modeling. By the fourth repetition of this entire sequence, the young girl was able to clap her hands at least five out of eight claps, much to the surprise of the aide. By the culmination of the research, eight weeks later, this child was fully capable of clapping the entire sequence in tandem with the aide. In my observation, it served to indicate her newly acquired ability to coordinate, motor plan, and organize the structured arm movements. By the time the research concluded after eight weeks of trials, this development carried over into her ability to hold a writing implement, and other hand and arm activities her OT was presenting, who determined that the progress resulted, in part, by the intervention that improved her mid-line orientation, proprioception and visual capacity to see her arms in order to better control her arm movements.

This intervention was also presented to several clients with Rett's Syndrome (not research-related), who, after many sessions, were becoming somewhat able to control some of their involuntary hand-clasping movements, and to temporarily redirect the stereotypic repetitive hand wringing common in Rett's Syndrome. This intervention was taught through hand-over-hand prompting, but after many sessions, clients usually attempted to clap without assistance. The parent in attendance was encouraged to repeat the intervention at home several times a day. The sequence takes a little over one minute of continuous participation, leaving little time or room for deviation. In my practice, I have never encountered the situation in which the client attempted to abort the task before completion. In addition to addressing the focus of objective (b), that is controlled, organized motor-planning and movement, this hand-clapping sequence derives progress in achieving objective (c), the continuous eye contact, memory of sequence, and task attention resulting from the intense nature of the required need for concentration and focus.

Transitions

Upon the completion of this session module, a brief interim activity serves as a transition to Modules 3 and 4 of the session—modules of full-body rhythmic movements for "quick responses" and sensory collaboration to increase motoric flexibility, body dynamics, and auditory processing skills. Various transitory activities can be developed based on ages, in-the-moment objectives, and the interests of the clinician and client, and always with the continued objective of obtaining "quick response" in motor-planning (proprioception and vestibular senses), auditory attention, and movement flexibility (enhancement of body dynamics). Below are several sample transitory activities that have served well in my clinical work:

Trampoline bounces

This transition works well with young persons from toddlers to early adolescents. Jumping is undertaken with the client holding (heavy) maracas, face down at the side of each leg, during jumps. The participant stands on a small mat awaiting a jump cue from the piano. Only after the "jump on" music cue is rendered will the participant jump onto the trampoline. Once on the trampoline, the client jumps as long as the music is playing. Upon hearing the music cease followed by the "jump off" sound cue from the piano, the client will quickly stop and jump off the trampoline, returning to the designated mat to wait again for the "jump on" sound cue. This task addresses vestibular reinforcement and auditory attention. Tempo of jumps are at the client's pace while the clinician improvises on the piano, reflecting that tempo at the same pace with the client. This intervention not only supports "balance," it sonically reflects the body motion and provides rhythmic auditory feedback from both the maracas pulsing at the sides of the client's body and the emphasized rhythmic tempo and beats heard in the piano's improvisation. This is entirely a *non-verbal* centering activity. Directions are given verbally only the very first time the intervention is presented, informing what the sound cue commands mean, and what will be the body's response.

Rest, water

Although many ASD clients undergo OT treatment involving trampoline and vestibular reinforcement, this music-based rhythmic intervention reaches a bit further, providing auditory feedback reinforcing vestibular activity. Remember that the vestibular system mechanisms are in the inner ear and depend on various head positions (see Berger 2002; Schneck and Berger 2006). Stimulating both sides of the inner auditory and vestibular ear canals can assist in securing and reinforcing corrective maneuvers for maintaining balance, also helping the head remain stable in an upward position. In addition, the anticipatory (attention) state of waiting to hear a musical cue has been observed to increase the speed of motor-planning for "quick response" commands by the cue: jumping off immediately, jumping on quickly, stopping (freezing on the trampoline), or continuing the jump while awaiting the music to cease and cue. In addition, the tempo and pulse support from the piano helps the client's rhythmic entrainment, further facilitating movement organization. Depending on the client's abilities and the clinician's developmental objectives, sometimes jump speeds can be "played with," altered to include faster music inducing quicker jumps, or slower pacing for jump and stop, jump and stop, reinforcing motor-planning and control. Since vestibular and auditory control are addressed in this intervention, it is effective for the music to vary jumping tempos from time to time, if only to keep the brain attending.

The transitory trampoline intervention need not take long, depending on the interest and energy of the client. The playfulness of this activity, the curiosity of not quite knowing when the cues will occur, and which actions will be required, the centering impact, and the fun of jumping, often can be desired by the participant (especially younger ones) for a longer time than necessary. Whatever the length (and in some sessions it might take longer than in others), the clinician will "cue" the conclusion, perhaps with a designated chord or glissando, the maracas will be stored, the trampoline removed, and water sipped by the client. **Note:** If a client is very young, is physically incapacitated, has difficulty jumping, or is laden with various paralyses, this activity can still be undertaken! I have presented this intervention by having the client seated on the trampoline, supported by caretaker, aide, or myself, who mounts the trampoline and does the jumping so that the client can bodily sense the rhythmic pulsations of a jump! In several cases this has led to the client trying to move (from the buttocks upward) in an effort to "jump," or bob back and forth, or side to side in rhythm. For a younger child who has mobility but as yet not the balance or knowledge of jumping, I ask the child to step onto (pretend jump) the trampoline, along with the caregiver or aide, who stands either in front or behind the child, holding onto hands, arms, or shoulders, jumping with/for the child. Other ways of physically supporting the child for jumps could be having the child stand leaning toward the caretaker/aide, the adult participant jumping as the child senses the movement and bounces. This eventually leads the child's brain to develop the jumping motor plan, which is quite complex. In short, nothing should deter the clinician from providing this fun transitory activity that supports vestibular and auditory processing.

You're a mirror, I'm a mirror

For any age, this transitory intervention addresses imitation, and can be done in silence, or with slow background music (CD or pre-programmed keyboard). The client is the "mirror", and the clinician looks into "mirror," and moves in various ways, including arms, head, high and low body levels, facial grimaces, and more. The client is to *simultaneously* "reflect back" the movements and facial expressions. The clinician is aware of segmentation, so that movements are not long and continuous, but rather slow, with pauses to give the client's information-processing speed a chance to absorb the information. After a few minutes, the role of "mirror" changes so that the clinician is now the mirror, with the client moving in various manners while seeing the "mirror" imitate. This short intervention accomplishes several objectives: eye contact, imitation, motor control, balance (if the activity is done in a standing position), and imagination. Scarves can be used in this exercise, and if imitation is a bit problematic, clinician and client can each hold one end of a scarf and "imitate" simultaneously one or the other's motions. (Do not have or use an real mirror since that would defeat the purpose of the activity.)

Relax, sip water

Another transition activity addressing body dynamics and creative imagine, for any age and diagnosis, follows:

A walk in the park

A transitory intervention is especially important for clients aged from childhood (age eight and up) to senior adults with ASD, Alzheimer's, psycho-emotional issues, ADHD, and others. Since objectives of Modules 3 and 4 involve spatial orientation, movement flexibility, and more, this transitory intervention includes guided movement imagery with piano improvisation. This intervention previews the more structured, upcoming movement activities, and aids imaging and less concrete thinking. The client is asked to imagine that the room is a lovely park, with a stream and a lake, birds in the trees, white clouds in the sky, and grassy and sandy areas beneath the feet. The clinician improvises slow, flowing, arrhythmic music (Debussy-like), and the client is invited to take a walk around the park. This continues for two to three minutes, when the music beings to change, becoming faster and a bit more intense; the clinician suggests the client imagines the presence of strong winds beginning to blow, the sky darkening, and the possibility of rain. This imagery can influence changes in movement dynamics, for example, stronger movements against the wind, different movements in sand rather than grass, head bowed if it's raining, and so on. After a minute, the music again begins to calm, and the "day" becomes lovely again. Movements are freely interpreted, using any space in and around the room, in any manner conceived by the participant. The walk concludes when the client "arrives home," the music reaching its final cadence.

Relax, sip water

The primary purpose of imagery interventions is to provide an opportunity for a client to sense and control his or her body in movement, motor plan dynamic changes of movement energies, use imagery to influence movement that parallels the energies heard in the piano improvisation, and control vestibular, auditory, visual and spatial perceptions through imagery—the "top-down" component of instinct. The image "script" described above is a sample of one of a myriad of possibilities, but always with the same objective in focus: attaining flexibility in body dynamics, imagining movement, and calling forth appropriate motor plans to reflect imagined scenarios. The clinician will know what types of images are best, based on assessed movement objectives, that is, the kinds of body dynamics being sought. It is the beginning of further body dynamics training to derive movement flexibility, replacing the pervasive stiffness and repetitive stereotypic movements in arms, legs, and head with new possibilities. Clients with ASD, in particular, have difficulty imagining abstract concepts due to their more concrete thought processes, therefore this short transitional exercise can help open the mind to new ideas. Any client—of any age, even with a walker or wheelchair—is encouraged to image walking movements, using support equipment in creative ways (e.g., twirling the walker, sway in the wheelchair, and other inventive ways to "walk in the park"). Many parts of the body move, in many directions. Movement *dis*abilities are not movement *in*abilities, even if physical prompting is required. The above suggested transition tasks preview the next session module.

Module 3: Fully-body movement gross-motor movements in and across space: Upper-/Lower-body organization

Objective (d): "quick response": upper-/lower-body motor-planning and coordination; rhythmic multi-tasking and movement
Objective (e): body dynamics: develop control of movement energies and flexibility
Objective (f): auditory focus and figure-ground training; continued breath control

Jaques-Dalcroze approached the teaching of movement and its reflection of music to even the earliest childhood (later followed into adult training as well) with "the automatic exercise of marching, for marching is the natural model of time measure" (Jaques-Dalcroze 2010a, p.17). He describes his approach as follows:

> By means of various accentuations with the foot, I teach the different time measures. Pauses (of varying lengths) in the marching teach the children to distinguish durations of sound; movements in time with the arms and the head preserve order in the succession of the time measures and analyze the bars and pauses. (p.17)

To the musician, this concept makes perfect sense. To the music-based clinician, this approach makes even more sense, because the objectives of entrainment and embodiment of rhythm are to organize sensory and physiologic function, and instinctive motor-planning and body dynamics, in order to derive functional movement and behavior.

Movement cues for quick response and auditory attention

Most Eurhythmic interventions for music-based treatments are non-verbal, other than the initial directives defining the meanings of the music cues and their required responses. The following movements are directed solely by sound cues:

- **moving forward:** verbal directive to begin moving either clockwise or counterclockwise around a circle: *music cue*—march music begins at 60 bpm
- **turn around and move in the other direction** (depending on which direction the activity moved, move the other way): *music cue*—(e.g. 2-note trill, upper register)
- **stop (freeze) go:** *music cue*—music stops, then continues
- **fall down** (meaning body goes down onto floor): *music cue*—glissando, high to low
- **stand up (rising from the floor):** *music cue*—glissando, low to high
- **march backward:** *music cue*—middle C played as four quarter-notes (or any other type of cue clinician prefers)
- **feet only:** *music cue*—left-hand music only, lower register

- **hands only:** *music cue*—right-hand music only, upper register
- **change tambourine hand—hold in other hand:** *sound cue*—clinician rattles a tambourine as march continues, indicating instrument to be switched to other hand
- **movement changes from march to gallop, skip, run, jump:** *music cue only*—music patterns change from 4/4 march to 6/8 gallop (quarter followed by 8th note), or 4/4 skipping (dotted quarter followed by 8th note), or running pattern (fast 8th or 16th), or staccato chords to indicate jumps.

Any of the above cues are sounded at random, interrupting an ongoing movement, to facilitate auditory attention, focus, and instant response. Obviously not all cues will be memorized in one session. The first few times that this intervention is presented, the clinician may call out, or sing, the instruction accompanying the cue, but this is eventually extinguished so that only the music provides the direction. And of course the clinician must also remember what the cues mean, because these do not change, and are repeated in the same manner, once they have been set.

The march—with tambourine in hand

Tempo for the marching "game" is again at 60 bpm, rather than the usual 120 bpm marching tempo, because a faster speed might inhibit the brain's ability to come up with prompt motor-planning responses. (I refer to this as a "game" which tends to be more entertaining to many young clients.) The objective is for the client to *hear* and *quickly respond* to the various music cues, as outlined above, calling for precise actions. The tempo can be increased gradually, at a later time, depending on client ability and intervention progress, but at first, the slower tempo allows the brain and muscular systems time to "think and do" while sustaining a steady march beat. Keep in mind that "information processing" in many diagnoses can be slower than in "typical" populations.

THE MOVEMENT

The client holds a tambourine (or Tom Boy 6" hand drum) in his or her hand, one hand securing the tambourine, the other tapping the instrument. This will later alternate upon hearing the cue to change hands. The marching activity is done with the tambourine simultaneously being clapped to the beat of the marching feet, in time with the music. This multi-tasking movement is very articulate, with each leg's knee bending and being raised upward (high, if possible) toward the chest (soldier-like), so that when the leg descends there is a firm accent on the floor. The piano, or keyboard, plays a march, with a pre-programmed march drum pattern (when electronically available) accompanying in the background, to support the beat. Actual march tunes can be used, such as "Yankee Doodle," "The Ants Go Marching (When Johnny Comes Marching Home)," or other tunes preferred and requested by client, all at 60 bpm. The more familiar the tune, the more entrained the system can become to the pulse and tempo of the march. The client is constantly vigilant awaiting the "cue" for further action. If the marching action and tambourine tapping are uncoordinated, that is, if arms and legs cannot rhythmically coordinate to pulse simultaneously, this intervention can be first undertaken in a *seated position*, with the legs being physically prompted by the clinician as the client taps the tambourine. This helps to "teach" the motor-planning required for coordination of the upper/lower body. This, then, is followed by standing up and performing the actual march movement in space, motorically. If the client still displays upper-/lower-body coordination difficulty, the clinician, caregiver, or aide will role model, marching alongside the client, or in front facing the client and moving backward as the client moves forward. This induces an *imitation* of the motions involved. For some, it may take many such repetitions, over many sessions, before the activity "clicks in." In the situation of the client being unable to fully execute this intervention, a limited number of cues can still be effective: the *stop and go, change tambourine hand, fall down and rise up*, and *turn around and move in the other direction*. If the clinician is role modeling or prompting, a whistle or other manner of sound "cueing" can be temporarily substituted for those listed above, unless a second person can role model so that the clinician continues to play keyboard. If an electric keyboard with pre-recorded songs is available, a march can be rendered to free the clinician for the purpose of prompting, as long as the tempo can be programmed at 60 bpm. For my research project (Berger 2012), as well as various client sessions, I have been able to do this, although cueing still required my reaching for keyboard tones.

When the clinician does not have to role model or prompt, the clinician is at the piano or keyboard playing a march, and will randomly render a cue, for instance a high frequency trill, indicating "turn and march in the other direction." The cue is given at any *unexpected* time, and not at the end of a phrase or song, so that it is always *a surprise* element. All of the cues listed above are rendered at varying times during the march (including the skip, gallop, run, described below), with quick responses observed and logged in order to track for progress. Some simple musical cues listed above include the trill indicating the turn around to march in the other direction (clockwise, or counterclockwise, as the case might be); glissando from high to low register, indicating "fall (or go) down"; glissando from low to high indicating "stand up"; sudden stop in the music, asking for "freeze"; middle-C tone, played as four quarter-notes indicating "walk backwards," and various changes of tempo or meter (see below). These are designed at the discretion of the clinician, as long as the client is informed of the meaning of the cue. Playing just bass tones on the keyboard (e.g., left-hand tones) indicates "move feet only, no tambourine," or unaccompanied melody in a middle or higher register (right hand only) indicates claps only, feet still (stop and clap tambourine only), or both hands playing piano means resume both hand and feet activity. This intervention can last as long as the clinician feels the necessity for repetitions. It is also important to have the client change hands for holding and clapping the tambourine. It is surprising how often a client is able to clap while holding in a preferred hand, and less able when alternating hands. Making this intervention a "fun" activity is key to success.

SHIFT OF ACCENT

For clients who are able, have surpassed and "graduated" from the simple marching exercise, this more advanced marching intervention is presented: the client marches for four 4-count measures, but claps a tambourine accent only on the first count of each measure; next four 4-count measures are marched with tambourine clapping not on the first, but now only on the second count of each measure; then again, and on the third count; and again on the fourth count, returning back to the first count for another go round, in the following manner:

ONE—2—3—4|ONE—2—3—4|ONE—2—3—4|ONE—2—3—4

1—TWO—3—4|1—TWO—3—4|1—TWO—3—4|1—TWO—3—4

1—2—THREE—4|1—2—THREE—4|1—2—THREE—4|1—2—THREE—4

1—2—3—FOUR|1—2—3—FOUR|1—2—3—FOUR|1—2—3—FOUR— return to...

ONE—2—3—4|ONE—2—3—4|...and so forth

This "shift of accent" intervention is rather difficult but keeps the client totally focused, concentrating quite intensely, without any audible counting, and further strengthens upper-/lower-body coordination. Meanwhile, musical cueing, as in the usual marching task, continues while musically emphasizing the required accented beat (e.g., a chord on the accented beat as the march music is played, or other ways of emphasizing the accent). This also keeps the clinician quite busy concentrating along with the client. The client has to concentrate not only on the counts in relation to where the body movement is, but must also *be prepared to hear a cue* during this multi-task, and respond precisely as directed by the music cue. Often the "turn around and go the other way" cue might appear before the completion of the four measures of a particular accent sequence, further instigating auditory acuity, motor-planning, and quick response. To complicate matters, the fourth line ends with the accent on the fourth count, and must immediately accent the first count—one—of the very next line! Yes, this is a challenging exercise. There is much going on in the brain and body in this multi-tasking intervention, but I have encountered many positive results from it, and it has been presented developmentally in even more difficult formats. For instance, instead of changing accent after every fourth measure, each change of accent occurs in *each* ensuing measure, thus:

ONE—2—3—4 | 1—TWO—3—4 | 1—2—THREE—4 | 1—2—3—FOUR|
ONE—2—3—4 | and so on

In addition, the tempo might increase from 60 bpm up to 120 bpm actual march tempo, alternating with tempos slower than 60 bpm. Memory is key in this intervention, and my clinical results were quite exciting, especially with clients of limited memory for academic learning.

Of course, all the other cues are still in play (turn the other way, fall down, etc.). While responding to those cues, the client keeps in mind which number he or she is or was in when that cue came, without interrupting task continuity and rhythm, in order that movement consistency adheres to the beat and tempo! This intervention works well with clients aged from pre-teen through senior adults (especially senior adults!), and is particularly helpful for people with ASD and ADHD, due to the need for concentration. For younger clients, the clinician must determine the applicability, and apply much segmentation to portions of the movement in a more simplified and apportioned manner, perhaps presenting only one part, such as the first line accenting only number *one*.

Another version that is applicable to younger children, as well as other ages, can be done with jumps on the accented count, continuing to march and clap tambourine on the rest of the counts, so that the accent is *JUMP*—2—3—4, clapping and marching on the 2—3—4. This motor-planning complexity involves coordination of upper/lower body, jump anticipation and preparation (body and legs bending, lifting, disconnecting feet from floor, etc.) while simultaneously pulsing on the tambourine. Difficult? Absolutely. But music-based sensorimotor clinical work is not about *easy*, but rather, about music and cues serving the role of "adequate stimulus," that "forcing function" for attaining functional adaptation, concepts we've learned about in previous chapters of this book.

CASE EXAMPLE 4

Remember Ronald from Chapter 5, who had difficulty exhaling slow, long breaths on the recorder? For him this marching "game" first began with a recorder in hand. Four sticks were placed in a row, on the floor, spread approximately 24 inches apart (approximately two feet). He was to step over a stick, stop and blow, take another step-stop-blow. Tempo was 60 bpm and music was a march tune. This was done moving forward, and returning again, in the same manner. Once the task was completed he began once again, this time holding the tone as he stepped over two sticks (i.e., left forward, right forward on the next stick, etc.). This was a bit more difficult, but the step-blow activity was continued at home on his staircase—step up-blow, vice versa. Along with the opening seated long-blows, after some six months, Ronald was beginning to show an ability to sustain a slow exhaled longer tone, which also influenced his expressive language, and could finally say "O-o-oh no-o-o-o" in slow exhale. The rest of the marching tasks and quick responses to musical cues (as described above) were very well executed, and he "graduated" to the shift-of-accent march with little concern. His ability to remain focused and track the counts while attending to the cues helped make major headway into his previously deficient motor-planning. Work remained on developing imitation and body dynamics.

CASE EXAMPLE 5

Gregory, a 12-year-old with ASD and with other undiagnosed issues such as extremely slow language, cognitive processing, and lethargic responsiveness, had been considered as "non-teachable." He did have expressive and receptive language abilities, but spoke very little, very softly, and seemed to be living in another world. In music-based treatment, Gregory presented with an amazing ability in rhythmic understanding! The first time that the Eurhythmics marching with tambourine was presented, Gregory became a different person, to everyone's amazement. Not only was he able to quick-respond to any musical cue, and seemed absolutely in control of his body, but he also immediately conquered the shift-of-accent intervention to the point where regardless of cues, he could turn on a dime, move in any direction, and stop/start without ever losing the count or the accent location of the count! Gregory was a student at a school for special needs students, and everyone was amazed at his abilities—things that would never have been discovered outside of music treatment. The more the marching was presented, the stronger his body awareness became. Interventions with this student included many tempo changes, fast to slow, many dynamic energies for developing body dynamics and flexibility of movement from strong/stiff to light/flowing. Teachers began to notice quicker verbal responses in academic work, and more interest in learning. Subsequently, Gregory asked to take "piano" lessons!

Galloping, skipping, running, and jumping

In addition to the march, this session module includes the gallop, or skipping (whichever is more suitable for the client), running, jumping or hopping, all dictated by the music changes (meter and patterns) that clients have been taught to hear and to await. The march is still the basic movement activity, but when the music suddenly changes to 6/8 meter with the rhythmic pattern of quarter—eigth—quarter—eigth, and the clinician plays triplets, accenting the first, third, fourth and sixth beats: **1**—2—**3**—**4**—5—**6**, the client now hears and recognizes this changed metered pattern as a *gallop* and immediately begins to gallop.

The *galloping* movement is a step to the side, slide other leg over (to close up), step to the side, slide other leg over, and so on, within the 6/8 rhythmic pattern. For many younger children, asking for "gallop like a pony" is a more familiar movement than a skip.

Skipping is a 2/4 or 4/4 meter, dotted quarter—eigth (**1**—2—3—**4**—**1**—2—3—**4**), which involves alternating legs, one leg step/hop (all with the same leg), alternating with the other step/hop. Many younger children have difficulty *alternating* legs and doing both step/hop with the same leg. It involves balance and shift of weight, therefore this action requires being taught a motor-planning strategy through segmentation of the movement. For this, the clinician will slow the pace and pattern, will teach skipping by asking for a hop with the same leg, and will speak or sing "step—hold—hold—hop (with the same leg)—step (with the other leg)—hold—hold—hop (same leg)—step(other leg)…and so on, at first in a slow, deliberate tempo, gradually increasing to reproduce a skipping action. Since this requires shift of weight from one leg step/hop to the other leg step/hop, role modeling side by side with the client is a practical way to teach the "skip," which is more complex in motor-planning than the gallop since it involves, as mentioned, a shift of weight stepping with *alternating* legs, and a bit more elevation for the hop.

Running in clockwise and counterclockwise directions is called for when the music becomes fast arpeggios or other running-notes configurations (8th or 16th notes), but still within the overall 60 bpm tempo, although it sounds faster and calls for faster movement. *Jumps* are called for when the music plays "jumping chords," staccato motifs, and so on.

Important to all the above interventions is the client's constant contact between *musical dynamics* and *movement energies*—for example, music for "light jumps," energetic or light "tip toe" running, heavy marching, strong, quick, free, bird-like flying (running) movement, and many other such musical cues using *dynamics*. For the majority of clients, the dynamic levels of piano or keyboard music will instinctively invigorate reflective dynamic movements of the body in space. Such interventions will eventually increase motor-planning and body awareness, because the music and movement are united in similar energies, further encouraging "quick response" to reflect the sound.

Summary

In all, the interventions in Session Modules 2 and 3 discussed in this chapter are predominantly *non-verbal*, allowing the music to dictate actions through sound rather than verbal directives, and enabling movements to indicate synchronization with the music. Each element of music has its role to play—from the four p's of *rhythm* (pulse, pace, pattern, perpetuation (continuity)), to *melody cues, harmony* (chords and key changes often used as cues), *timbre* (different keyboard timbres can become cues, if available—e.g., flute for "go the other way," etc.), certainly *dynamics* for movement, and *form* (structure and repetitions). The only verbal directives are those advising the client about which actions are cued by what music. In the interest of clarifying directions the clinician might ask questions such as, "What do you think the music is doing?", even if the client is unable to respond, as a way of developing more imaging via musical content. Through these activities and quick response, sensory systems instinctively coordinate once the brain is "taught" the strategy of how to execute interventions. These modules focus on upper-/lower-body coordination through multi-tasking rhythmic activities. They also involve auditory training—listening for cues, and responding precisely to what the music is requesting. These are basic in Eurhythmics training for musicians, but in treatment, these kinds of exercises serve an even broader purpose, as is described here. These interventions address multiple ASD characteristics and needs simultaneously, within an entertaining atmosphere. Emotionally the client is challenged but not "threatened," so other than some temporary "stress" in compliance with a requirement and learning to execute the activity, the general demeanor of the participant remains calm and enthusiastic. That said, the rest is up to the music, and instinct.

CHAPTER 7

Free To Be Me

In the preface of her book *Rhythm and Movement: Applications of Dalcroze Eurhythmics*, Elsa Findlay declares that the most exciting thing about Eurhythmics is its demand for total involvement by both the teacher and the participant. (Findlay 1999, Preface page). This is precisely the same in music-based treatment, which is why Eurhythmics is so adaptable in treatment.

The music-based clinician is, in fact, a teacher of sorts, helping the brain and body to learn new, more functionally adaptive, options and manners of COPING. While a neurotypical (NT) person learns behaviors through imitation, a neuro-developmentally-delayed person must be taught how to imitate, and to reassign instincts toward more functional behaviors. It is the close involvement of the music-based clinician during Eurhythmics interventions, the being and doing with the client through every aspect of the rhythmic movements, that gives rise to the development of new sensorimotor options. Without the presence of *live*, in-the-moment, improvised music accompanying reflective movement, it would be difficult for many of the elements of music to be effective catalysts for sensory regulation, systemic coordination, anxiety reduction, and the many objectives clinicians hope to achieve. Elsa Findlay (now deceased), former Chair of the Department of Eurhythmics, Cleveland Institute of Music, led the way to working with young persons in the mid-to-later part of the twentieth century, in her work with children in Cleveland, and through her book, *Rhythm and Movement: Applications of Dalcroze Eurhythmics* (Findlay 1999). Her book carefully outlines approaches and activities for teaching children rhythm, dynamics, phrasing, and other elements of music through movement. Several of the interventions constructed and described in the chapters of this book are adaptations of approaches adopted from recommendations by Jaques-Dalcroze and Findlay, who was taught directly by Emile Jaques-Dalcroze.

In adapting Eurhythmics exercises to music-based sensorimotor treatments, clinicians require clear treatment objectives in order to understand what and how the various exercises can address and achieve, never losing sight of the ultimate goal—attaining the COPING ability of the client(s). In addition, as already stated, recorded music is not quite as effective as live, in-the-moment presence of music and music-making participation that is directly connected to a client's demeanor, physiological and emotional needs, movements, and direct contact with the clinician and music. So far, Part Two of this book has presented session modules and plans for a systematic approach, interventions being directed and focused on motor-planning, sensory interactions, and destressing the amygdala, HPA axis, and musculoskeletal systems. We move now to the final modules of a session, encouraging independent thinking, creative output, language, and overall "freedom of expression." As in any educational approach, the school teacher is in charge, with self-expression enabled through various tasks and assignments that call for self-expression (i.e., story writing, special projects, holiday greeting cards, etc.). But first, the student must follow a structure set by the curriculum and administered by the instructor, so that learning will take place and can progress in an organized, sequential flow. The Eurhythmics-based clinical modules outlined thus far in this book are somewhat similar—they serve as the "curriculum" consisting of various *training* objectives, with the clinician organizing the sequential (developmental) session flow, with interventions addressing particular objectives, and with the client (the "student") following the training routine. It is through such *systematic*, evidence-based clinical modules that progress can be observed, tracked, and logged, both per session and over the long run. As the teaching and learning progresses, and the physiologic systems are able to "organize" more efficiently, the clinician can continue addressing several most important human factors: independent thinking, language, and creative self-expression. The last session modules aim to provide the "student" the opportunity to apply (intuitively, for the most part) the training toward independent thinking: creative self-expression, making choices, rhythm, language, through improvised music-making jointly between clinician (teacher, or "other") and self (student).

Module 4: Instrumental and rhythm improvisations, seated or moving. Drumming and/or various rhythmic instrumental and movement interactions

Objective (g): sense of self, rhythmic internalization, mirroring (imitative responses), creative self-expression (also expressive language), and task organization

Now that attention has been given to reducing survival-anxiety, systemic organization, sensory regulation and interactions, auditory and visual attention, motor-planning, following directions, eye contact, memory, rhythmic embodiment, and body dynamics through movement activities, it is time to lead the client from the strict structure, to free self-expression, perhaps with just a bit more rhythmic persuasion and improvisation for influencing imaginative thinking. This session module is when the clinician can provide various interventions that highlight independence, self-awareness, quick response (this continues throughout), language, and musical preferences of the client. Below, the reader will encounter several sample interventions that have been presented to clients in my own clinical work. Activities are interchangeable and the clinician can surely develop many other tasks, depending on clinical assessment and current client needs. As long as the first three session modules have been conducted in a *systematic* manner, these last two modules can be freer, and can include areas that may not have been covered earlier (such as exacting expressive language interventions), and music and movement improvisation.

Language transition to drumming activities

Having just completed many movement activities, it is time to relax for a minute, replenish oxygen in the cells by drinking water (again, and always), and continue with a seated activity. Throughout my book, *Music Therapy, Sensory Integration and the Autistic Child* (Berger 2002), I share many rhythm intervention ideas, most based on Eurhythmics training for children. One particular exercise I continue to present, and one that has been very successful in enhancing language skills, involves a kind of segmentation of words by reducing them to the rhythms of their syllables, in a task I call "Drum Speak." This is fun, and similar to some Melodic Intonation Training concepts (though Dalcroze and Ms. Findlay preceded that). In brief, Drum Speak services as a very nice transition to the ensuing drumming activities of this module. The language objective is to segment (remember segmentation of movement?) a sentence into the rhythmic expression in syllabic form. A bongo or conga drum is placed between the client and the clinician, and all conversation is clapped out on the drum. With young children, I have used the song, "One, Two, Buckle My Shoe" so that the tapping rhythm is quarter—quarter—trip-o-let—quarter: the precise rhythm of the syllables in the rhyme. The clinician speaks the first stanza, the client speaks the second, the clinician the third, until the rhyme is completed and begins again, this time with the client starting. There are many other words, sentences, lyrics, and nursery rhythms that can be spoken while simultaneously tapping the syllables on the drum. Question and answer is undertaken in rhythmic actions; invented song lyrics or poems can be presented similarly; if the client reads, story lines in books can also be tapped out syllabically on a drum. This "drum speak" serves to slow the spoken language down, giving the brain more time to process, remember, and articulate words. This intervention can transfer to using various instruments for dramatizing words, still expressing in rhythmic syllable manner. A xylophone can "drum speak" to a clave, for instance. As a transitional activity, a few minutes of session time is usually long enough to achieve its purpose without belaboring the experience. Once concluded, the next drumming segment can proceed.

A note of interest: In Eurhythmics music classes for children, simple sentences such as "It's time to go to bed," "Yes, mother, yes mother, I'll go to bed" are clapped and spoken in rhythm, and the rhythmic notation of the sentences are put on the board for students to identify which notation reflects which sentence. As a cognitive intervention, this particular type of activity has been applied to several clients with Asperger syndrome with whom I worked, with much enthusiasm and success.

Continued rhythm embodiment

Objective (g) focuses on independence of thought, and addresses additional concerns through some interventions that continue attending to quick response, motor-planning, improvisation, memory, creativity, and redirection of fight-or-flight responses. To reinforce rhythmic entrainment for attaining physiologic organization and rhythmic embodiment, the hand-clapping intervention presented at the start of the treatment session (see Session Module 2), is now adapted as a *drumming* activity. Two drums (not floor drums, but snares or other standing drums) *A* and *B* are set approximately 18–24 inches apart. A cymbal can be placed between and behind the drums, set back so that the client must extend the arm to reach and strike it. The client will *sit* in front of the two drums that are spread apart, with mallets in hand. Mallets that are weighted with drum-stick weights and have thicker hand grips are preferable, in order to continue providing proprioceptive information regarding arm positions and motor-planning needs to the brain.

Drumming

This intervention begins first with the client freely playing the drums and cymbal, to a tune requested by the client. Any tempo, song, pre-recorded tune on the keyboard, Blues on guitar, or other music (including rock) serves the purpose, which, for the clinician, is to observe client's ability in organizing limbs, holding mallets appropriately, playing drums according to his or her impulses and interests. The clinician will often notice that the playing might always be loud and dynamically uncontrolled, repetitive, perhaps rather rigid, containing few if any patterns and contrasts. This "free drumming" activity may indicate further needs. For instance, if the client continually releases or drops a mallet, it can indicate inappropriate proprioceptive information—the brain does not know how strongly to hold the mallet, how much to fold the hand around the mallet to securely grasp the item, which arm functions better, and so on. Once the "free drumming" tune ends, the clinician provides a more structured rhythmic drumming, incorporating bi-lateral arm coordination (as was an objective in the hand-clapping segment), mid-line crossovers (also a repeat of the hand-clapping segment), and dynamic energy variance: loud and soft playing for increasing dynamics of limb movements. (Indeed, every intervention has physiologic objectives.)

The following intervention reflects part of the rhythmic hand clapping sequence presented earlier in the session. Here the pulse begins at 60 bpm, by now a familiar pace for the system, but might increase, depending on ability, cue, or clinician interests:

4/4   1 2 3 4   1 2 3 4
       ♩ ♩ ♩ ♩ | ♩ ♩ ♩ ♩

1. Eight quarter-note beats (i.e., two measures in 4/4 meter), played with parallel arms (bilateral) open and set apart, one over each drum, to beating both drums *simultaneously*.

2. Eight quarter-note beats played by *alternating* one beat per drum, left-right-left-right (bilateral alternate).

3. Repeat 1 (bilateral parallel).

4. Eight quarter-note beats—alternating arms crossing mid-line, left arm reaching across body to play drum A, right crossing to drum B (bilateral alternate), with last beat striking on cymbal (if available).

Stop, repeat

Piano (or guitar) music and polyrhythmic (electronic) background (if available), accompanies this activity and emphasizes the pulse. Any music, improvised or electronically pre-programmed, in any genre (Latin included), in 4/4 meter, can be used. Although the tempo begins at 60 bpm, it can increase intermittently to ensure auditory attention and motor-planned response. When a pre-programmed or improvised selection is applied on a keyboard in which tempos can be altered, the clinician can be freed to play percussions that will add polyrhythms enhancing this task. This provides auditory multi-perception attention, since the client is hearing a tune and counter-rhythms while sustaining the pulse in various ways of playing dynamically (loud, soft, crescendo, etc.). An interesting bilateral issue that often arises is the inability to use both arms in precisely the same tempo; often, instead of a unilateral "thump…thump…" in which both drums sound as one, there is a "ka-thump…ka-thump…" with one arm striking the drum sooner (or later) than the other arm. In such cases, the clinician may want to work with the arm that is late, to strengthen the proprioceptive information, motor plan, and to increase the speed of action on the delayed side. Precise *unanimity*— both arms striking the drum at precisely the same time—is an added objective of parallel arms playing. Additional work and physical prompting for this imbalance may be required. The client's OT might also be informed of the discrepancy, if it has not been detected.

Additional drumming

It is important for the client eventually to be able to develop the ability for inventing or sustaining rhythmic "patterns." When a client is able to improvise and create rhythmic patterns, on any instruments, it is an indication of creative-inventiveness, independent thinking, interest in curiosity, exploration and an ability to conjure rhythmic and tonal *musical images*. The clinician can assist the client to release and explore these instincts in several ways. For one thing, employing 3/4 meter rather than the usual 4/4 meter presents a unique opportunity to *shift accents*, and to develop simple hand patterns for drumming. Several simple patterns in 3/4 meter that I have used, organize the drum beats in the following way: beat one is struck on drum *A* (with whichever hand services that drum), followed by beats two and three played on drum *B*, with the other hand, so that arms play alternately but each arm executes a different pattern. A music cue then dictates a switching of action, after some four-measure phrases, so that drum B now plays beat one, and drum A plays the remaining beats two and three. In other words, the pattern would be: *left—right—right* |*left—right—right* for several measures, and vice-versa, *right—left—left* for several measures (it doesn't matter which hand begins, as long as the alternation of arm patterns is applied). This exchange involves very quick response and motor-planning in order not to lose the beat. The musical "cue" signal is rendered at random by the clinician, who can inform the client that the piano's right-hand music (mid-to-upper register) will parallel the right-hand drumming of the client, and the left piano hand will reflect the left-hand drumming. Thus, the client will *hear* the piano's switch in registers and musical motifs (as a similar cue directed earlier that called for feet-only or clapping-only in the march intervention). The difficulty is that the *cue is random* with no advanced warning of when to quickly switch arms and pattern without loss of the 3/4 pulse. Again, auditory attention and motor-planning for prompt response are required to successfully stay on target. Indeed it does also require a rather proficient clinician with equally regulated motor-planning and proficient piano skills!

Advancing this 3/4 time drumming intervention is to play two 8th notes (♫) for beat one on drum A, followed by two quarter-notes (♩♩) completing counts two and three on drum B, or any combination of such patterning, at the discretion of the clinician. A musical cue again designates this alternation of arms and pattern. Additional patterns of increasing difficulty can be designed by the clinician, on a developmental basis of ability, or, the client can be asked to invent or further modify the 3/4 drumming pattern, with the ability to recall and sustain his or her newly invented pattern for a length of time (e.g., four-measure phrases). Many percussion instruments can also be added to this type of intervention, with patterns involving several instruments such as claves, wood blocks, bongos, triangles, cymbals, and others. The objective continues to be auditory attention, creativity, motor-planning, quick response, task invention and attention, self-organization, rhythmic independence, and interdependence. This intervention can further address arm movement imbalances, devoting extra patterns and repetitions to be played by the "slower" arm of the "ka-thump." My research (Berger 2012) indicated that overall, this particular drumming intervention was the most enjoyable and easiest to execute, after all the previous activities. In sessions, by the time this activity is presented, the brain and body have navigated many rhythmic challenges. (In several non-research-related cases, I presented this task just after the opening breath-control intervention, and the client was less successful performing this activity than when it was presented again, toward the end of the same session, after other rhythmic movement tasks.)

CASE EXAMPLE 6

Eric was seven years old when he began working in music-based treatment. Diagnosed as being in the middle of the ASD spectrum, Eric had absolute pitch, no expressive language except for a word here and there ("no," "yes," "stop"), and presented with fight-flight behavior, high stress, and basic inability to sit still for any length of time. But once the session began, with the recorder, claps, marching, etc., he became more attentive, less erratic, and displayed his *innate* rhythmic and pitch-recognition abilities. Over many sessions with me at his school (five 40-minute sessions a week), he became quite proficient in this drumming task, as well as in quick responses to musical cues for changing hands, sustaining patterns, and more. His abilities were such that a new, fairly difficult, intervention was created but addressing motor-planning, auditory acuity, memory, and much more. The intervention was as follows:

Three drums were set in front of Eric, along with a hanging cymbal and triangle. Eric, seated, was asked to name three recognized nursery songs (I called them out, and he would nod or say "yes" when selecting). The objective was that when song *A* was heard, drum *A* would play quarter-notes with parallel bi-lateral arms simultaneously on both drums (♩♩♩♩); when song *B* was heard, drum *B* would play 8th notes (♫♫♫♫) one with arm, alternating on each drum (bilateral alternate arms); when song *C* was heard, drum *C* would play yet a third pattern with arms alternating—one plays a quarter-note, other plays two 8th notes (♩♫ ♩♫); when the piano played a chromatic ascending scale, the cymbal would crash when the scale stopped, and when the clinician played only right-hand in the very upper piano register, the triangle would be struck. These five cues and manners of playing not only required complete attention and instant changes, but also memory for which is what. Of course, none of the songs were played to the end, but rather would stop at random, and one of the other songs or instrumental cues would immediately begin. Eric not only had to remember which tune designated which drum, but also the pattern to be played on that drum! This task was executed in an absolutely fantastic manner by Eric, who, if piano changes came too soon, would call out "Stop! Stop!", motioning to me that I wait until he reorganized! The sum of this intervention was Eric's total self-control, organization and eye focus (he never took his eyes off me at the piano), and complete engagement with the task. The sense of achievement he felt was indicated by the smile on his face as he completed the activity and left the room with his aide, who was astounded at Eric's self-control. **Update:** Now, many years later, Eric is still basically non-verbal, but has learned to compose music and play piano, and is hired to play piano at a local nursery school, writing and playing music for young children!

This case is documented on a DVD that has been presented at many conferences, as an example of how memory and rhythmically challenging "quick response" interventions serve to help a client self-organize motor-planning, pay attention, and give eye contact (Eric never took his eyes off me during this task), because the curious brain has the motivation to excel! Eric's ability to self-regulate, evident in his calling out to me to "Stop!" because he needed to reorganize, was met with enthusiasm by his academic team who, up to that point, felt he was difficult to reach! Indeed, this is an advanced level intervention, and has been applied in my work with many older students and adults, persons with various brain traumas, dementias, and so on, precisely because of the required mental and auditory acuity and prompt response. Clinicians need not be concerned about presenting difficult interventions. In fact, interventions that continue to challenge can draw upon innate abilities that may not otherwise be readily observable or available. This "Three-Drum Plus Game" was presented to other clients, with many repetitions and excellent results. It need not always begin with five instruments—the intervention first can be presented as the two-drum intervention outlined above, with a gradual increase in number of instruments, songs, and rhythmic patterns. The objective is, indeed, enhancement of recall dictating body actions, as suggested by La Mettrie (Wellman 1992; see also Chapter 6), and motor-planning, among other things (i.e., task attention, etc.). This particular intervention always is and was presented late in a session, after clapping and Eurhythmics movements utilizing brain-mind-body interventions.

Improvisation

This is the most "inventive" portion of a treatment session, also leading toward the final concluding module. Any client, of any age, can improvise. Instrumental training or skills are not required. Tonal imaging (as in vocal toning) and sound organization is a skill available to any client, with clinician facilitation and role modeling. Several approaches can set into motion a client's improvisation (thinking in sound) skills. Below are some ideas, and there are many!

INTERVENTION: Q & A

The client is on one instrument, preferably a keyboard or tonal instrument (e.g., xylophone), while the clinician is based at another instrument, perhaps also a keyboard, xylophone, or guitar. The "game" rules are that one person's instrument asks a question of the other person's instrument, and the other person's instrument replies. *This is a purely non-verbal discussion.* Usually the clinician will begin, in order to role model the intent, and the client will respond. On any instrument this becomes challenging, but also intriguing, to the client who may be non-verbal without realizing that he or she can still "communicate"; or a very verbal client may not realize the effectiveness of non-verbal communication. Whoever began the activity as the inquirer now changes to become the responder.

Some verbal discussion can ensue, depending on status, age, and needs of the client. Whether verbal or totally non-verbal, this improvisation task is simple, revealing to the clinician, and often quite satisfying to the client. Of course this Q & A improvisation can be undertaken with drums, which is often simpler and more common, but with use of melodic instruments language prosody and inflections can be brought into play. If at times, *verbal* identification and discussion of the Q & A is undertaken after the musical improvisation, it provides the opportunity for the clinician to work on the client's self-recognition and language articulation of thoughts and feelings, and ability to express and interpret both verbal and non-verbal expressions. This can be a follow up to non-verbal Q & A expression.

INTERVENTION: Q & A ON PIANO AND OTHER INSTRUMENTS

This is a similar idea to above, but the client sits side by side with the clinician at the piano or keyboard, or shares a metallophone with the clinician. One begins playing piano sounds representing a question; the other responds with an answer. Whoever began the questioning later switches to become the responder, as in the above activity, so the client has the opportunity to experience both sides. This task on the keyboard, with both persons sitting side by side in close proximity, can be more difficult since closeness is often uncomfortable for clients, and the piano tends to be intimidating to some, especially to adult clients. This keyboard-based Q & A can therefore be undertaken on two separate keyboard instruments—piano and electric keyboard, if available, with one person at one keyboard and the other at the piano (or second keyboard). The piano asks a question, the keyboard answers.

This activity can also be undertaken with persons sitting with two different instruments, for instance, a xylophone and a recorder, or other combinations, as long as the Q & A is basically non-verbal. As in the above, it can be followed with discussion. For language-delayed clients, this improvisatory task can include pitches and melodic contours (rendered by the clinician and imitated by client) replicating verbal expressions and inflective melodies. Many persons with ASD cannot detect a statement as being a question with the voice rising, vs. a command, when the voice descends in pitch. This particular improvisation using instrumental "inflection" can begin to alert the brain for tonal inflections related to questions vs. commands. It is a step further into the "ear training" and comprehension of language objective. (This activity can also be undertaken with "neurotypical" piano students, to enhance non-verbal, musical self-expression).

FOUR-NOTE IMPROVISATION

This is improvisation on a piano, keyboard, or metallophone. The client is shown four keys or tones on the instrument, and is asked to make up a song using only those four tones. They can be played in any way, with any hand, in any registers of the instrument, repeated, and so on, but only those four tones can be played. The most successful tones I have designated are: D—F—A—C. I have not encountered a case in which the client was unable to remember the location of these tones, but if such a problem arises, then two tones with simple locations can be selected (such as C before two black notes; and F before three black notes).

The idea is that the client plays those four tones *in any manner he or she desires*. If in a group session, various other tonal instruments (i.e., xylophone, metallophones, chimes, hand bells, wind and string instruments, etc.) can be part of the band, with the same designated notes (all others are removed to limit confusion). While the client is playing, the clinician is improvising on a piano or other melodic instrument (violin, cello, sax, xylophone, etc.), using only the same four tonalities. The clinician will surely notice that in those four pitches are the D minor chord, and the F major chord, allowing for many harmonic sequences involving those two keys, along with a 7th chord, and some potential for intervallic dissonance. This improvisation is completely free, without any structure. Beginning and ending is determined by the client. The clinician simply follows, and guides in a subtle manner.

VOCAL AND VERBAL IMPROVISATION

This is one of the more difficult, self-conscious improvisation tasks. It was earlier addressed in the opening of the session through humming into a kazoo. A less intimidating approach to vocalization is to have a story book that the clinician can "sing-read," and have the client render vocal sounds supporting the story segments. Instrumental improvisation by the client can supplement vocalizations, helping the client to become a little less self-conscious. If the client has expressive language and can read even a simple book, he or she can "invent" the tune and "sing-read" the words in the book. Singing a story book by inventing the "story song" has been a pleasant and successful intervention toward the conclusion of a session. Vocal improvisation also addresses language deficits, when client and clinician sing-talk information, stories, and other themes encouraging verbal content. Verbal improvisation is also helpful in cognitive and language development. One such "improvisation" uses the song, "This Old Man" during which each stanza asks for a new word or words. For example:

This 'ol man, he played one,

He played knick-knack on my _____ (drum, thumb, strum…)

With a knick-knack, patty-wack give a dog a _____ (leash, rub, bone…)

This 'ol man came _____ home (singing, flying, humming…)

Each blank space per stanza requires a different new word—for example, "give a man a *book*," or "this 'ol man came *flying* home," "*laughing* home," and so on. Inasmuch as quick recall is required in order for the song to flow uninterrupted, the mind is called upon to think quickly of the next word. There are many other such opportunities for recall, vocalization, and pragmatic language skills to increase.

Of course there are many other ways for vocal improvisation to be exercised, including "toning," singing one's name in various ways, "sing-talk" in operatic-like conversation, or even just humming along to movement, or imagining the inventing of technology or machinery that makes different sounds. It is important every now and then to include vocal improvisation toward the end of a session, whether with or without language.

KAZOO-TALK VOCAL IMPROVISATIONS AND INTRODUCTIONS

An extension of the opening kazoo activity, here participants will have *a non-verbal conversation* by humming the tones and inflections of a question or sentence while directly facing the person to whom the tones (words) are spoken. The recipient of the sentence or question hums into a kazoo to respond in the same manner. Humming is less threatening than outright singing, at first. This can proceed to singing an invented way of introducing one's self by name (without kazoo), which is echoed back by the group, if in a group activity. One can also hum one's name into a kazoo as a way of introducing one's self by name. This activity has been used in adult groups as an introduction and way of helping to remember participant names. Feeling states can be "sung" or hummed non-verbally, and can be followed by some discussion with older, verbal adults with ASD and others (the clinician needs to consider that such talk therapy can be uncomfortable and cause anxiety in a music-based treatment session).

MOVEMENT IMPROVISATION

Many ideas for improvising movement abound, from "tell me how you feel," to "walk in the park or on a beach," to "move like an animal," or movement just to explore moving parts of the body in different ways. Essential to movement improvisation is the freedom to move in many directions and manners, with client and clinician jointly participating, perhaps to CDs of various kinds, or with someone else at an instrument (piano or guitar). When the clinician participates in movement improvisations with the client, it indicates support and "equality" among participants, thus providing a sense of comfort and joint "fun." This is not "dance" time, although dance movements, such as shaking, clapping, dance-floor-like movements (samba, congo, rhumba, bebop, etc.) are acceptable, as long as dynamics of movement, use of space and levels, and full-body motions are included. Evidence of rhythmic embodiment arises in this activity, which can then be logged as "progress" in any evidence-based document. If rhythm is not visible, it is yet another indicator of sensory work required further. Movement *imitation* can be explored. Now the clinician will imitate client movement (as in the "mirror" transitional activity presented earlier). Also, movement about the room can be imitated and encouraged—freely swirling, leaping, dynamic angular movements reflecting "angular piano or instrumental sounds"; sharp movements (i.e., staccato), lyrical movements, silly walks and hopping, and various interchangeable energies in the "body dynamics" objectives. Most clients will need clinician (or aide) role modeling for movement "invention" ideas. Destructive movements, such as kicking something, flailing an object, or other injurious movements are inadmissible. (In general, male teenagers are less enthusiastic with movement improvisation unless they can move like "Ninja" characters, which is restricted in my clinical setting because it infers "threat" and violence.)

The overall objective of movement improvisation is, once again, to follow and reflect the music stimulus. However, moving in silence can also be effective, enabling the imagination to activate silently, without obtaining ideas from the sound. Actions such as moving in a storm or against the wind, or running from danger (or a Ninja character) can be done in silence, or just with percussion accompaniment.

SPACE WALK

Although this is not an "improvisatory" movement, as such, it addresses motor-planning in a unique manner, and has entertained many male clients particularly. This involves moving across a room (or designated space), in a decreasing number of steps, beginning with ten steps to cross the room from the starting point. Music accompanies and counts the number of steps. Pace is again at 60 bpm, or slower, depending on client ability. The client is asked to cross the room *in ten steps*, no more, no less. Returning to the starting point, the client now takes only nine *steps*; returning across the room, client takes eight *steps*, and so on, until fewer and fewer steps are required. Of course by the time client is at the four steps and fewer stage, it becomes more unlikely that the area will be crossed (although one of my clients refused to stop and took a flying leap across the room for the one step count!). The challenge is that the weight and distance between legs and leg weight-transfer must change with each count in order to cross the room. This automatically calls for the correct body alignment and motor plan to execute the task. There are no further verbal instructions, other than the progressive decreasing counts. A piano or instrument "keeps count and pulse"; there is a one-count break between crossings, but the instinct to achieve this activity is quite active, with the mind consumed with concentration and step count.

OLD MCDONALD HAD A BAND

This final movement recommendation is an intervention I have often described but will repeat here for clinicians who may not have read my other books or attended any of my previous lectures. The objective of this intervention is a *think and do* ultimate quick response Eurhythmics and auditory focus activity. The song used is the familiar "Old McDonald," but instead of a farm, he had a "band." Instruments are set about the room, in a circle, some instruments free-standing (such as a snare drum), others on chairs (such as triangle, claves, xylophone, single bell tones, etc.). The client is at the center of the circle, on a "waiting mat." The clinician is at the piano. The clinician advises the client that the song will be sung as usual except when the stanza, "and in that band he played the…" comes, the client will move immediately to one or more of the instruments in McDonald's band to sound that instrument. BUT—which instrument is to be sounded will be determined by a *musical cue*, non-verbally. The clinician devises specific cues identifying particular instruments, for instance a trill for shaking a tambourine, a bass motif indicating playing the bass drum, glissandos indicating playing on the xylophone, and so on. Once the cues are provided and logged in the memory of the client, the song begins. Sometimes just one instrument will be played, sometimes two or more, and the song will conclude with a decrease in tempo indicating the end is near.

Although this activity appears to be complex, any client aged seven and older (to adults) can learn to execute it quite efficiently. Because the song is familiar, the objective continuity—that is, to immediately respond in order for the song to continue uninterruptedly—calls upon instinct to "do" no matter what, and it is almost as if the brain and body forget what they cannot do, and proceed to act at once! Such is the nature of instinct, as in the fight-or-flight response, although this is not a survival-anxiety behavior of that sort. It can be looked upon as a kind of "survival" behavior, because the brain/mind want to achieve the task stimulated by the music and the lyrics! This particular intervention (which I have shown in a DVD) has served very well in movement interventions for motor-planning and quick responses. The timing of information processing seems quickened in this type of intervention.

CASE EXAMPLE 7

Vanna, the adult female with ASD that we met in Chapter 5, whose mother excitedly told me her daughter could suddenly blow, was riddled with "fear" and anxiety, and required constant calming and assurance of safety. Vanna had absolutely no expressive language and eventually learned to hum into the kazoo. Vocally she was inept, unable to imitate any pitch, and very monotonal when making vocal sounds. Cognitively, Vanna was said to function as an eight-year-old child. Her early session activities required much prompting and role modeling, but her enthusiasm for executing any task was always high and evident. In the march activity Vanna required prompting, while marching in a seated position, to coordinate rhythmic synchronization between arms playing the tambourine and legs marching in time. When seated Vanna was able to coordinate upper and lower movements, but when in actual march movement, her legs moved faster than the tempo and pulsations of the tambourine. (When the tempo was faster than 60 bpm, the upper-/lower-body coordination was closer to tempo, but at 60 bpm, the coordination was difficult.) Most problematic, however, were her inflexible body movements—rigid, fearful, flat-feet walks, and so on. This called for extensive repetitions of movement interventions addressing the increase of body dynamics and leg flexibility. We spent many sessions on learning to Take a Walk in the Park—moving lyrically, flowing, stopping to image smelling flowers or looking at birds in the tree. Because Vanna loved to "dance," some of her favorite rock songs were used, either CDs or pre-programmed on electric keyboard, and we could dance together. Vanna was able to "mirror" my movements, so my role modeling various actions served to decrease her rigidity, because it served also to calm her continual distressed demeanor. Vanna was compliant. She would nod as if understanding the directive and image. Whether or not Vanna really understood was irrelevant. Her interest in imitating what she saw me do in this session module involving movement articulation, served her well. By the time the session was completed, her walk in exiting the room was entirely different to when she entered.

I bring Vanna into the movement intervention discussion to underline the importance of the clinician analyzing a client's movement abilities and undertaking exercises that can address and alter for the better one's body movement. Emotions and feelings are logged into muscles and body movements. Movements are indicative of how one is feeling, at any given moment. Vanna's entrance into the treatment session was always with a tense body, shoulders raised, legs stiff, eyes looking all around the room, fearful as to what might be approved or disapproved of in her behavior. I never truly knew how her group-home aides, or those driving her to the session, treated her prior to bringing her, but her "fear" demeanor was very obvious—looking at me as if asking whether I approve or disapprove of something she is doing, and so on. But as the session progressed through recorder and breath control for calmness, and as the rhythm and movement activities progressed, Vanna was able to sense her abilities, and her interest in copying me and executing new movements. By the end of each session, her sense of self and safety, indicated by her smiling facial expressions, head nodding in approval, and sign language asking for more and more of a music-making activity (she loved playing drums), replaced the fearful behaviors and body tensions observed when she entered the session. Often, upon exit, her various aides would remark that Vanna's sense of *comfort in her body* and calm demeanor would extend for several hours beyond the treatment session. However anecdotal this is, it nonetheless validated my continuing to further interventions along this rhythm and movement protocol. Because Vanna was extremely rhythmic (except when trying to coordinate her upper/lower body in marching), her drumming activities were always successfully executed, with the exception of the 3/4 pattern, that mostly required my prompting by gently tapping her upper arms, from behind her, with her permission to do so. She also had the opportunity to freely drum, and could keep perfect metronomic time with the beat. Eurhythmics activities were perfect for someone like Vanna. She loved rhythm and rhythmic music.

Module 5: Closing the session, seated

Objective (h): reducing energies of session; winding down of activities and return to calm; some singing, instrumental improvisation, creative invention

Now that a client has experienced a full, structured treatment session, and has been working tirelessly to enhance sensorimotor functions, the closing of the session is less intense, but still taking into account the goal of reaching a functional level of COPING. Closure can include actually learning to play piano, or selecting a favorite book or song, and singing a usual "goodbye" song either used always to end a session, or that is familiar and requested by the client.

A word about solfeggio

The third area of training described by Jaques-Dalcroze's Eurhythmics concepts is *solfeggio*. For musicians, this is the sight-singing portion of ear training—the ability to sight-read music through words indicating tones. In clinical work, the objective is not necessarily to train for "sight-singing," but has another interesting function, as the following case example will describe.

CASE EXAMPLE 8

When Anna came for treatment, she was 11 years old, home schooled, with expressive language (used only in very limited ways, not always in full sentences, little pragmatics), had absolute pitch (which I envied), and was very specific about her music requirements. Anna required that whatever I played on the piano had to be in the key of F major. Over the years of working with her no one could determine why or what about the key of F major was the requirement, but the reasons were irrelevant. With Anna, before beginning the recorder breath-control activity I would sing my invented "Hello Anna" song—which Anna immediately memorized, both lyrics and tune, but which I had to present in the *key of F*. If not, Anna would bellow "F! F! F!", and reach over to strike the F key! Okay, so "hello in F," although occasionally I would play in D minor, or in the key of Bb (which contains an F), or in F#. Anna's perfect pitch ability would immediately detect the "incorrect" key, and again she would dictate that I play in F major!

Since Anna had such good auditory function, perfect pitch, and pitch detection, and since Anna constantly improvised on the piano, both at home and in our sessions, (chords and all!), I suggested the possibility that Anna could be taught to read music and to play the piano. She nodded in approval, so from that point on, a typical beginners book of some method was purchased, and we began actual lessons as part of the concluding module of her treatment sessions. I showed her where on the piano and on the staff the "picture of Middle C with a hat" is found, then "D" and "E," and so on. As long as I could write, in pencil, the letter of the notation, she could deliver the piano piece. Without the penciled cue, she was unable to define the notation!

This went on for several years. Anna was becoming quite able to play songs, using both hands and both treble and bass clef notations, as long as I penciled in the letters of the notes. However, I suspected that (a) she knew more than she was willing to admit; and (b) was quite able to learn to read music without the penciled-in letters. In my frustration, one day, I decided that rather than the letters C—D—E—F—etc. to identify the tones, I would refer to each by its solfeggio name: do—re—mi—fa, and so on. Yes, I penciled those onto the notes, with the intention of extinguishing that as soon as I believed Anna would recognize the pitches without my scribble. Hark! One day, as I sang the "Hello Anna" song, I decided to play it in the key of G major, thinking it was close enough to F that she might let it pass. Indeed NOT! She reached over, pounded the F key on the piano, shouting "F! F!" When I didn't respond, she shouted "Fa! Fa!" What a surprise! No longer was it "F" but now, Fa. She also ran to the electric keyboard, sat down, and played all the Fa notes up and down the registers. Breakthrough! I was now sure that Anna knew how to read music notation because the solfeggio words made more sense to her than the alphabetical letters! This way, each tone had a "real" name, and she was able to sing the pitch (since she had perfect pitch) calling it by its solfeggio name! Left-hand chordal tones were also identified by solfeggio names, and Anna hence required less and less penciling, and was able to sight-read (even sight-sing) a new piece immediately!

This case illustrates the importance of teaching solfeggio words for identifying pitches, on any instrument, rather than alphabetical letters. Solfeggio is included within Jaques-Dalcroze's Eurhythmics training program philosophy, and can provide a unique service to persons with special needs studying an instrument. Consider this: when tones are identified as alphabetical letters, it is an abstract concept that can be quite confusing to a student with "concrete thinking" and an inability to generalize or attach new meanings to familiar things, just as pretending to "walk in the park," although the room is not a park, can be difficult to image. Alphabet letters are taught in an entirely different context—the alphabet letters are combined to spell *words*—"D" for dog, "C" for cat, and so on. Associating alphabet letters with *pitches* is an abstract idea, and such thought processes are very difficult for someone with ASD, or others, to comprehend, who are unable to transfer meanings and intended labels from one use to another! As Anna illustrated, although she could not verbally explain to me why she was having difficulty learning to identify notes with alphabetical letters, her sudden ability, through solfeggio definition that the white key before the two black ones is named "Do," was logical and clear. The solfeggio system of "fixed Do," where the tone of "Do" is always C, a concept used in the study of solfeggio in France, is the best system for those with ASD and others, since "Do" only identifies pitch "C," and no other. Most Dalcroze training programs use this "fixed Do" approach to solfeggio sight-reading. For Anna, whenever I tested her notation reading skill by pointing to a note on the music page asking her to sing and say what pitch it was, she would immediately say "Sol" if the treble clef notation was on the "G" line, and so forth. This was something she could never do in prior sessions without this information. A final note of interest about Anna; her all-time favorite operatic aria was (is) Mozart's angry "Queen of The Night" from *The Magic Flute*—and by the way, that aria (on her CD recording of it, at least) is in the key of F (minor)! This client not only loves this aria, but can sing the entire thing, in the German language, and with all the difficult key modulations!

The idea of applying solfeggio to pitch recognition in clinical practice and instrumental learning is not, necessarily, to teach "sight-singing," as in the training of "typical" musicians. Rather, and especially for clients with perfect pitch who can immediately sing or recognize a pitch, working with solfeggio labels to identify pitches can shed light on some remarkable abilities. Before my experience with Anna, it had not occurred to me that solfeggio would be functional in treatment, and I sadly think back on how it might have assisted many clients such as Eric, and others. This said, I encourage music-based clinicians to present solfeggio-related information to any client, but especially to those with absolute pitch who might enjoy "reading music," even if not studying an instrument. Arnold, the piano player with ASD that we encountered in Case Example 1, Chapter 5, who has absolute pitch, practiced the piano while seated at a desk, whenever the family traveled on vacation, because he applied his learned solfeggio words to sight-reading the material (even Bach Preludes!). Several other clients not sampled in this book who are studying instruments (e.g., cello, violin) in their local schools, often bring their instruments and music sheets to our sessions, seeking assistance in reading the notation. At such times, we "sight-read" the notation through solfeggio; that secures their understanding of the music, although in school alphabet letters are still used for identifying pitches. One cello-studying client once came to the session complaining that the teachers kept referring to a pitch as a "D," rather than "Re," and he taught his stand-partner the solfeggio names for the pitches so that his partner (a "typical" child but also confused between "D" for dog, and "D" for pitch designations) could have a better way of learning to read music! In vocal improvisation activities, the use of solfeggio designations as "lyrics" can reduce inhibitions or resistance to singing. Improvisations need not be complicated—*Do-Re-Mi Mi-Re-Do*—and several variations of those, are simple but motivating for vocal invention. Of course the solfeggio song from the Rogers and Hammerstein show, *The Sound Of Music*, can always be sung, although I personally prefer not to do this since the words in the song are translated to stand for certain things (Doe, a deer, etc.). In my practice, solfeggio labels define specific pitches, and nothing else.

Summary

We have now covered the basic areas of Eurhythmics training, applying concepts of music-based sensorimotor goals and objectives, for ultimately attaining COPING skills in ASD and other special needs populations. We discussed a structured modular approach to sessions, articulating progressive interventions based on adapted Eurhythmics concepts as developed by Emile Jaques-Dalcroze. Those concepts include: rhythmic exercises, improvisation, and solfeggio and the capacity for "quick responses" to music and music cues to yield enhanced motor plans, auditory acuity, and embodiment of rhythm for good body organization, dynamics, phrasing, movement, cognitive attention, and emotional comfort. Although the structure progresses in the manner discussed thus far, it does not preclude client interests and choices. A participant can select a particular activity, a different order of modules, or total disinterest in any undertaking, that could alter the order of procedure. However, as long as the clinician can adapt whichever action or task a client wishes, and satisfy a treatment objective, a change in session flow can still achieve purposeful results. The "clinical eye" of the therapist will determine how to "modify" an objective and still obtain desired results. After several sessions of familiarity with routine, most clients willingly follow an established flow, but from time to time, this could change, due to many factors (health, mood, etc.), and the clinician can flow easily with changes. The client's comfort and choices are important in any session, as long as treatment objectives can be addressed in some manner. It is pertinent that each module be represented, in the best interest of the client and ability of the clinician, maintaining the recommended flow within the overall session structure. In the case of client resistance, activities can always be modified but still retain an "objective," even if an intervention can only be presented briefly at a time.

Session modules and interventions described here in this Part Two of the book have taken up much time and many pages, and reading the material, which may be new for many clinicians, may take even longer to assimilate. Interventions may only last 30 to 60 minutes, but the "clinical eye" of the therapist takes much observation and instant response. Interventions always need to be clinically purposeful, with *accountable treatment results*, physiologically, psycho-emotionally, and cognitively. In applying an intervention the clinician must know *why* and *what* the intervention represents, and *what results* are sought or expected (anticipated). Logging of some of the structured interventions is crucial for tracking progress. In Appendix 1A the reader can view a sample session-rating scale for several of the rhythmic interventions discussed throughout this part of the book, and also addressed in my research (see Berger 2012). Many additional tracking logs can be developed, following activities such as "improvisation," task attention (how short, long, etc.), task creation and organization, and other interventions. The music-based treatment environment is the clinician's laboratory. Any and all clients are research "subjects," especially clients with sensorimotor issues and survival-anxiety, regardless of age or diagnosis. Therefore, the treatment process can be looked upon as being continuous research into the curative elements of music—which ones are significant, in what manner of application, with what results. In sum, all *structured* approaches to music-based treatment are, after all, not hit or miss, but rather, *systematic* application of exacting music elements for addressing explicit needs and behaviors. Therefore, treatment sessions and interventions are well designed and well structured, achieving unambiguous results as *evidence-based* accounting. After all, ongoing music therapy is an accountable *treatment*, not simply a momentary therapeutic entertainment.

The well-trained music-based clinician understands the difference.

CHAPTER 8

Observing With a Clinical Eye

A goal without a plan is just a wish.

Antoine de Saint-Exupery (1900–1944)

The above quotation from Saint-Exupery (French author of *The Little Prince* 1943) hits the nail on the head, so to speak! A goal without a plan is indeed only a wish: a desire that cannot become reality unless steps are taken to develop actions ensuring the attainment of the desire. In clinical work, this goes without saying. In treating any diagnosis through music-based interventions, the goal ("wish") must be carefully assessed and defined, objectives well articulated, music elements and human physiology properly understood, and observations very rigorous for developing treatment plans leading to reaching the goal. In culminating Parts One and Two, it is worth reiterating some thoughts expressed in the Prelude:

> ...the world is not perceived as a series of independent sensory experiences to which the integrity of each modality's "snapshot" view is preserved intact in its own location in the brain; rather, there is an interweaving of different sensory impressions through which sensory components are subtly altered by, and integrated with, one another. The product of these integrative processes is perception. (Stein and Meredith 1993, p.xi)

Furthermore, "The integration of inputs from different sensory modalities not only transforms some of their individual characteristics, but does so in ways that can enhance the quality of life" (p.xi).

Quality of life presumes that a person is comfortable within his or her body, and that COPING faculties are intact. When addressing sensory, emotional, cognitive, and behavioral interactions through music-based treatment, assessments of observed behaviors from a physiological perspective, are undertaken by clinicians with trained *clinical eyes*. In this manner interventions can be focused to address more than just *symptoms* of a diagnosis. The astute clinical eye, paired with a calculated understanding of goal and objectives, can help lead to possible treatment of *causes* that are shaping behaviors. Behavior, after all, is communication. When a presenting demeanor is associated with physiological contingencies possibly manipulating behaviors, the music-based clinician gains profound insight into which interventions could directly address what this "communication" is revealing. However, developing goals and objectives explicitly for music-based treatment, other than being entertaining and fun, is not simple. In the music therapy profession thus far, goals and objectives have often been borrowed from psychology, or assessments of allied clinicians, school-developed academic and behavioral programs (e.g., IEPs), or borrowed from other treatment modalities. However, using an outsider's goals and objectives as music-based treatment dismisses the opportunity to treat *with* and *through* music itself. Instead, music becomes a kind of accompaniment to the objectives of others. This is unfortunate, because while goals of allied clinicians can certainly illuminate particular issues currently arising, and how their areas of treatment plan to address those, the music-based clinician must evaluate what music—specifically, *music*, the acoustic intervention—can *add* to the overall treatment plan. Although music treatment may, every now and then, encompass supplementary treatment areas, the music elements, in and of themselves, are unique resources not readily available in other treatments. Although one wishes that music were included in efforts of allied therapies, we clinicians have six discrete music elements serving as treatment tools, and this is understood and taught (hopefully) in music therapy training programs. I tend to refer to these elements as "pharmaceuticals" prescribed for various human agendas (though this analogy has often been greeted with disdain). The approach to treatment described throughout this book provides sequential, "treatment prescriptions" and session modules for addressing particular functions through some of these music "pharmaceuticals" (e.g., rhythm, dynamics, timbre). The beauty of this is that these elements combine in an *aesthetic* way, impacting emotion!

A school administrator once asked me to explain how music therapy fits into an educational setting, and why this service should be included: what are the goals specific to *this* intervention that are not already covered through OT, speech, and cognitive services? My response was quick and simple: "music therapy goals are based on factors that *prepare* the brain and body for learning by addressing needs such as environmental, auditory, attention, focus, and emotion—areas that the other services do not venture to address!" I graciously informed the ominous powers seated around the conference table that learning cannot, and *will not* take place while the system and brain are busy elsewhere dealing with survival (see also Schneck and Berger 2006; Tennant 2005). Allied clinicians do not treat survival-anxiety, repetitive behaviors, nor auditory and attention deficits. Having said this to "them," some questions for us are: "Why and how does music prepare the mind and body for learning?" "What are *we* doing that is different and goes beyond what allied services do?" Our music-based objectives surely are not academic goals ("...child will count; read" etc.); surely not directly speech goals ("...child will pronounce 'th'; will describe his clothing" etc.); certainly not OT and PT goals ("...child will thread a chain of beads...child will toss a ball into a net..."). While music-based treatment objectives may be supporting and even incorporating some of the objectives of allied clinicians into our treatment, we understand that clinical music addresses physiologic necessities from a broader, *holistic* perspective (or so we like to believe). That means that music energies, through its six elements (rhythm, melody, timbre, dynamics, harmony, and form), can address many mind-body functions to regulate the system and prepare it to receive, process, and retain information more contextually. Why? Because music requires *no semantic translations*, and the elements immediately resonate with body functions (emotions, energies, tensions, movement, etc.) that can be altered, depending on how music elements are applied.

In several of my published papers on the subject of developing goals and objectives, I propose the analogy that the clinician can think of *goals* as describing a final destination—that which needs to be changed and altered in order to reach *the end of the road*, *objectives* as the various roads to be travelled for reaching the end destination, and *interventions* serving as the vehicle(s)—the specific music elements in treatment strategies and approaches that will help the vehicle navigate the road toward the *goal*: the final destination (see Berger 2009, 2010). The importance of understanding how to define and develop goals and objectives cannot be underestimated. These are precisely what differentiates music activities from being *therapeutic* recreation, entertaining pastimes, or performances, to music as a *therapy*—a treatment protocol to reach a long-term end result. In the Eurhythmics-based sensorimotor treatment protocol presented over the previous chapters, music-based treatment is the means to reaching a "destination." None of these extra-medical services will "cure" a major diagnosis, but the goal of treatment with music and rhythms—the establishment of COPING abilities through objectives and interventions that can drive a person toward that goal—remains unique to the music-based therapy profession.

The last seven chapters have explained that we humans are instinctively *emotional* animals, with brains obtaining information only through its seven sensory systems, processed in a sequential flow from stimulus in context, to perception interpreted by emotions that ultimately succumb into corresponding responses. We have come to realize that even psychology is physiologically driven, that sensory systems are interactive, one influencing another, and that presented ASD behaviors communicate ongoing survival-anxiety, fight-or-flight responses, driven by sensory over- or under-load, mis-communication, and inefficiencies causing auditory distress, and unfortunate information processing resulting in erratic and stressful brain-body reactions. We discussed ASD movement deficits that could be contributing factors to a poorly developed sense of self, and limited social and cognitive skills. Music has been defined as *energy*, and energy as a life force, with each of six music element's energies available for addressing brain-body coordination. Most important, we briefly reviewed some information-processing brain functions, and especially the activation of the HPA axis in survival-anxiety (fear) fight-or-flight response, and axis responsibility in the creation and secretion of catecholamines that are destructive to cells and organs when continually present in higher amounts. Now that we understand the structure of the proposed Eurhythmics-based sensorimotor clinical work for systematic treatment approaches, with the goal throughout of attaining functional COPING skills, levels of Calm—Organized—Paced—INtegrated—Growing (maturing) standard of living minus stress, stereotypical behaviors, or survival-anxieties, we can reply intelligently to administrative staff, parents, and others about *what* music-based treatment is, and *how* it contributes clinically to the treatment team. So, if a speech pathologist is working on verbal enunciation, the music-based intervention will involve the recorder, kazoo or harmonica for oral-motor and breath control, the addition of melodic contour replicating language prosody and inflection, and fill-in songs recalling and intoning vocabulary, and more, thus supporting *but not "copying"* speech pathology. The same is true for the work in body movement that can help the system rhythmically organize and become paced and balanced, even as the OT is looking for muscle tone and motor-planning, because music-making activities involve the whole body, and quick responses in Eurhythmics interventions addressing muscle tone through body dynamics and use of variable energies, and motor-planning. Yes, the music therapist is a team player, but not as a duplicator of, or accompanist to what others are doing. In fact, it has been my experience that most often other clinicians seek the advice and input from music clinicians to help shed light on their own problem solving. In all, the clinical eye of the music therapist will observe and support the development of holistic interventions that address the brain, mind, and the body. This will result in adaptive sensory function, and a positive relationship between client and clinician, since Eurhythmics-based activities involve the equal participation of the clinician with the client, as described in previous chapters: in movement activities, instrumental improvisation, singing, mirroring, physical prompting, and other interactions.

Case example analysis

Let us take a look at a case example that required a very keen clinical eye in order to assess abilities and contributing factors of particular behaviors. While perusing the description, readers are encouraged to think ahead about what behaviors might have indicated, which sensory system(s) appeared to be impacted, and in what order the COPING objectives needed to be administered, in accordance with the information attained thus far in previous chapters. (This case has been presented often in many of my conference presentations, and is pertinent to our discussion of "clinical eye.") The following information represents actual in-session behaviors logged over an assessment period of four 45-minute individual sessions in the private music therapy studio.

CASE EXAMPLE 9

Female child, five years old. Diagnosis: pervasive developmental disorder/not otherwise specified (PDD/NOS); limited expressive language, good receptive language; general cognitive delays; some eye contact; may have absolute pitch.

Description: child loves music; will sing all lyrics to any song she knows; uses some, but very little language. Will request for specific needs (food, drink, etc.). Loves drums, and will be *perseverant* on playing drums; is compliant and can be directed with prompts. She occasionally smiles when pleased, provides eye contact, and will connect with parent and siblings. Can be directed, will accept prompting, but learns best through *role modeling* by others. Child currently attends regular kindergarten, and is receiving speech pathology; occupation therapy; applied behavioral analysis (ABA). Parent indicates that although child is basically cooperative with others, she prefers to be left alone, and will interact only in a limited brief manner with others.

Clinician observations during initial 45-minute assessment sessions:

1. Child *smiles* when hearing children's tune.
2. References therapist each time child approaches an instrument; however, does not reference when engaged in joint music making.
3. Prefers drums; uses primarily right hand; continually drops mallets.
4. Develops excellent rhythmic patterns on drums; sustains pulse intermittently but if both hands used, pulse sounds like "ka-thump; ka- thump..." right-left, the left arm being fraction slower than right.
5. Strikes xylophone primarily with right hand; shows little exploration of sounds on xylophone.
6. Difficulty playing designated tones on xylophone.
7. Seems troubled by certain sounds, e.g., tolerates loud gong but not loud piano; likes recorder, but dislikes kazoo.
8. Does not imitate what therapist is demonstrating or doing on an instrument.
9. Little curiosity about variety of instruments around the room.
10. Jumps on trampoline for short periods, but does not like to hold maracas; cannot clap cymbals while jumping; prefers to hold someone's hands while jumping; jumps with straight legs (knees are not bent especially when landing).
11. When sitting next to therapist at piano, child *looks away* as therapist plays.
12. Is non-possessive of objects (one can remove an item she is involved with, and she will not demand return of it).
13. Has difficulty jumping with, and landing on two feet.
14. In "Jack Be Nimble" task in which child's cue to jump is when lyrics say "jumped over the candle stick," child has difficulty waiting until lyric cue is reached, and difficulty timing prep-and-jump sequence.

Given these observations, and based on what has been presented throughout this book, what clinical assessments can be made about this child's functionality? What objectives can be designed to address some of the listed presenting modes? Let us take a look at some of the individual observations and reflect on what the responses may be communicating:

1. Child *smiles* when hearing children's tune
   What assumptions can be made?

   a. Probability: brain is tracking linked sounds because she is recognizing the song; or *something* in this tune is recognizable and pleasing to her; she finds this particular sensory information to be "safe" and entertaining.

   b. Possibilities but perhaps inaccurate assumptions: she may be recognizing the actual melodic contour and deems the tune as being familiar, she likes the timbre of the presenting instrument(s) and/or voice rendering the tune; OR—is unaware of the timbre(s) but follows just the melody or rhythm or lyrics…OR…she's receiving an entirely different sensory perception (maybe is experiencing a good taste in her mouth, or seeing nice color designs?).

   c. Unknowns: *What* about this tune is she relating to? Melody? Rhythm? Harmonic flow? Timbre? Particular pitches (e.g., mostly high or low; scale or skips; lyrics)? Will she *consistently* recognize and respond to this tune if presented in other formats, e.g., other instruments, a cappella vocal; new keys? *What* is she actually perceiving when listening to this tune? Other sensations? Visuals? Tactile? Tastes?

In my very first session with this child, the parent informed me that this girl absolutely *hated* the song "Twinkle, Twinkle Little Star," or its alphabetic version. The parent advised that at no time should the child be presented with that tune, either sung with lyrics or simply played on an instrument. It had not been determined by anyone why this particular song would be so upsetting. The cause for this was left undetermined. As in treatment for allergies and phobias, it was determined (by me) that many presentations of this tune might extinguish whatever dislikes, fears, or other sensory issues the child might have in the presence of this song.

2. References therapist each time child approaches an instrument, but not when engaged in joint music making:

    a. Possible assumption—is insecure, seeks adult approval; may be fearful that she may not be allowed to touch/play/participate without adult permission; other unknown reasons. (By the way, this is the kind of referencing behavior encouraged by Relationship Development Intervention (RDI) practiced by many speech pathologists, though RDI is not referenced in any clinical reports for this client.) It could also be a result of the ABA training in which her expectation may be some kind of "reward."

    b. Does *not* reference therapist when engaged in joint music making perhaps because she may be unable to multi-task-process sensory information: visual + auditory + motor plan + + ??

3. Prefers drums; uses primarily right hand; continually drops mallets

    There are several possibilities here. To begin with we know that:

    a. Drums do not require linear linkages of "melodic" tones and contours, making rhythm information somewhat easier to invent, and for the senses to process.

    b. Drums provide deep proprioceptive input through vibrations that she can sense through her hands/arms and throughout her body.

    c. May be most familiar with this instrument that may be more commensurate with her instinctive needs and interests; her system may require and/or prefer rhythmic organization above all else.

    d. She may be *synesthetic*: maybe she processes pitch frequencies of tonal instruments less comfortably, or through cross-processing with other senses. What if she actually tastes pitches and it disturbs her?

e. Uses primarily right arm:
      i. perhaps weaker in left arm (uncoordinated muscle tone)
      ii. may lack mid-line orientation
      iii. brain may not know she even has a left arm, and if so, where it is.
   f. Continually drops mallets: clear indicator of uncoordinated proprioceptive information in brain: how much to grasp, what is the object, how much energy is required to adjust grasp in playing; *also*: indicates LOW muscle tone which is one result of inaccurate proprioceptive information processing.

4. Develops excellent rhythmic patterns on drums; sustains pulse intermittently but if both hands used, pulse sounds like "ka-thump; ka-thump…" right-left, left a fraction behind right (arms uncoordinated in parallel movements)
   a. Possibilities: hears rhythm inside her head; brain can instruct arms to execute what she hears in her head; may be hearing and repeating rhythmic patterns of word syllables she may be hearing in her mind.

Rhythm controls this child's behaviors, and appears as well to help coordinate her physical actions and reactions. Through the session, as long as rhythm was present, her system was able to entrain to the pulse. This enabled her to stay calm, stay on task, and sustain a pulse very well for the length of the task, which could be indicative of her system's ability to quickly "adapt" to the environment through "entrainment" activities. Cognitive implications of this rhythmic organization is that in school, educational materials might be provided to her within a rhythmic structure. Language input to her from others should be rhythmic and well paced—*not too fast*. The ka-thump drumming with parallel arms clearly indicates (and confirms) low muscle tone in her left arm, lack of appropriate proprioceptive feedback from her body's left side to the brain, and the inability to coordinate bilateral arms in parallel movements. Any drumming intervention will require physical hand-over-hand prompting to "teach" the brain how to coordinate both arms moving simultaneously.

5. Strikes xylophone primarily with right hand; shows little exploration of sounds on xylophone

    Again, *low muscle tone* and insufficient motor-planning issues in left arm; does she even know she has a left arm? Where is it? Does she know what she needs to do to use it? As for "little exploration of sounds on xylophone," here again, since the xylophone is a tonal "pitch" instrument, we question whether there could be extenuating conditions that cause discomfort with tonal instruments. Is she comfortable with "pitch"? Does she hear melodic contours in her head that she'd want to duplicate? Do various timbres interest her? Does the sound irritate?

6. Difficulty playing designated tones on xylophone

    Here we encounter an important possible *visual tracking* issue, and *eye-hand coordination* problems. Child could not easily find the designated tones on the xylophone, nor could she consistently follow her arms as they moved about to find and play the pitches. Tones were marked with color dots, so when asked to play on the "red dots," or on the "yellow happy faces," she was unable to consistently find and play those pitches, with either of her hands. Yes, it could be a form of resistance or disinterest, but in that case, she would have balked, complained, or completely avoided the task. However, she sat and attempted to comply, but for a fleeting moment, before returning to the drum. Therefore, it was determined that some visual and/or auditory infraction was preventing the execution of this task. Interventions would be required to address this—perhaps through learning to play piano, or a familiar tune on the xylophone instead of random tones? The discomfort with tracking her arms and locating the pitches implicates mid-line orientation problems, and even basic resistance to structure, though with her ability to invent structured rhythms, this was unlikely.

7. Seems troubled by certain sounds, e.g., tolerates loud gong but not loud piano; likes recorder, but dislikes kazoo

Timbre processing issues! Questions: What is her actual *perception* of certain sounds? What does she actually *hear*? Do both ears work stereophonically? She did not like using the kazoo—was that a dislike of oral vibrations and the timbre distortion of her voice? What about tolerance of overtones? Is her auditory system selective in preferring one register or timbre over another, as in high vs. mid or low? Again, is she *synesthetic* regarding certain timbres or pitches? Is this a reason she abhors the song "Twinkle Twinkle Little Star," or the instrument or voice that originally presented this song?

8. Does not imitate what therapist is demonstrating or doing on an instrument

    Clinical eye will observe and ask: Is there a problem with prefrontal lobe "mirror neurons"? Does she even understand *self* and "*other*"? Are there problems with her imitative motor-planning? What is her *visual perception*? What does she really "see" or visually perceive? And, does she see more than is there? Images unseen by others? Images emanating from sounds? Many questions that could lead to erroneous assumptions. Does she "see" (perceive and process) what I am doing?

9. Little curiosity about variety of instruments around the room

    Does she consider the environment safe for exploration? Does she understand that various items are, in fact, music-making instruments? Does she *discriminate objects* and labels well enough? What is her level of *self-presence* awareness within any setting? From her constant referencing of an adult, is she able to make independent decisions or is she awaiting directions or approval? Has she been directed by others all her life so far? And if so, might that be altered through interventions involving more creative exploration? Disinterest in "making" music, or undertaking creative expression, could also be the result of related language deficits, since she was basically non-verbal, or at least, disinterested in verbally communicating. Organizing a thought—"stream of consciousness"—and expressing it pragmatically could be a major problem, and rhythmic drumming can fill that communication void. In fact, is she instinctively already doing this? Her drumming self-expression shuts out the rest of the world, and does not generalize into forms of expressions in other abstract ways, such as through making various random "sounds" on instruments other than drums.

10. Jumps on trampoline for short periods, but does not like to hold maracas; unable to clap cymbals while jumping; prefers to hold someone's hands while jumping; jumps with straight legs

   Here we encounter *vestibular insecurity* with *visual implications*. Her spatial sense may be distorted; her sense of "upright" may be problematic; motor-planning for jumping and vestibular corrective maneuvers seem problematic; maraca sounds may be distracting and further demonstrating the child's inability to multi-process sensory information. She presents with erratic upper-/lower-body coordination—motor-planning deficits that are inhibiting physical multi-tasking. This was confirmed by the parent who offered that the child's physical therapist and OT also reported physical multi-tasking problems. The child required holding someone's hands during jumping, and did not flex her leg joints while jumping, which further indicated vestibular insecurity, motor-planning deficits, and "fear" of disengaging from the ground.

The remaining four observations, 11 through 14, described at the beginning of this case, further stimulates one's clinical eye in assessing this child's treatment requirement. In summary, her sitting next to clinician at the piano but looking away when clinician played (see observation 11) questions her ability to multi-task both hearing and seeing simultaneously. Did she look away because she was "tuning out" the visual in order to hear? Did seeing distract hearing? Motions of the clinician playing, the black and white keys, books on the piano rack, and other items may have been an overload of visual information distracting adequate listening ability. Seeing and hearing are multi-sensory tasks.

Being non-possessive of objects (see observation 12) or easily relinquishing an object implicates a limited sense of possession—self/mine/yours—or a lack of commitment to an item. In other words, all items have the same value to her—one is not more important than another—a "take it or leave it" attitude. Or, none are important altogether. Is the easy relinquishing of an object a signal that child is in continual "fear" of reprisal if not compliant in relinquishing an object? Is this communicating something about home or school life?

The child's difficulty jumping with, and landing on, two feet (observation 13) further addresses vestibular insecurities, and again bilaterality and motor-planning issues, as noticed when her arms had problems simultaneously playing drums. Does the brain know that both legs belong to this body? Right/left coordination seems to be lacking, so does she know she has two sides to her body? And finally, in the "Jack Be Nimble" task (observation 14) in which the child's cue to jump was when the song lyrics reached "jumped over the candle stick," the child had difficulty waiting until the lyric cue was reached, and also presented with difficulty timing the prep-and-jump motor sequence.

Two questions the clinician needs to answer when assessing a case presenting with many problems, are: i) Given these observations, what information about the child's functionality can be drawn? and, ii) In what priority order do treatment objectives need to be considered based on this information? Obvious areas of function immediately pop out: breath control to relieve anxiety and connect with the clinician through recorder; structured rhythm activities in both seated and moving positions as described in Eurhythmics exercises; vestibular and proprioceptive motor-planning issues need addressing through "quick response" activities forcing the brain to call for immediate and better organized movements; prompting for bilateral arm movements; creative exploration on tonal instruments and joint music making with the clinician; vocalization and "singing" if possible, and much more. Treating through Eurhythmics music-based interventions as described is a natural structured approach addressing many of this child's current needs. Since her auditory system appears intact, music (which she loves) is the ideal intervention, and rhythm the best resource, since rhythm has been the key to this child's ability to organize. In addition, all other therapies and academic instructions need to incorporate a form of rhythm in order to sustain this child's attentive abilities. All her "social and language skills" seem dependent upon rhythmic interventions.

In reviewing this case, although answers are complex, and many clinicians can reach a variety of different solutions, when thinking physiologically and Eurhythmically from a "clinical eye" vantage, many answers begin to appear. This child's survival-anxiety is instinctively controlled by a recessive, withdrawn, isolating demeanor, the opposite of "fight-or-flight." Her "flight" is through withdrawal, a kind of "freeze" effect often experienced in frightening circumstances. As soon as a form of adult "approval" is garnered, this child proceeds about her drumming business, separating herself from all, with no further contact. Her motor-planning, proprioception, vestibular, and visual senses are functioning with inadequate interactions, so that her movements and corrective maneuvers (such as in her jumping, or bilateral playing) are limited. She needs to hold on in order to jump. She does not "imitate." She moves erratically and with rigidity. She does not tolerate much tonality and shows signs of possible synesthetic sensory cross-processing.

In sum, the goal of COPING and the objectives and activities presented throughout Part Two provide highly effective opportunities to modify this child's behaviors. As for the "Twinkle" song issue, it was resolved as follows: after presenting it once, in its usual form, with the child closing her ears, shrieking and humming an atonal sound until I suspended playing the song, I decided to investigate what she might actually be *perceiving* that distressed her about this song. So one day, I decided to play it with an altered meter and key signature, and began playing the song as a 3/4 time Waltz tempo, in the key of C# major! I did not sing the song lest she recognize the lyrics and become troubled. I just played it, quietly, lyrically, and slow-waltz like. No negative reaction! In fact, she sat down in a chair near the piano, looked at me, smiled, and allowed the entire song to be played twice through. Did she recognize it? The answer was unclear, but during her breath-control exercises with the recorder, I often played this song in slow 3/4 time, in the key of G major, and she enjoyed blowing the designated recorder-blowing pattern, which I had slightly modified to accommodate the 3/4 meter. Eventually I gradually returned the song to its 4/4 meter, but continued to play it in many different keys. The "allergy intervention" seemed to work, because never again did she find this song problematic.

Most of the other activities presented in the structure in earlier chapters, were successful in redirecting this child's responses toward positive interaction and COPING. We worked together for several years before she and her family moved elsewhere. Her progress, physiologically, emotionally, cognitively, and even socially, increased by such large percentages that school personnel often requested observing her in music treatment sessions. Apparently she verbally communicated with me more than with others, although much of our sessions were non-verbal interactions, movement, rhythm, and creative improvisations. Her OT and PT incorporated various suggested rhythmic activities (such as bouncing a ball onto a tambourine rather than into a basket, etc.) that ultimately changed the child's manner of moving, jumping, seeing, and even multi-tasking. While music-based Eurhythmics treatment does not take all the credit for the child's progress, it can be said that the majority of movement and music-making work played a major role in modifying this child's deportment and emotional well-being.

Conclusion

Conclusion? In fact, there are no "conclusions" to the music-based clinical work, nor to the information presented in this section of the book. We do not *conclude*. We *commence* absorbing new, clinically rigorous and physiologically astute concepts about what music, and music-based treatment, means, how music elements contribute to brain-body connections, how carefully and *systematically* to approach teaching the brain new options for responding to various stimuli, and how the astute "clinical eye" of the music clinician who comprehends the factors he or she is observing, will amalgamate the information into selecting objectives that reach the COPING goal. Since we emotional animals respond *instinctively* first and think afterward (bottom-up/top-down), treatment described herein proposes creating *new* instincts (new homeostatic settings), trading negative perceptions for better alternatives. The most important point to understand is that humans, like animals, depend exclusively on sensory feedback systems informing brains about the planet, the self, and others. When that function operates sufficiently, the feedforward results (brain to body) present more functional behaviors. Otherwise, anxiety becomes pervasive, flooding the system with lethal chemicals, and subsequent responses resemble "fight-or-flight." In such HPA axis-driven reactions the brain is incapable of learning. Erratic or inaccurate multi-sensory interactions also impede such functions as socialization, language, self-awareness, and other skills.

Addressing physiologic/sensory irregularities is the *first priority* on the road to COPING. Well-articulated assessments of sensory and emotional needs, and development of pertinent goals and objectives, with targeted interventions that apply music and movement interaction to address various modes of incorrectly-driven behaviors, *precedes* addressing cognitive and social proficiencies. After all, the role of the clinician is primarily to guide the client toward self-organization and the ability to remain Calm—Organized—Paced—INtegrated—and Growing: to cope (adapt) in a comfortable manner. Once that becomes the new normal, other conduct will fall into place.

Part Three
PUTTING IT ALL TOGETHER

CHAPTER 9

Eurhythmics for Treating Other Diagnoses

As we begin to amalgamate the information presented in the book, it is helpful to recall the basics: that humans are emotional animals and responses are first instinctive. That means, responses to sensory system information are basically automatic, with reactions based on homeostatic set-points; thinking enters afterward to explain and figure things out. The brain's knowledge of external and internal events is derived from electric signals from any or all of the seven sensory systems. The sequence is that a stimulus, in context, converts to "action potential" traveling into the brain where perception, shaped by emotion, results in a response. The brain does not "see" or "hear" or "touch-feel," and so on, per se, but rather receives and perceives these feedback sensory signals, triggering neurons to communicate with each other and activate neurotransmitters and the CNS for a feedforward response. These sensory systems work *in tandem*, multi-modal, in an interactive multi-sensory activation based on homeostatic settings of the system. The brain and body are not separate entities. Animals function in a unity of brain-body events, holistically, provided that all systems are operational. Sensory systems monitor both external and internal occurrences. *Exteroception* refers to the monitoring of external events through vision, touch, audition, smell, and taste, while *interoception* monitors internal events through proprioception, the vestibular system, and also smell, taste, and audition depending on event (e.g., we taste inside of our mouths, and can "hear" our stomachs gurgle). In as much as we are emotional animals, the amygdala, thalamus, hypothalamus, and related regions of the brain's limbic area consult regarding the safety or danger of all incoming information. Perceiving the information as being "safe" means that no survival actions are required. The brain may then continue further processing, coding, and storing the information. Judgment of danger is good in that it is an important survival alert that activates the HPA axis (see Chapter 2), flooding the system with catecholamines (cortisol, noradrenaline, etc.) to prepare the body for fight-or-flight. However, on an ongoing basis, if information is mostly misunderstood or considered threatening, survival-anxiety becomes a constant state of being, with the amygdala and HPA axis continually flooding the system with catecholamines in preparation for fight-or-flight. This is not good because chemicals, such as high levels of cortisol, can destroy cells, muscles, organs, and more.

Reviewing the paradigm: Teaching as treatment

Neuroscience research on brains of musician vs. those of non-musicians, as discussed in earlier chapters, has been indicating that the brains of musicians are more efficient and better organized in information processing than are the brains of persons who have not had musical training. Most important is the active participation with music, along with movement and "ear training." As discussed earlier in the book, making music is a multi-sensory physical activity directly involving the auditory and motor cortexes joined by proprioceptive, vestibular, visual, and tactile information required for locomotor and non-locomotor motions (hand-clapping, foot tapping, "dancing," drum-beating, piano playing, etc.). The sense of taste is sometimes also involved in music making along with oral-motor activities (e.g., singing, blowing wind instruments). Thus music-making, whether instrumental or vocal, is a whole-brain-*whole-body* activity, implicating at least five, if not all seven, sensory systems and interactive brain areas. Furthermore, auditory and motor cortexes are highly interactive in the presence of music, music-making, and strong rhythms (see Gran and Brett 2007; Janata and Grafton 2003; Patel 2006, 2008; Warren, Wise and Warren 2005; Zatorre, Chen and Penhune 2007). What's more, the described Eurhythmics-based sensorimotor treatment modules support the idea that treating the brain and body through rhythm, breathing, and movement interventions is analogous to *teaching* the brain new, "automatic" response options to bring about systemic organization and alter homeostasis for the better. In short, clinicians are teaching the brain "a new normal," just as music educators teach the brain new functions. When such "teaching" is approached in the same manner as training the brains and bodies of musicians, it can also change the brains of special needs populations, bringing about many positive sensorimotor and physiological interactions, steering the system away from anxiety to yield efficient functional adaptation—COPING: Calm—Organized—Paced—INtegrated—Growth.

This paradigm—treatment as teaching through rhythm and movement—is not limited to working only with people with ASD. As suggested in previous chapters, and in various references, many other diagnoses fall into similar sensorimotor, emotional, and movement shortcomings. For example, there is a neurologic and genetic association between ASD and Parkinson's disease, often resulting in the need for similar movement and rhythmic interventions addressing parallel issues (Hollander *et al.* 2009; Ridgel, Vitek and Alberts 2009; Wright 2011; Yochum and Wagner 2009). What's more, sensory processing, anxiety, locomotor, and non-locomotor movement setbacks are similarly indicated in diagnoses such as PTSD (Eckberg 2000; Levine 1997; Macnaughton 2004; Ogden, Minton and Pain 2006; Payne, Levine and Crane-Godreau 2015; van der Kolk, McFarlane and Weisaeth 2007, 2014; Weber 2008), Parkinson's and stroke (McIntosh *et al.* 1997; Nolano *et al.* 2008; Nombela *et al.* 2013; Thaut 2008; Thaut, McIntosh and Rice 1997; Thaut *et al.* 2007; Zabriskie 2010), cerebral palsy (see Altenmüller *et al.* 2009; Kwak 2007), Alzheimer's, other dementias, and typically functioning ageing populations (Hutchison and Balota 2003; Li *et al.* 2001; Pai *et al.* 2003). Many other physiological, psychological, and psychiatric diagnoses, including schizophrenia, bipolar disorders, depression, Angelman and Rett's Syndrome, stroke, and fetal alcohol spectrum disorders, all contain similar needs for calming, rhythmic, and movement intervention, and COPING, since various movement irregularities and deviant behaviors often produced by various health conditions cause continuous states of hyper- or hypo-arousals that impact responses to external and internal sensory stimuli, yielding recurrent survival-anxiety (fear). This results in the brain and body's inability to COPE adaptively with present, previous, or ongoing circumstances. The paradigm upholds that music, especially rhythmic movement, and music vibrations comprise adequate stimuli, in various roles as forcing functions, urging the brain and body to "learn" functionally adaptive options in response to sensations. This is applicable in any music-based treatment protocol, since music *forces* movement and change, without requiring semantic definition, directives, or interpretation. A paper by van Vugt and Tillmann (2015) reminds readers that "Music and speech are skills that require high temporal precision of motor input" (Abstract, p.54). They continue to suggest that given the poor temporal resolution of somatosensory information that drives motor learning (i.e., motor-planning), auditory feedback contributing to the control of *timing* helps the system correct "error-signals" of perceived timing errors. For our purposes, research results of this investigation supports the idea that auditory feedback, and the embodiment of rhythm (for our practice, including locomotor and non-locomotor Eurhythmics interventions) are necessary for teaching the brain temporally precise timing, whether for language or body movements.

Eurhythmics-based sensorimotor interventions go further, getting "right to the quick," as the colloquial expression states. Eurhythmics in music-based treatment of sensorimotor functions "gets to the quick" through quick response calling for immediate action. This technique addresses not only symptoms of observed inadequate movements, but also probable *causes* driving some of those characteristics. Of service to the paradigm and technique of Eurhythmics-based clinical work are two hypotheses reviewed below.

Hypothesis 1

Eurhythmics-based sensorimotor interventions will redirect fight-flight survival-anxiety behaviors in ASD and other diagnoses, and bring about calm and functional adaption through rhythmic embodiment that can organize the system and yield COPING skills.

This hypothesis supports the opinion that characteristics of ASD, on any level of the spectrum, as well as many other childhood and adult diagnoses, indicate a state of instinctive perpetual survival-anxiety (fear) and ongoing levels of distress, whether intense or mild. Such a state harbors a hyperactive amygdala and HPA axis driving fight-or-flight behaviors. This pervasive state of being is possibly attributed to inadequate sensory processing. Based on this hypothesis, clinical music for sensorimotor organization must begin by first attending to the calming of brain-body systems. This is done through breathing and rhythmic non-locomotor (i.e., seated) and locomotor movement interventions that can organize the body and sensory interactions, ultimately reducing anxieties, and preparing the brain and body for further learning. In addition, "ear-training" interventions can bring about astute auditory function, as it does in the training of musicians.

Hypothesis 2

Eurhythmics-based sensorimotor interventions for rhythm embodiment can enhance "quick response" motor-planning of movement while correcting several movement inefficiencies in autism, such as dynamics, sense-of-body and self, that limit social skills, language and relationship development, cognition, and general well-being.

Hypothesis 2 suggests that movement deficiencies are innate and pervasive in ASD and other diagnoses, are often unaddressed or indirectly included in music-based treatment, and that this inefficiency impedes the learning of social skills, imitative movements, eye contact, sense of self, knowledge of self and others, and communication (language) abilities. Therefore, Eurhythmics-based treatment interventions involving body movement and rhythmic embodiment, addresses movement as a priority (after calming the system), in an integrative, holistic manner, to develop body dynamics, automatic motor-planning through quick response to music cues, eye contact, and many other observed behaviors of ASD and neurophysiologic characteristics of other diagnoses. The clinician creates the music environment through improvisation, the client reflects that music through breath control, rhythm, and movement. The predominantly non-verbal interplay between clinician and client, brings about calm, organized, instinctive motor-planning, upper-/lower-body coordination, and much more, as has been shared in previous chapters.

Eurhythmics in treating other diagnoses

The Eurhythmics-based sensorimotor clinical music treatment technique presented in Part Two, outlined five distinct modules addressing the goal of COPING for a Calm—Organized—Paced—INtegrated—Growing demeanor. Objectives and interventions describe the intentions of each intervention, with the session flowing in an arch-like manner, beginning with Module 1 seated, breathing and rhythm exercises, flowing through Modules 2, 3, and 4 moving and music making, applying locomotor interventions, instrumental and vocal improvisation and drumming structures, concluding with Module 5 seated, for end-of-session decrease of energies to exit in calm.

Throughout the book readers are provided with extensive references to support and illuminate various sensorimotor and movement characteristics, not just of autism, but also of many similar neurophysiologic diagnoses, so that the reader can draw on the extant information available, beyond that discussed throughout this book. In the section immediately preceding this one, the select references provided, among the myriad that exist, suggest ongoing research in sensorimotor and neurologic brain-body functions diagnosed in many medical issues and diseases, not just ASD, and that this is far-reaching and worthy of further investigation by the music clinician. Continued research can aid in understanding both the science of illness and diagnoses, and the science of music and rhythmic interventions. Much of the information underscores the thrust behind the evolution of this Eurhythmics-based sensorimotor music therapy treatment technique. The information below, largely based on aforementioned research and references, further supports the need for this structured music therapy technique to address physiologic and emotional functions of clients in *any* diagnosis. We must begin with the brain-body emotional relationship.

Eurhythmics in psychodynamic therapy

As we music clinicians know, a wide variety of clinical music treatment protocols are rooted in the history of psychodynamic talk therapy, based in theories in psychology (i.e., cognitive-behavioral, Jung, Freud, etc.). Many music therapy training programs are ingrained in psychology theories, psychoanalytic techniques, and psychoanalysis, concerned with such psycho-emotional features as the role of "transference" and "counter-transference," and the "therapeutic relationship" between client and clinician. As important as these aspects are when a trained psychoanalytic clinician treats emotional and psychiatric functions, it does often preclude attention to the *physiologic* constraints responsible for deviant behaviors, particularly the over- or under-loaded sensory systems. To repeat the words and concepts of Dr. William Wundt in his book *Principles of Physiological Psychology* (1902; also review Chapter 1): "Physiology is concerned with all those phenomena of life that present themselves to us in sense perception as bodily processes." In short, even psychology is physiology. A person cannot be "talked out of" a poorly behaving physiologic system that is causing psycho-emotional problems. It must be somatically experienced—a body sensation. And because music was created by humans with elements that the body understands—periodicity (rhythm, cycles); tonal frequencies (pitch, melody); complex frequencies (overtones, timbre, harmony); structure (form)—the body immediately understands the message in music. In a statement by neuroscientist Antonio Damasio on a record jacket of a Deutche Grammophon recording of Schubert *Lieder* (date and other information unavailable), this scientist/Schubert lover confirmed that:

> The universal power of the greatest music—and some of the greatest music is Schubert's—comes from a prodigious coincidence: such music fits like a glove into the secret codes with which the body transmits its signals to the brain, and because body codes and music codes are the same, the brain treats the messages of that music as if they were coming from the heart, not the ear.

The presentation of Schubert *Lieder* for clinical body work most likely is not undertaken (although research into this would be very interesting), but other ways of reaching the brain and heart through the ear and body are ideal ways of approaching psychological problems. Let us review some diagnoses for which Eurhythmics-based sensorimotor movement interventions can be applied in psychodynamic treatment.

Post-traumatic stress disorder

Survival-anxiety and *fight-or-flight* responses are prevalent and pervasive in *observed* behaviors of PTSD, schizophrenia, obsessive compulsive disorders, paranoia, depression, anxiety, and any other types of emotional anguish, across all age groups. Potentially, music and movement can obtain excellent results, non-verbally. In treatment for PTSD, several psychotherapists have thankfully moved from talk therapy exclusively, into treatment approaches that combine sensorimotor and body awareness through both non-verbal and verbal therapy, recognizing that many psychological behaviors are, indeed, sensory-driven, and that trauma is retained in the body. Body movement interventions as psychotherapeutic treatment are being undertaken more and more. It is understood that the body retains and displays anxiety—muscle tensions, distorted body positions and movement (e.g., shoulders high, neck stiff, facial frowns). These characteristics need to be alleviated, but talking them away is not enough.

Dr. Pat Ogden and colleague Dr. Kekuni Minton, at the Sensorimotor Psychotherapy Institute based at Naropa University in Boulder, Colorado, advise us that "Sensorimotor Psychotherapy is a method that integrates sensorimotor processing with cognitive and emotional processing in the treatment of trauma" (Ogden and Minton 2000). Clearly the importance of integrating sensorimotor processes with other functions is critical in achieving adaptive levels of COPING, for any age group. In the Abstract of their paper, Drs. Ogden and Minton further explain that "Unassimilated somatic responses evoked in trauma involving both arousal and defensive responses are shown to contribute to many PTSD symptoms and to be critical elements in the use of Sensorimotor Psychotherapy."[1]

---

[1] Their paper and those of several others, are available through the Institute at http://sensorimotorpsychotherapy.org/articles.html.

Music-based clinicians and other readers working psychodynamically with PTSD victims of trauma, abuse, and dysfunctional families, of any age, are encouraged to investigate sensorimotor psychotherapy, and perhaps include some of the concepts into Eurhythmics-based music treatment.

Several other prominent clinicians working with sensorimotor and somatic psychotherapy approaches include Dr. Peter Levine (1997) at the Somatic Experiencing Trauma Institute in Colorado[2], and Dr. Bessel van der Kolk and colleagues (2007; van der Kolk 2014) at the Trauma Center at Justice Resource Institute in Massachusetts.[3] Of particular interest about sensorimotor and emotion work through the body in PTSD is that behaviors and physiologic problems parallel fight-flight symptoms, survival-anxieties, similar to reactions encountered in *autism*, and other diagnoses. I am sometimes tempted to consider ASD as a form of PTSD, as suggested in earlier chapters, replacing "Post" with "Pervasive," since it appears as an ongoing traumatic stress discomfort (TSD) based on similar pervasive sensorimotor deficits. In ASD, traumatic stress may not result from any particular *previous* episode, but is an inherent continuous (pervasive) event. Survival-anxiety incorporating the body and muscle function, and the fight-or-flight responses, is driven in PTSD, ASD, and elsewhere by the HPA axis, the vagal nerve and CNS that Dr. Stephen Porges discusses in his *Polyvagal Theory* (2011). Anxiety functions proprioceptively and vestibularly, tensing muscles and joints and implicating balance, along with auditory and visual emotional perceptions. While talk therapy and other psychotherapeutic interventions (e.g., cognitive-behavioral) achieve some success, those that include body and rhythm work are alleged to bring about more frequent and permanent coping skills in these trauma diagnoses.

For the music-based clinician who seeks to work in a *psychodynamic* manner with PTSD and other emotionally-driven behaviors, several of the Eurhythmics intervention modalities put forth in Chapters 5 and 6 can be easily adapted and modified for treating PTSD at any level, from children to adults and combat veterans. To begin with,

---

2   www.traumahealing.org.

3   www.traumacenter.org/about/about_landing.php.

Module 1 using a recorder or other wind instruments for breath control is an important way to initially reduce anxiety and bring about a sense of calm. Multi-rhythmic movement interventions involving upper and lower body responding to rhythmic and emotional music cues provided by the clinician (as suggested in Modules 2–4) can be modified to instigate various sensations and emotions, while increasing body sensation awareness in which the client can sense muscle tensions and changes that occur through the activities. These types of intervention can then be discussed and analyzed. Full-body Eurhythmics movement (slow walks, shift of directions, and other such activities), song writing and instrumental co-music making with a clinician within an arc-like flow of Modules 4 and 5, including some of the approaches of Analytical Music Therapy practiced by music therapists Mary Priestley (1994) and Benedikte Scheiby (Scheiby and Pederson 1989; Scheiby 2015), will address psycho-emotional pain and sensorimotor organization. Eurhythmics interventions are especially effective in childhood PTSD because movement activities are familiar and fun, while reducing survival-anxiety behaviors and releasing body tensions. Perry and colleagues (1995) suggest that approaches to treatment must underscore the persistent state of fear that a traumatized child experiences, and therefore interventions should first be concerned with minimizing anxiety and regulating the arousal system. This is precisely what Eurhythmics techniques discussed earlier seek to achieve in the person of any age with ASD, so there are many similarities involving survival-anxiety behaviors in both ASD and PTSD populations (see Rothschild 2000).

Other physiologic and psychiatric diagnoses

For many other psychological, psychiatric, and brain damage diagnoses, including schizophrenia, obsessive-compulsive disorders, manic depressive bipolar diagnoses, dementias and Alzheimer's, the same behavioral symptoms are observed—the sensory systems are uncoordinated with information perceived incorrectly by the medicated or diseased brain, much anxiety pervades, and outbursts, labile emotional reactions, and fight-flight responses are the norm. In schizophrenia, for instance, there is minimal self-awareness, as in autism. Furthermore, autism and schizophrenia in many ways resemble each other's behaviors and existence, in that both exist in a basic sense of dis-embodiment and social dysfunction (Stanghellini 2009; Stanghellini and Ballerini 2002, 2004). Recall that Jaques-Dalcroze was influenced by a psychology colleague and became involved in Eurhythmics work with persons of psychological and emotional distress (see Chapter 4). So indeed, many of the Eurhythmics, movement, and improvisational activities outlined in the Modules 3, 4, and 5, are very adaptable for sensorimotor music-based treatment for schizophrenia, and patients with psychological and psychiatric needs. Modules 4 and 5 could include not only instrumental, but also vocal improvisations and song writing reinforcing memory, body sensations, and events.

Speaking of music rhythms, an interesting paper by Wolf Müller and colleagues (2014) at the Psychiatric Institution at Herford Hospital in Bünde, Germany, describes a pilot study investigating whether long-term exposure of psychiatric patients to music that was individually adapted to brain rhythm disorders associated with psychoticism could act to ameliorate psychiatric symptoms! Without going into all the details here, what is interesting is that after the 18 months of exposure to specifically designed and selected music, the researchers found that not only were psychoticism and paranoia ameliorated, but to their surprise, also psychotic and phobic *anxieties* as well, compared to the control group (see Müller *et al.* 2014). So clearly brain rhythms impact brain and body, and vice-versa, and given brain plasticity and brain's rhythmic function (Buzsaki 2006), Eurhythmics interventions, which go beyond just listening to CDs, but participating in rhythmic playing and moving, can change perceptions and behaviors of psychiatric populations, through consistent applications over longer periods of time.

For many of the above diagnoses, the Eurhythmics-based treatment goal would be the ability to COPE—that is, to be Calm—Organized—Paced—and Engaged—while many of the treatment objectives entailed in the interventions would still apply, with age-appropriate modifications and expansions. Many if not most of the tasks are viable, in one-on-one treatment, as well as in group encounters in hospitals or health-care settings, so the music clinician might consider incorporating Eurhythmics technique modules into psychiatric clinical practice.

Parkinson's, stroke, cerebral palsy, and other movement incapacities

There is no doubt that rhythm has been playing a key role in movement rehabilitation for Parkinson's and other physical incapacitations. There has been extensive research on Rhythmic Auditory Stimulation (RAS) indicating that structured rhythmic movement interventions bring about excellent rehabilitation in Parkinson's, stroke, and other physically incapacitated patients (see Hausdorff *et al.* 2007; McIntosh *et al.* 1997; Thaut 2008; Thaut *et al.* 1997, 2007, among others). Proposed here is that with the inclusion of Eurhythmics interventions to already existing rhythm treatment and forced exercise (Ridgel *et al.* 2009) more can be accomplished. Eurhythmics-based interventions described can serve as a form of "forced" exercise, as described in the Ridgel paper (2009). For example, one particular intervention conducted with several of my clients with ASD was the step—blow, step—blow, not only enabling the pacing and vestibular and cerebellar (movement) cooperation of balance of the step-stop-blow…step-stop-blow exercise sequence, but blowing into the recorder during the stop increased breath control and balance as well. This could work well in some Parkinson's movement interventions. In many instances of Parkinson's, the brain must have time to organize proprioception, vestibular, and cerebellar interactions, since walking is a fall-rebound shift-of-weight motion. In addition, the music for Eurhythmics movement interventions for Parkinson's would eliminate much extraneous auditory information (such as song lyrics, orchestrations, various timbre), so that the brain could concentrate purely on a the pulse, pace of movement (tempo), and simple rhythmic patterns (not the tick-tock of the metronome), so that the brain remains attentive. As the movement rehabilitation begins to take hold, multi-tasking movements such as marching and clapping (or playing tambourine) to a familiar march (Sousa, Yankee Doodle, etc.), and other new movement activities (stop-start-change directions, etc.) for balance and shift of weight would be supported by improvised keyboard to which the system responds. With Eurhythmics interventions, the gait training would follow the module sequences described in earlier chapters, beginning first with seated position, legs moving in rhythm to the march (without vestibular concerns), while hands beat a tambourine to further embody the pulse and pace. The sequence modules described in Part Two would function similarly for Parkinson's as for ASD and other characteristics, with modification considering age and ability of client/patient. To repeat, many, if not all, the Eurhythmics treatment exercises are applicable or can be modified while keeping the sequence flow, for Parkinson's, ALS, cerebral palsy, wheelchair confined patients, and stroke and language rehabilitation, aided by the inventiveness and inventive adaptability of the music clinician.

A note about Eurhythmics and disorders of consciousness

There seems to be no available research on music and rhythmic movement interventions for patients in vegetative or minimal states of consciousness. However, it is not inconceivable that co-treatment between a music clinician and a physical or occupation therapist could, through hands-on prompting, infuse the brain with certain sensory (proprioception), auditory, and tactile rhythmic information to somehow teach the brain what needs to be relearned, that could also bring about some levels of arousal states. Rhythmic music and prompted movements could impact on the state of consciousness, given the assumed plasticity of the brain. We will leave this thought for future research and potential application of Eurhythmics activities for this population.

Eurhythmics for the "typical" ageing population

The risk of falling due to weakening muscles, decreasing visual and auditory acuity, and slowing of proprioception and vestibular sensory information processing are deficits that can endanger the senior adult, physically and psycho-emotionally. Corrective interventions are especially important for this population, and merit special application of Eurhythmics-based treatment with multi-tasking movement activities such as are detailed in earlier chapters. Free movement, as in some of the transitional interventions described in Chapters 6 and 7 (slow walking, change of directions, imagery in movement, etc.), alternating with structured, rhythmic multi-tasking movements, such as marching or sliding while shaking maracas, playing tambourine, blowing a recorder, extending arms in various directions, and so on, and responding to rhythmic music rendered by piano improvisation, are excellent training tasks for regaining "quick response" motor-planning, balance, and agility, without risk of falling. The multi-tasking reflection of rhythms and improvised piano music and its impact on the ageing populations is being researched, several concluding that not only does rhythmic movement strengthen and become secure through Eurhythmics multi-tasking activities, an increase in cognitive ability and general betterment is also derived (Hars *et al.* 2014; Trombetti *et al.* 2011). Research is progressing in several ongoing projects being conducted at a Geneva hospital and will be published shortly.[4] Eurhythmics-based music and multi-tasking treatment for the ageing population is at the forefront of music and geriatric wellness, and holds many opportunities for music clinicians who can learn and apply Eurhythmics in music-movement services for the betterment and well-being of the growing senior population. Eurhythmics exercises described in our previous chapters are similar to those being provided to seniors by a few clinicians with Dalcroze backgrounds, so there is room for further development in clinical work by creative music therapists.

Eurhythmics-based music/movement interventions can play a major role in rehabilitation of many diagnoses, as discussed above, in addition to autism. Consideration of survival-anxiety factors along with typical body-rhythm pace of clients (too fast, too slow, inconsistent, and more) will account for the type of rhythmic intervention presented, and the multi-tasking requirement thereof.

---

4   The research is undertaken in collaboration with the Institute Jaques-Dalcroze in Geneva, Switzerland, the international centre for Dalcroze training www.dalcroze.ch/the-jacques-dalcroze-institut, accessed on 5 June, 2015.

A very fast-paced system may need slowing (often observed in PTSD); a very slow system may need speeding; a rhythmically erratic paced system (as in an emotionally labile person) may need consistent rhythmic organization based on emotional moods. There is much to consider, indeed, but keeping Eurhythmics interventions in mind will give way to many excellent treatment interventions within the technique and modules discussed. Ultimately, the goal of COPING (or, to COPE) always remains the target.

A brief look at related movement theorists

For the interest of the reader, various important contributors to movement interventions will be briefly mentioned. Most have had impact upon the dance profession, although many of the concepts of movement can be adapted, or may have been included in Dalcroze Eurhythmics activities, since Jaques-Dalcroze was already in existence and practice across the world. The main difference between Dalcroze Eurhythmics and other body movement contributors is that music and rhythm are fundamental elements in driving movement. Still, some investigation of other movement theorists could be applicable in interventions and needs articulated throughout the book.

Rudolf von Laban (1879–1958)

Hungarian-born Rudolf Laban is considered to be one of the major important figures in the history of dance, dance education, and also music education's incorporation of rhythmic movement. Overlapping somewhat with and influenced by the work of Eurhythmics and Jaques-Dalcroze, Laban was intrigued by movement and believed that everyone should be trained in movement as a way of learning to develop self-awareness and creativity. His writing and those of his followers (Abril 2011; Laban and Ullman 1971; Moore and Yamamoto 2012) ascertains that there are four main factors involved in locomotor movement: time, space, flow, and weight. In addition to the body movements in time and space within a certain flow and use of energy, there are eight unique body actions that make up the movement vocabulary, either individually or in compounded manner. These are: floating, gliding, wringing, pressing, flicking, dabbing, punching, and slashing (Abril 2011). Of interest in Laban's concepts are the similarities in movement behaviors of ASD and other movement deficit populations. Clinicians observe several of the listed actions, especially wringing, flicking, pressing, and sometimes punching or dabbing, in uncontrolled stereotypic self-stimulating upper-body movements, with whole-body variations of the energy, flow, and so on. (Several YouTube clips demonstrate some of Laban's movement analysis. I suggest that readers further investigate this online.) For muscle tone, occupational therapists often ask clients to push, or pull: actions defined by Laban (for other purposes). Laban's major contribution to the world of dance is his effort-shape analysis ultimately enabling its translation into dance notation. Laban Notation, which undertakes to completely notate choreographic works, based on his movement analysis (effort-shape) of the above mentioned vocabulary, is the major efficient notation of dance currently available. To date it is the only way that dance works can be retained specifically for future restaging, since just filming does not provide the expanse of energies and body phrasings required by the choreographer.

As for Eurhythmics-based sensorimotor treatment in ASD, combining with Laban movement exercises appears to be ideal in music-based treatment formats. David Frego, Chair of the Music Department at the University of Texas in San Antonio, is a major exponent of and trained in Dalcroze Eurhythmics. He has written extensively and conducted many workshops in support of Dalcroze Eurhythmics in music education, as well as in music-based treatment. His article on Dalcroze in therapeutic settings (Frego 2009) supports much of the ideas expressed in Laban's work, as well as in Eurhythmics-based music treatment. Laban worked in tandem with movement teacher Imgard Bartenieff, and resources for investigating Laban/Bartenieff's work are extensive. Online sites and YouTube films are available and recommended for readers interested in further exploring Laban/Bartenieff movement methods to add in clinical work. Many training centers exist, and a major training center and library in the

United States is housed in Brooklyn, NY.[5] A new and important contribution to Laban movement education and clinical work is titled, *The Moving Researcher: Laban/Bartenieff Movement Analysis in Performing Arts Education and Creative Arts Therapies* (Fernandes 2015). This is a very helpful reader for the music-based clinician in understanding movement as education and treatment. Although Laban/Bartenieff is based in dance, and dance therapy, Eurhythmics-based treatment, though not at all "dance," incorporates much of the movement analysis upon which clinicians can determine objectives and interventions for body awareness, proprioception, energy (dynamics), and much more, in treating ASD and many other diagnoses.

Moshé Feldenkrais (1904–1984)

Another important contributor to movement and wellness concepts was Moshé Feldenkrais, an Israeli physicist and engineer who at one time was a research assistant in the lab of Frédéric Juloit-Curie, in France. In 1933, Feldenkrais connected with Jigoro Kano, the founder of judo. He became a good friend of Kano, who encouraged Feldenkrais to study Asian martial arts, judo, ju-jitsu, and such movement activities. Skipping a description of his war-time activities during the Second World War, we move to post-1946, when he continued his studies of judo, and the scientific nature of the sport. He also connected with information on Alexander Technique, and others of the time, involved in body regulation. In 1945, he published the book, *Body and Mature Behavior: A Study of Anxiety, Sex, Gravitation, and Learning* (Feldenkrais 2005). Subsequently, he began to develop his particular method of movement healing, which he referred to as the Feldenkrais Method. It was basically designed to improve human function by increasing self-awareness through movement. His teaching philosophy was that increasing a person's kinesthetic and proprioceptive self-awareness of movement could yield increased function, pain reduction, greater self-ease, and pleasurable movement (see his papers in Beringer 2010). This is precisely similar to Peter Levine's somatic experience and Pat Ogden's sensorimotor psychotherapy discussed above in treatment of

---

5   www.limsonline.org/, accessed on 5 June 2015.

traumas. Therefore, it seems logical that the Eurhythmics-based music clinician could employ some of Feldenkrais's movement approaches, with the interaction of Eurhythmics movement, that would well address sensory issues (proprioception and motor-planning).

The Feldenkrais book that I found extremely informative in relation to psychotherapeutic treatment is his *Body Awareness as Healing Therapy: The Case of Nora* (1977), in which he describes his method of work with Nora, an elderly psychiatric patient, and the results he obtained through his movement interventions. On the website of the Feldenkrais Guild of North America[6] his movement technique called "Feldenkrais Method of Somatic Experience" that subsumes several sensorimotor connections, is described and filmed, including reading resources and more. Rather than encumber the reader with many more references and information, I draw attention to many listings about Feldenkrais on the web, and through internet research, readers will encounter excellent details and YouTube viewings of how the Feldenkrais Method operates. It is something well worth investigating, with the potential of integrating some of the movement techniques in Eurhythmics-based sensorimotor and movement treatment of ASD, Parkinson's, and others.[7]

Frederick Matthias Alexander (1869–1955)

Finally, a brief note about the Alexander Technique. Since this particular movement training is more widely known and used in the performing arts and in sports, it is only given brief mention here. Frederick Matthias Alexander was an actor—Shakespearian, at that. His technique resulted from his discovery of how his body carriage impeded his vocal transmission; he recognized that he was always in a contracted body demeanor, stiff-necked, head held back, and so on. On tour with the theater, he became more and more aware of head carriage and tightening of upper musculature, how it impacted on his speech, and how it appeared in other actors.

---

6   www.feldenkrais.com, accessed on 5 June 2015.

7   See also www.feldenkraisboulder.com/article-content.asp?edition=18section238article=33/.

He worked on his body and began to sense that perhaps he could help others improve health and wellness through improved body carriage, different ways of holding the body comfortably upright, prone, or seated. Thus began the Alexander Technique (Alexander 1995; de Alcantara 2011), which is widely applied to musicians and performing artists, among others.

There are differences among the techniques of Alexander, Laban, and Feldenkrais. Laban is the only one who employs music to support and enhance the eight body energies his technique outlines (see above). Another difference is that the movement approaches of Laban and Feldenkrais seem more aesthetically, sensorimotor, and psycho-emotionally based, whereas in Alexander Technique, there is basic concern with the carriage of body and limbs, and how musculoskeletal areas are used, and it includes more clinical hands-on prompting and body correction by the instructor. This is not to compare the quality of the interventions. All are equally valid in body-centered movement treatment for personal wellness. Alexander Technique seems to be more concerned with movement corrections and less with sensory-emotional self-expression. All three systems are worthy of further investigation by the music-based clinician since each can contribute unique ways of supporting and altering movement inefficiencies in any population. In addition, clinicians could benefit from training in any of these techniques for their wellness.

Although Alexander Technique is also mind-body, it may be somewhat less adaptive to Eurhythmics-based music treatment for ASD because it implicates more use of instructor directives, and more hands-on prompting, whereas the objective of Eurhythmics treatment is the development of free expression and "quick response" corrections of motor-planning stimulated entirely by music. In addition, hands-on correction in autism could add to client stress and anxiety. There is one self-published book discussing autism and Alexander Technique, but the treatment is not music based and the clinician is not a music therapist. However, it may shed some light and ideas for readers interested in combining Alexander with Eurhythmics treatment. The book is titled *Autism and Alexander Technique: Using the Alexander Technique to Help People on the Autism Spectrum*, written and self-published by Caitlin Freeman (2014) who identifies herself as an autism specialist, service provider, and faculty member of the Theater department of Point Park University in Pittsburgh, Pennsylvania. Other than this short book, there appears to be little writing about use of Alexander Technique with special populations, although it may be applied but clinicians have not written about the treatment.

In sum, again the reader is referred to further online research, because there are volumes of books on Alexander Technique, including many sites and YouTube clips demonstrating various exercises and activities that may be of further interest to the reader. Let us keep in mind that Laban trained with Jaques-Dalcroze and incorporated many of the music/movement/sensory concepts; Feldenkrais focused on somatic and psychological experience within movement—whole-body sensations; Alexander was concerned with the carriage and muscular flexibility of the body, and efficient motions. Jaques-Dalcroze Eurhythmics is a unique design for full embodiment of rhythm and music; the main purpose of the system is for internalizing and reflecting music events through the body, which, as treatment, can produce changes and sensorimotor adaptations in autism and other special needs populations.

Final thoughts

The main point in this chapter is that regardless of diagnosis, the *sensory systems* and the *body* must be addressed in any treatment approach to so many neurophysiologic diagnoses and characteristics. Survival-anxiety is inherent in most diagnoses; the body remembers trauma, fear, and survival-anxiety that prevents calm and coping. The Eurhythmics-based sensorimotor music therapy structure and technique presented in the previous nine chapters provide the opportunity to bring about a sense of wellness and betterment through a systematic clinical procedure, with interventions focused on the physiological derivatives of many emotional struggles accompanying physical and mental difficulties, along with the observed resulting behaviors. This is not just effective for autism, but also for many other neurophysiological, sensory, and medical problems. It is hoped that the information will be helpful in the practice of music-based clinical work.

Coda: **C**are, **O**rganization, **D**evelopment, **A**chievement

> *Do not be astonished by new ideas; for it is well known to you that a thing does not therefore cease to be true because it is not accepted by many.*
>
> Baruch Spinoza, philosopher

Well, we have come to the end of our book. It has been a long process in the writing and research, and surely an even longer process in the reading and amalgamation of the information. It may take several readings to digest all the information. I would like to suggest that music-based clinicians seriously consider adopting the techniques described for Eurhythmics music-based sensorimotor treatment, because they are dedicated to addressing important physiologic issues of autism behaviors that require direct, focused, and repeated interventions. What matters is the consistency with which interventions are administered from one session to the next. The five modules described are intended to flow in the sequence described, and be repeated in the same manner from session to session. It is equivalent to skills training and practice.

The goal for Eurhythmics-based treatment of autism is to bring the system around to an adaptive level of COPING. Objectives within the modules specifically address issues that need interventions. As long as the modules and objectives remain dedicated to the overall goal and objectives sequenced and described, the interventions within the modules can vary, be expanded or decreased, by creative clinicians who will invent many rhythm-movement-improvisation interventions beyond those sampled here. Important is the *consistent repetition* of interventions, with developmental increases to strengthen gains made in treatment.

This technique of Eurhythmics-based music treatment for autism attends to some of the *causes* driving the observed symptomatic behaviors. Socialization and communication are important, but secondary to treating survival-anxiety and commensurate behaviors such as ambient hearing, auditory insults, peripheral vision, erratic movement, and other observed fight-or-flight behaviors. When *un*observable causes of behaviors are attended to, observed resultant behaviors will revise. As for the client-clinician relationship, so often focused upon, the most important relationship in music treatment is that of the client *to the music in the room, his or her own music making,* and *the body*. The client-clinician relationship automatically results from joint music making and movement interactions. Socialization, eye contact, and the rest will increase once the client begins to feel comfortable in the body.

I encourage clinicians to trust the music, more than words! By "teaching" the brain and body new options, in a similar manner to the way musicians are taught, the possibility of deriving progress and positive changes is strong. Ear training, rhythm, and the elements of music and movement are excellent treatment resources, and when the clinician uses a particular music element for a particular movement or need, changes will be observed over time. Music elements such as tempo should not be random, but rather, conscientiously calculated and applied—fast, slow, medium—whatever the assessed needs require. Tonality, dynamics, timbre all have individual roles to play in asking the system to respond in certain ways. And of course, rhythmic pulse and pattern—not just any rhythm, but rhythm for a particular purpose. Also, improvise…improvise…improvise! In-the-moment music means something "new" and unexpected in the moment—new sounds, new texture, new rhythm, new melody and harmony—all teaching the ear, brain, and body to process new events comfortably. Use keyboard and piano for strong vibrations and resonance.

Advice: Will clients resist or oppose participation as described? Will clients be unable to blow a recorder, or move about the room? Indeed they will. My advice to clinicians is to *be persistent*—gently—and patient. Resistance or inability are not deterrents, just indicators that revisions and adaptations may be required. All the information presented throughout the book is actual, not philosophical. Interventions and session flow have been, and continue to be, practiced as described and my experience has been that amazing results can be achieved! Yes, it takes time and patience, by both the client and clinician, but ultimately, things fall into place and become the "norm." Will the clinician flow through all five modules in a session? Perhaps not—so careful *selection of objectives and interventions* will be required, with the exception of the "calming" element which needs to be present in every session. In my own clinical work, there were times when I felt that the session was wasted because I was unable to flow with the modules. *Solution:* tomorrow is another day! I never lost sight of what was needed, so waiting it out to return to routine was useful. In the end, music-based treatment is *cumulative.* One day more or less will not impede progress. (When I used to worry about my child missing a day of school, my dear father used to say, "So what? So she'll be smart a day later!")

A note about the appendices: In addition to an intervention progress rating scale, session behavior rating scale, and a sample session report, I have added two of my previously published articles from a music education journal. One shares information about a clinical session I had with a dementia client, and the other talks about understanding the child with special needs in school music classes. This latter one I've included for music clinicians who work in schools, and who can advise teachers and music educators about how to understand, work with, and redirect behaviors of children with special needs.

The References and Further Reading list are extensive, and readers are encouraged to obtain and read some of the research and other materials listed, in order to further knowledge of physiology, ASD behavior, Dalcroze Eurhythmics, and more.

Finally, my selection of the Spinoza quote at the top of this chapter was deliberately chosen for two reasons: first, Spinoza is one of my favorite philosophers whose ideals resonate with mine; second, the quote articulates a truth—do not be astonished by the new ideas as presented in this book. We are emotional beings functioning largely on instinct. *That is a truth.* The brain modifies and codes sensory information in order to make sense of the environment; seven sensory systems interact and cross-process in order to derive functional adaptation; music is an adequate stimulus in the forcing function role to yield changes. *These are all truths,* whether or not the new information presented throughout this book is accepted or denied. What matters is not to be in agreement with the information, but to *hear* it, *dissect* it, *understand* it, *learn* from it, *pursue* it further, and *make it useful* in treating populations for wellness and coping. I use the letters of the word "coda" to stand for Care—Organization—Development—Achievement because it succinctly defines what the music-based clinician strives for.

In the end, I have loaded you down with much information and hundreds of references. I have shared with you my knowledge, and what I believe to be a necessary and important treatment technique for well-focused, Eurhythmics-based sensorimotor music therapy. For me this was a labor of love.

The rest is up to you.

APPENDIX IA

Intervention Progress Rating Scale

Name .... Date ....

	Rep. 1	Rep. 2	Rep. 3	Rep. 4	Total
RECORDER BLOWING (160) Tempo:					
8 short blows					
4 long blows					
8 short blows					
4 long blows					
8 short blows					
4 long blows					
8 short blows					
4 long blows					
Did not undertake/complete task					
CLAPS (160) Tempo:					
8 hand claps					
8 lap claps (parallel arms)					
8 hand claps					
8 lap claps (alternate arms)					
8 hand claps					
8 foot stomps (alternate legs)					
8 hand claps					
8 cross-over lap claps					
Did not undertake/complete task					

	Rep. 1	Rep. 2	Rep. 3	Rep. 4	Total
MARCHING TASK (20) Tempo:					
Sitting/tambourine (w/prompt)					
Sitting/tambourine (no prompt)					
Marching w/o tambourine (prompt)					
Marching w/tambourine (prompt)					
Marching w/tambourine (no prompt)					
# of reps to full time					
DRUM TASK (80) Tempo:					
w/prompt; w/o prompt; w/role model					
8 beats parallel arms					
8 beats alternating arms					
8 beats parallel arms					
8 beats cross-over					
Additional information:					
RATINGS: (420 total possible rating) 0 = did not/would not undertake 1 = hand-over-hand prompting but incomplete 2 = complete; hand-over-hand a must 3 = will do with some prompt/role modeling 4 = independent with role model only 5 = full sequences entirely independent					
Total points acquired for session:					

Task Performance Rating Scale: 0—5 points per repetition at 60bpm. Numbers in parenthesis signify total points available for task after 4 repetitions in the session.

APPENDIX 1B

Session Behavior Rating Scale

OVERALL BEHAVIOR RATING—CURRENT SESSION

Name_____ Session #_____ Date_____

Rating: 0–5 with 5 being best/most positive

	1	2	3	4	5
A. Overall session demeanor					
1. Ability to sustain organized movement					
2. Ability to follow directives					
3. Ability to stay on task					
4. Ability to wait quietly for next repetition (1 minute)					
5. Ability to wait quietly for next task (2 minutes)					
6. Ability to provide visual attention to task and/or clinician					
7. Requires behavior reinforcers during session					
8. Level of repetitive behavior/self-stimulation need during session or task					
B. Overall task execution (including motor-planning, prompting, etc.)					
1. Ability to follow beat and stay on pulse					
2. Ability to imitate actions of task from role model					
3. Requires continuous physical prompting for task execution					
4. Level of resistance to physical prompting					

SESSION BEHAVIOR RATING SCALE

	1	2	3	4	5
5. Level of resistance to undertaking task					
6. Ability to recall task and/or sequences					
7. Requires redirection or reminder to remain on task					
C. Overall physical/sensory constraints					
1. Level of upper–lower body coordination					
2. Level of motor-planning ability					
3. Level of expressive language ability					
4. Ability to control movement at slower pace (vestibular)					
5. Level of mid-line orientation/crossing					
6. Level of general auditory sensitivities					
7. Level of bilateral upper-body coordination (without physical prompting)					
D. Overall response to Music Therapy Treatment					
1. Remained calm and attentive during session					
2. Smile indicating enjoyment during session					
3. Task(s) enjoyed best overall: blow					
claps					
marching					
drumming					
	Sum of Scores per items_____					
	Total overall score _____					
	Top Total Score Achievable: 140					

Summary: Overall Behavior Rating During Sessions
Name_____ Session#_____
Date_____
TOTAL SCORE AND COMMENTS:
_____
_____
_____
_____
_____
_____

APPENDIX 1C

SAMPLE BRIEF REPORT OF CLINICAL WORK AND RECOMMENDATIONS FOR A CLIENT

The following brief report indicates clinical work with an adult ASD client in their mid-40s, upon completion and discontinuation of Music Therapy services (for various reasons). It was intended to advise their carer or aide that portions of exercises could and should be continued, with assistance, for the benefit of the client, in order to preserve the progress gained over several years of Music-based treatment.

DORITA S. BERGER, PhD, MT-BC, LCAT
THE MUSIC THERAPY CLINIC
Board Certified Music Therapist NY
Licensed Creative Arts Therapists
27 Chipmunk Lane, Norwalk, CT 06859
203-853-4426
dsberger@mags.net

June 3, 2014

Re: Music-based treatment for X
From: Dr. Dorita S. Berger, PhD, MT-BC, LCAT

To whom it may concern,

X has been experiencing music-based treatment for several years, at my Music Therapy Clinic in Norwalk, CT. I would like to review some of the work and progress we have accomplished, and to urge that music experiences should not be discontinued. What follows is an outline of the procedures that persons involved with X can undertake simply and in productive ways.

Overall Review

Several areas of treatment (objectives) have been focused upon during each 45-minute music-based treatment session, as recently itemized:

- Reduction of anxieties and fears.
- Accurate vocal and verbal imitation.
- Increased appropriate non-directed organizational skills: organization of self, organization of environment, task organization, etc.
- Decrease and redirection of stereotypic behaviors.
- Fine and gross motor skills: development of good posture and generally comfortable gross and fine- motor movement planning; development of body dynamics in movements.
- Sensory coordination.
- Cognitive development: number concepts, identification of letters, colors, words, etc.
- General psycho/emotional well-being (having fun!): identification of feelings and emotional states and self-esteem.

Recommendations

1. X is riddled with fear and anxiety, therefore many times during the day, she should have an opportunity to "relax to music," radio, CDs (using the ear-phones) or to reduce anxieties. Also deep breathing through blowing the recorder, and drinking water to redirect stress, is IMPORTANT.

RECOMMENDATION: 5 or 10 minutes every now and then during the day, X simply sits or lies down comfortably, listening to quiet music (lullabies, etc.) before undertaking any other activity, so that her system releases tension and is relaxed for further action.

2. For accurate vocal and verbal imitation, X has learned to blow into a recorder and hum into a kazoo, in order to help develop appropriate use of her vocalization skills. After over a year of work, X now understands and blows her recorder, and can imitate sound patterns produced by another person who is blowing along with her. She also understands that to derive sound from a kazoo, one must produce sound through humming (use of self-voice) into the kazoo. She loves to try doing that, and is successful deriving some kazoo sounds at each "practice."

   RECOMMENDATION: It is important that X continues practicing the blowing of a recorder—copying how the aide does it—and continues to try vocalizing through a kazoo. Since she is quite familiar with this routine, it should be continued with a staff member who does not need music experience, but simply sits opposite X and enjoys joint music making through the kazoo and recorder. This activity should be continued on a *daily basis*, a couple of times a day, if possible (e.g., in the car or before or after a meal).

3. Redirection of repetitive and stress behaviors includes the ability to self-direct, and undertake some enjoyable music activity. X loves to play xylophone, and also loves to do drumming, so some fun and familiar music can be played on a CD, so that she can play along. She has an excellent sense of rhythm, and will sustain this task for as long as music is playing. She is very familiar with this routine.

   RECOMMENDATION: Select a down-time during her day, take out the xylophone, and the drum/cymbal, put on one of her favorite CDs, and have a joint session of playing with the music. The xylophone activity can also be used to calm X. Select a slow song (e.g., lullaby, or other third-stream quiet flowing music), and play along with her on the xylophone. This will reduce stress, redirect anxiety, and entertain X with her own progress of playing along with staff and CD. In the studio she has been known to continually smile when undertaking this task.

4. Body movement, posture, flexibility of movements, body directions (up, down, high, low, side, back, etc.) have been worked on through movement and "dance-type" of activities from the very first session. X will try to imitate another's movements, whether flowing a scarf, raising arms above head, jiggling body, etc., so if staff undertake to "dance" with X, she will try to imitate movements, which can help release body tensions and create a level of flexibility of movement.

RECOMMENDATION: The CD titled *Kids In Motion*, which can be obtained through Amazon, and is not very costly, should be used several times a week. Tracks 1, 2, and 4 in particular have been successfully used as background music to jazzy movements. A staff person undertaking this activity with X can move in many different ways (arms high, side, low), which X will try to imitate. Dancing and movement organized in this manner does help her develop a sense of body flexibility, and a positive sense of self, which is currently lacking in X, contributing further to her anxieties and insecurities.

In general, other objectives listed above will be addressed if X continues participating in music activities each day. Because several of the above asterisked objectives require clinical knowledge, they are not addressed here, except to indicate the importance of continued interaction with music activities that will yield positive behaviors at home.

OVERALL RECOMMENDATION: Music activities should be part of daily routine for X. From simply blowing a recorder and kazoo several times a day, to structured activity on the xylophone and drum, to quiet listening to music, it is highly recommended that a simple routine can be followed and conducted by any staff member, on a daily and weekly basis, in the following sequence:

1. Blowing recorder and humming kazoo (5-6 minutes), rest, drink water.
2. Clapping hands, knees, shoulders, sitting and stopping with feet, to a rhythmic beat of rhythmic music (6–8 minutes).
3. Improvising music on the xylophone; playing random tones, both hands parallel and alternating; playing on the designated tones with yellow happy faces stickers on them, in order to involve simple eye tracking and focused playing (10–12 minutes).
4. Movement—dancing to *Kids In Motion*, or jazzy CD (15 minutes).
5. Drumming to fun songs (5–10 minutes).
6. Concluding with "down-time" relaxing, listening to slow quiet songs.

In conclusion please know that structured music activities time is very important to continue for X. It is not only a matter of various developmental considerations, but also for quality of life. After all, there is a person inside of that body, and that person is alive and responsive. Music-based interventions have been known to help make positive changes in chaotic and unfocused behaviors. There is extensive research in this area, and staff are encouraged to find some of the many papers on this subject.

It is assumed that music activity will continue. It is hoped that a structured music time will be part of X's routine with staff, parents, and others undertaking joint music activities *on a daily basis*, as listed above.

Thank you for your attention and compliance in continuing Music Therapy treatment for X. I am pleased to be consulted if further needed.

Respectfully submitted,

Dr. Dorita S.Berger, PhD, MT-BC, LCAT

APPENDIX 2

MUSIC SOOTHES THE RAVAGED BRAIN

(Article reproduced from *TEMPO* magazine, October 2013[1])

Collette walked into the room with a frown on her brow, a look of doubt and confusion on her face, and fear in her eyes. She scanned around the room as she sauntered toward the couch, dragging her legs in a very unstable walk. Collette was grunting sounds of disapproval, resistance, disturbance. Mumble…mumble…mumble…mumbling some low-tone jumbled commentary we could not understand. She gazed intensely at my face expecting a response to her gibberish chatter. I did not understand what she was trying to communicate, but I smiled and continued singing "Hello Collette" to the tune from Hello Dolly. It took some 10 minutes to settle her comfortably onto the couch on which she would remain during our session.

Collette has been suffering from Dementia with Lewy Body (DLB) for several years, progressively losing speech, cognition, motor control, self-care skills, and more. Dementia with Lewy bodies overlaps clinically with Alzheimer's and Parkinson's diseases but is more associated with the latter. Within DLB, the loss of cholinergic (acetylcholine-producing) neurons is thought to account for the degradation of cognitive functioning, as in Alzheimer's disease, while the loss of dopaminergic (dopamine-producing) neurons is thought to account for the degradation of motor control, as in Parkinson's

---

[1] *TEMPO New Jersey Music Educatiors Association Jounral*, October Issue, 62–63. Available at www.academia.edu/4975113/Music_Soothes_The_Ravaged_Brain_TEMPO_NJMEA_Magazine_October_2013.

disease. Thus, DLB is similar in some ways to both the dementia resulting from Alzheimer's disease and the movement problems of Parkinson's disease. Collette's demeanor resultant from her diagnoses is/was generally morose, unresponsive, quite stubborn and feisty, resistant to any new undertaking, fearful of crowded environment, and frightened when her friend Laura was not immediately available. I was told that she is very difficult to handle, has very little self-care skills, can be quite belligerent and moody. Added to this is Collette's continual loss of expressive language. She mumbles gibberish continually and incomprehensibly to others, though it often seems as though she understands what it is she is trying to convey. These characteristics are inherent in the dementia diagnosis. It is unclear how self-aware Collette is regarding her condition and behaviors. It is also unclear whether she can still read or fully comprehend complex spoken language. In addition, her information processing and responsiveness is extremely slow, and she can be quite unresponsive to directives much of the time.

Music Therapy has been known to have positive impact on several dementia symptoms, including long-term memory retrieval, movement organization, self-awareness, and some cognitive abilities. Mood shifts are common in patients with dementia, predominantly triggered by inner systemic fear responses. Music has been known to calm systemic fear responses. There has also been some research on music's ability to influence and help increase dopaminergic neurons. Music indeed has a great influence on movement, and has been known to induce organized movement activities throughout the body, from heart rate to rhythmic head swings, shoulder bounces, to fancy hip and foot work akin to "dancing."

So there we were, Collette, her colleague Laura, my music therapy assistant Christine, and another music therapy colleague, Bruce, about to experience a 1-hour music encounter once or twice a week, over a period of three months. What was designed as a one-on-one music therapy session was, in reality, a group encounter with Collette being the center of attention, and the rest of us participating together in a "group music making session." In fact, this format hit upon a very unusual and one-of-a-kind situation: Collette had the advantage of observing and imitating non-diagnosed persons (i.e., "typically functioning" individuals) surrounding her in making music.

This was quite interesting, because most of the time, such diagnosed persons meet in group therapy sessions with other diagnosed persons, who may or may not provide "positive role models" to be imitated during music-making. In addition, the only person receiving attention from this "group" was Collette, who indicated strong awareness that she was the center of the attention, by her smiles, exaggerated responses, fleeting eye movements focused on each of us from time to time, and other indicative gestures. In all, five persons partook in this activity, with occasional additional one or two non-diagnosed visitors, increasing the size of this group from time to time. Therefore, although the focus was one-on-one, with activities and music selected specifically to address Collette's diagnosed issues, the sessions felt more like "party" than therapy, which served to calm Collette's "fear" and anxiety.

My clinical goals for Collette were:

1. Reduction of "fear" response (5+ minutes quiet listening to start session);
2. Consistent engagement musically and jointly with us;
3. Organized rhythmic movements, such as pulsed hand-clapping, marching, dancing (even when seated), drumming, playing xylophone in tempo, etc.;
4. Breath control (blowing recorder in pulsed tempo), vocalizing (singing) and language use (recalling lyrics and fill-in songs), rhythmic speaking;
5. Verbal response to simple questions (i.e., "did you like this song?", "what's your favorite song?", "which instrument(s) would you like to play?"...etc.)

My notes from the first session, after Collette settled onto the couch, and we four circled in chairs around her, were as follows:

Hello Song: Hello Collette (to tune of Hello Dolly). I was at the piano, Bruce and Christine held guitars, Laura had a tambourine. Placed before Collette were a pair of maracas, a tambourine, and a small 5-tone xylophone (wooden) with a mallet. We sang and played "Hello" to each member of this quintet and noticed Collette able to look to the person to whom we were saying "hello," and she smiled as we continued around the group. We then continued with "Getting to Know You" (The King and I), directed toward each member of the group, beginning with Collette, who recognized this song. She smiled and mumbled something unrecognizable to the rest of us, but she was trying to communicate, making eye contact when directing her "mumble" to someone specific.

As we continued singing and emitting much musical sounds and energies, Collette first played tambourine for a short time, then took the maracas and began shaking them in pulse with the song. Basically, Collette used only her right hand throughout her playing activities. She then held one maraca over the standing drum (a conga) and began to beat a specific pattern along with the song: ////////// (quarter-quarter-quarter-2-eighths, repeat). Collette was very focused on playing this pattern, and continued playing even as we brought the song to a close. Soon we continued with just rhythm and Collette maintained her own patterns, being totally engaged in the music-making. As she ended, she picked up the maracas and shook them into a finale!!

The session continued, and by now some 45-minutes had elapsed. Added to the session was a sequencing task ("Pass The Shaker"), which was difficult for Collette. We also undertook to march, but in a sitting position…and this, too, was difficult for Collette who seemed resistant to lifting each leg in a march tempo. (Things to work on in future sessions). We concluded with singing "Michael Row Your Boat," which she thoroughly enjoyed, smiled, and attempted to repeat the word "Hallelujah" quite clearly, smiling throughout. The last few minutes of the sessions provided quiet relaxation music (I played Keyboard) to allow a calm-down conclusion. We were done with the first meeting—and Collette was now reluctant to leave!

The results of this first session indicated that my clinical goals seemed well-targeted. Collette "came into herself" during this session, and displayed what was left from the ravages of this illness—quite a bit was left! When I asked her to use more of her left hand to play, she clearly stated, "It hurts, I hurt it" ! She did allow me to prompt her as we worked on the use of the left arm. In all other respects, she could control her movements at least in playing the rhythms; she could track the melodies and even attempt lyric inclusions; she could enjoy a portion of "normalcy," smile, awareness of the rest of us. By the fourth encounter (virtually the 4th hour of meeting), Collette was entirely engaged in this activity. My notes are as follows:

Session four, Collette was highly responsive today! She entered the room which was already filled with the "Hello Collette" song (being played by me) as we all sang the greeting to her! Walking into the music environment made a big difference in Collette's desire to participate. She smiled, looked at each of the four of us, and did not rush to the couch. Instead, Collette stood and "danced" to the music, moving from side to side, alternating legs, smiling broadly, picking up and shaking the maraca (again right hand only) in perfect rhythm! This focused activity continued for at least 10-plus more minutes, and finally we concluded the "hello," and helped Collette settle onto the couch—same arrangement as in previous sessions, same instruments before her.

In this session, I attempted to do more playing of the recorder (we each had one), but Collette had great difficulty understanding how to put it in her mouth and blow. However, she sang the pitches we were producing, instead, and smiled in awareness that she was imitating the pitches we were playing on the recorder!!! Obviously Collette was engaged!

Her all-time favorite activity was playing the 5-tone xylophone. Her focus on this (which we have on video) lasted more than 20-minutes. She use her right arm predominantly, but said, clearly..."I should use the left hand......" ! Surely we were obtaining some small breakthroughs. Collette seemed much more lucid and understandable in this session, and was extremely appropriately engaged throughout.

We sang a tune suggested by Christine, with adapted lyrics, "I don't want to work, I just wanna beat the drum all day." It was amazing to observe Collette's energy output here, as she beat the drum! She was totally engaged. Laura played the xylophone with her, then took some video of the activity (through the I-phone).

It was an excellent session, and obviously this woman was displaying some changes back to parts of her that could function "normally." She even spoke in a less mumbling manner. Not only was Collette enjoying the music-making, but the group interaction as well. External energy that music provides is an important stimulus to keep the brain and body appropriately engaged. And rhythm was and is the admission ticket to her (and anyone's) brain. The more we used rhythm, the more creative and responsive Collette became, developing and sustaining clear rhythmic patterns, and making continuous eye contact with her own playing on the drum.

We had twelve hourly sessions in all, over three months, and although there were times when Collette was less motivated to participate, the musical energy often prevailed and induced her to do "something," however minimal. Collette was never given specific directions, except once in a while a request to blow recorder, or use the left hand. Otherwise, the music took control of the activities in which Collette engaged. Our final session was in the form of a holiday party. We played, sang holiday songs. It was difficult to say good-bye (she is bi-coastal and was leaving for the West Coast), but all told, it must be said that the music treatments were able to bring out the working portions of Collette's brain.

What's more, one must conclude that creating a gathering of "normal" members of a group may provide better opportunity for progress in brain-injured patients. A person with dementia needs role models to recreate "normal" imitative behaviors. Collette copied our movements, manners, and language. This is not unlike the "inclusion" trend for diagnosed children attending school, in which parents prefer to have the child in a class with typically functioning children rather than a closed classroom only for children with various diagnoses.

Perhaps an advocacy group for adult inclusion should be considered. In any event, there is no mystery about the fact that music plays an important role in bringing out the working parts of the human system, as Collette and other clients clearly demonstrate. The energies, vibrations, pitches, timbres, and music-playing processes involved have no competitors in resonating with, and driving a system toward response.

Science is simply verifying what musicians have known for centuries—that indeed music soothes the ravaged brain.

(Names have been changed to preserve confidentiality and anonymity).

APPENDIX 3

UNDERSTANDING THE INCLUDED SPECIAL NEEDS CHILD IN MUSIC CLASSES

(Article reproduced from *TEMPO* magazine, May 2013)[1]

Once, at a middle school where I was providing music therapy services, a band instructor came frantically seeking me for advice on how to handle a special needs youngster whose parents insisted their son participate in band, and in the upcoming school concert. The student, whom I was treating at the school, had Angelman Syndrome, which is a neuro-genetic disorder characterized by severe cognitive, developmental and language disabilities, sleep disturbances, sometimes seizures, jerky movements (especially hand-flapping), and most of all, an unusually happy demeanor with frequent smiling, audible laughter, and spontaneous and uncontrollable involuntary vocal outbursts, such as "aaaahhh," "eeeerp."

The band instructor was anxious because the school Principal insisted on compliance with parental requests. This student had been placed in the band, seated in the percussion section, and given an occasional triangle, or maracas to play. But with a concert coming up, the instructor did not want the student to participate on stage, fearing that the frequent involuntary vocal outbursts would disrupt the performance. What could be done? Since I had

---

[1] TEMPO New Jersey Music Educators Association Journal, March Issue, 68–69. Available at http://issuu.com/njmea/docs/maytempo?mode=window&pageNumber=70.

been providing clinical services to this student, I was well aware of his abilities, interests and behaviors. In clinical work I require students to have recorders for developing better breath control, and also to have kazoos into which to hum. The kazoo activity provides fun, vocalization practice, and redirection of vocal outbursts. So I suggested that this student bring his kazoo to band rehearsals and ultimately to the performance, so that his vocalization compulsions could be redirected into the kazoo—an activity we often practiced in our music therapy sessions. Although the student was cognitively deficient, he was able to understand this directive because it was a familiar activity that he enjoyed.

The student was told that his role in the band was to "play" kazoo, and that he would keep it in his mouth throughout the performance! I guided the student's aide on how to observe potential precedents to outbursts (that were usually triggered by unmodulated excitement), and to guide the student on when (or when not) to "play." Even if the student was to vocalize into the kazoo throughout the performance, the sound would not carry nor be heard by others in the band or the audience. He was placed standing behind the trombones, near the percussion, and everyone was thrilled to enable this student's participation at his level of ability. The concert went well, and everyone was satisfied!

In my years of providing music therapy services to schools, I have come to understand that "inclusion" is education's ongoing buzzword. However, although "inclusion" can provide many positive educational experiences for special needs students, many music instructors find themselves at a loss in ways to resolve the many issues that arise, and that often result in the student being ejected from the class. Rather than expelling a student from class, there can be other solutions and alternatives to solving situations that rely upon educators being sufficiently knowledgeable and skilled at understanding and redirecting behaviors and problems. Music educators might benefit from in-service workshops and training on techniques that can diffuse problems that arise. I have been consulted often on issues in choruses, orchestras, bands, and general music classes in which students with Autism Spectrum Disorder, ADHD, Down or Angelman Syndrome, and other diagnoses, were included.

Basic Considerations for Music Educators

Music educators, whether classroom, instrumental, or vocal instructors, are not expected to be music therapists in identifying specific problems or fully understanding physiological and psychological deficits. However, certain factors are important to understand. Music, itself a strict discipline, involves an acoustic environment, and learning requires organized cognitive processes on the part of the student. Music education also requires a student's healthy sense of self and self-organization, knowledge of his or her body, and a coordination of sensory information. These basic areas of function are most often deficient in the diagnosed student, resulting in erratic behaviors, fear and fight-or-flight responses, an inability to focus and concentrate nor understand specific multi-layer directives, auditory and visual processing difficulties, and much more.

The first factors to be considered are the aspects of sound and auditory processing that might be problematic. Most childhood diagnoses have various levels of auditory processing deficiencies that implicate expressive and receptive language delays, fear of certain sounds, comprehension difficulties, and related problems. The music, or the instruments, may be too loud or too quiet. The room may cause reverberations or amplification of the sound's characteristics, causing sensory disturbances. Fluorescent lights, (that emit very high frequency pitches and appear visually as strobe lights for someone on the Autism Spectrum) could be causing bodily and sensory discomforts. Perhaps the timbres of the music, musical instruments, or teacher's voice, are being processed inaccurately, or with discomfort. Auditory deficiencies could include an inability to determine auditory figure-ground, or sound location. The student could be on sensory information overload due to too much auditory and visual stimuli. Visual or auditory systems may not be tracking sequentially, thus perceiving information inaccurately. Although the student sees and hears, the brain may not be receiving and perceiving the stimulus correctly. The brain may not know what's "me" and what's not (inaccurate proprioceptive processing). These are just a few of the deficits in the adaptive malfunction of a diagnosed person. When teachers consider these possible contributors to inappropriate behaviors, they will realize that emitting the student from class will not necessarily result in better behavior upon return, because the environment itself does not change, therefore discomforts will recur and the behavior cycle may continue. One cannot assume that what is being presented audibly by the instructor is what is being perceived by the included student.

In the classroom, the music educator is often unable to stabilize the included special needs student, and with some 35 students in the class, obviously the instructor cannot always take the time (or may not understand the problem) to consider alternative solutions. Added to this is often the inability of a student's aide to understand or redirect, in a positive manner, responses resultant from diagnostic characteristics. I have observed that redirection of behaviors, (key word, "redirection") is illusive, and often not well managed. Being sent from the class is not "inclusion." Several things might be given consideration:

- Seating arrangement—considering the acoustic nature of music instruction, some awareness of auditory and sensory processing function of the included student would be helpful. This information is often available from other clinicians on the IEP: speech pathologists, OT, Music Therapist (if available), parents and medical records. Some of the following can then be explored: perhaps the student would do better when seated in a location of the room where reverberations are minimal (perhaps further away from the sound source); perhaps the student does not have to sit alongside other string or brass players, or singers, but rather, can sit (or stand) in an area of the room where auditory insults would be less intense, or the out-of-tune player or singer is not immediately in the ear of the student. (Many ASD students have absolute pitch—often a major contributor to auditory discomforts).

- Class duration—a 30 or 40-minute class may be too long for the student to handle. I advise teachers and aides to allow the student to participate in time increments: participation in the first 10 to 15-minutes (depending on the length) of a class, then proceeding to a quiet area elsewhere, for 10 or 15-minutes to continue one-on-one repetition of the instruction, and returning for the concluding segment of the class. Two positive redirections of student stress can occur with this type of schedule—first, there is an immediate change of pace and environment that redirects attention, and second, there is a one-on-one opportunity for reinforcement of the information being taught before returning to the group. (Even orchestras and bands have "sectional rehearsals.") The suggestion of time increments has served many students (and classmates) well, because shorter attention time can reduce fears and anxieties, limit compulsive outbursts, provide a better sense of self-esteem, and is a positive alternative.

- Instrument selection—special needs students should be allowed to enter instrumental training—even if limited. When a student is able to choose his or her instrumental interest, that is a positive. However, not all selections are commensurate with a student's ability to handle or learn the skill. Here a consultation with a music therapist could be beneficial. I have often redirected a student to an instrument (or choir) which, based on my assessment, would be a better selection. It should not be assumed that because the student cannot handle a particular instrument, there is no ability for another instrument. One of my extremely musically gifted clinical clients, with keen absolute pitch, was first told he would not be admitted into any instrumental training program due to his diagnosis! After my discussions (and urging!) with the music faculty, he was reluctantly placed in the violin class, which indeed was quite difficult and unsuccessful for him. I implored that the cello, or the double bass would better suit his interests as well as his sensory needs. Indeed, he was subsequently moved to the cello class in which he became so proficient that he was placed as first chair cellist in the orchestra in that first year of music. The following year he decided he preferred the double bass, and immediately became principal bassist in the school orchestra! Difficult? Yes, but given his perfect pitch acuity, he almost does not have to read music! (He is currently 10 years old and on the Autism spectrum.) Playing double bass has become this child's identity.

Grading ability and progress from a Music Therapy perspective

Although there are specific curricular requirements for music education, I have not often encountered an alternate curriculum suited for included students. Many special needs students are simply inserted because of "inclusion fever," but may never achieve required curricular success. The Angelman Syndrome student described above surely learned much about music, tempo, observing a conductor, waiting and turn-taking, taking direction, and generally participating with others in the music-making activity. These are positive learning aspects resulting from the student's participation in music classes, but it is unlikely that he will read music notation, partake in sight-read or sight-sing, or develop instrumental proficiency skills. Therefore an adapted music curriculum and academic criteria for grading music knowledge required by the general music curriculum would be useful. Grading would require flexibility and modification in order to accommodate gains based on a student's "ability," rather than disability, and different rubrics for determining "progress" would be useful. This involves rating progress based on an understanding of the characteristics of a diagnosis and resultant behaviors, and an adaptation of teacher expectations and agendas.

In a future article I will share some information about my Triple A Approach for teacher leadership skills, from the music therapy perspective. The approach is based on the music clinician's assessment of self, strengths and deficits, goals and objectives, and knowledge used in treating clients. The information can be useful for music educators as well. Meanwhile, I suggest giving the included student a chance to practice developing music skills at the level of the student's ability, with modified expectations, and with supportive opportunities based on understanding important physiological characteristics that may be limiting the student's functional adaptation. As clinicians, music therapists are interested in treating a person's "abilities," rather than focusing on the disabilities. It can be the same for music educators who can enhance abilities and make "inclusion" a successful learning opportunity.

REFERENCES

Abercrombie, H. C., Kalin, N. H. and Davidson, R. J. (2005) "Acute cortisol elevations cause heightened arousal ratings of objectively nonarousing stimuli." *Emotion* 5, 3, 354–359.

Abril, C. R. (2011) "Music, Movement, and Learning." In R. Colwell and P. Richard (eds) *MENC: Handbook of Research in Music Learning*, Vol. 2. Oxford: Oxford University Press.

Alexander, F. M. (1995) *The Essential Writings of F. Matthias Alexander: The Alexander Technique, The World-Renowned System of Mind-Body Coordination*, Selected and Introduced by Edward Maisel. New York, NY: Carol Publishing Group.

Alexander, G. E., DeLong, M. R. and Strick, P. L. (1986) "Parallel organization of functionally segregated circuits linking basal ganglia and cortex." *Annual Review of Neuroscience* 9, 1, 357–381.

Altenmüller, E., Marco-Pallares, J., Münte, T. F. and Schneider, S. (2009) "Neural reorganization underlies improvement in stroke-induced motor dysfunction by music-supported therapy." *Annals New York Academy of Sciences* 1169, 395–405.

Amaral, D. C. and Corbett, B. A. (2003) "The Amygdala, Autism and Anxiety." In *Autism: Neural Basis and Treatment Possibilities*. Novatis Foundation Symposium, 251, 177–197.

Amos, P. (2013) "Rhythm and timing in autism: learning to dance." *Frontiers in Integrative Neuroscience* 7, article 27. Available at http://journal.frontiersin.org/article/10.3389/fnint.2013.00027/abstract, accessed on 4 June 2015.

Atigh, A., Akbarfahimi, M., Alizadeh, M. and Rad, M. M. (2013) "The effect of musical movement activities on the balance function of autistic children." *Journal of Kermanshah University of Medical Sciences* 17, 8, 483–491.

Baloh, R. W. and Honrubia, V. (2001) *Clinical Neurophysiology of the Vestibular System*. New York, NY: Oxford University Press.

Baron-Cohen, S. (1995) *Mindblindness: An Essay on Autism and Theory of Mind*. Boston, MA: MIT Press.

Baron-Cohen, S., Tager-Flusberg, H. and Cohen, D. J. (eds) (1994) *Understanding Other Minds: Perspectives from Autism*. Oxford: Oxford Medical Publications.

Baron-Cohen, S., Tager-Flusberg, H. and Lombardo, M. V. (eds) (2013) *Understanding Other Minds: Perspectives from Developmental Social Neuroscience*. Oxford: Oxford University Press.

Beck, D. L. and Bellis, T. J. (2007) "(Central) auditory processing disorders: overview and amplification issues." *The Hearing Journal* 60, 1, 44–47.

Berger, D. S. (2002) *Music Therapy, Sensory Integration and the Autistic Child.* London: Jessica Kingsley Publishers.

Berger, D. S. (2009) "Developing music therapy goals and objectives." *VOICES on-line: A World Forum for Music Therapy 9*, 1. Available at https://normt.uib.no/index.php/voices/article/view/362/285, accessed on 4 June 2015.

Berger, D. S. (2010) "On Developing Music Therapy Goals and Objectives in the Treatment of Autism Characteristics." In S. Brooke (ed.) *The Use of Creative Therapies with Autism Spectrum Disorder.* Springfield, IL: Charles C. Thomas Publishers.

Berger, D. S. (2012) "Pilot study investigating the efficacy of tempo-specific rhythm interventions in music-based treatment addressing hyper-arousal, anxiety, system pacing, and redirection of fight-or-flight fear behaviors in children with autism spectrum disorder (ASD)." *Journal of Biomusical Engineering 2*, Article ID M110902, doi:10.4303/jbe/M110902. Available at http://omicsonline.com/open-access/biomusical-engineering.php, accessed on 4 June 2015.

Berger, D. S. (2013a) "The sensory systems, eurhythmics and sensorimotor music-based interventions for autism and neurophysiologic characteristics." *Dalcroze Journal 40, 1, 16–23.*

Berger, D. S. (2013b) "Music soothes the ravaged brain." CMTE online journal. Available at http://cmteonlineclasses.wordpress.com/2013/04/23/music-soothes-the-ravaged-brain/, accessed on 4 June 2015 (also published in *TEMPO New Jersey Music Educators Association Journal*, September 2013).

Berger, D. S. and Schneck, D. J. (2003) "The use of music therapy as a clinical intervention for physiologic functional adaptation." *Journal of Scientific Exploration 17*, 4, 687–703.

Beringer, E. (ed.) (2010) *Embodied Wisdom: The Collected Papers of Moshe Feldenkrais.* Berkeley, CA: North Atlantic Books.

Blasing, B. E. (2015) "Segmentation of dance movement: effects of expertise, visual familiarity, motor experience and music." *Frontiers in Psychology 5*, 1500.

Blumenthal, A. L. (1975) "A reappraisal of Wilhelm Wundt." *American Psychology* November, 1081–1088.

Brennan, J. (2003) *History and Systems of Psychology*, 6th edn. Upper Saddle River, NJ: Prentice Hill.

Brett King, D., Viney, W. and Woody, W. (2009) *A History of Psychology: Ideas and Context* (4th edn). Boston, MA: Pearson Education Inc.

Buzsaki, G. (2006) *Rhythms of the Brain.* New York, NY: Oxford University Press.

Collins, P. (2004) *Not Even Wrong: Adventures in Autism.* New York, NY: Bloomsbury.

Corbett, B. A., Mendoza, S., Abdullah, M., Wegelin, J. A. and Levine, S. (2006) "Cortisol circadian rhythms and response to stress in children with autism." *Journal of Psychoneuralendocrinology 31*, 59–68. Available at www.ncbi.nlm.nih.gov/pubmed/16005570 , accessed on 4 June 2015.

Cytowic, R. E. (1999) *The Man who Tasted Shapes.* Boston, MA: MIT Press.

Cytowic, R. E. (2002) *Synesthesia: A Union of the Senses.* Boston, MA: MIT Press.

Damasio, A. R. (1994) *Descartes' Error: Emotion, Reason and the Human Brain.* New York, NY: Grosset/ Putnam Books.

Damasio, A. R. (1999) *The Feeling of What Happens: Body and Emotion in the Making of Consciousness.* New York, NY: Harcourt Brace & Company.

Damasio, A. R. (2003a) *Looking for Spinoza: Joy, Sorrow, and the Feeling Brain*. New York, NY: Harcourt, Inc.

Damasio, A. R. (2003b) "Feelings of emotion and the self." *Annals of the New York Academy of Sciences 1001*, 253–261.

Damasio, A. R. (2003c) "The person within." *Nature 423*, 227.

Damasio, A. R. (2010) *Self Comes to Mind: Constructing the Conscious Brain*. New York, NY: Pantheon Books.

Damasio, A. R. and Maurer, R. G. (1978) "A neurological model for childhood autism." *Archives of Neurology 35*, 777–786.

Damasio, A. R. and Maurer, R. G. (1979) "Vestibular dysfunction in autistic children." *Developmental Medicine and Child Neurology 21*, 656–659.

Day, B. L. and Fitzpatrick, R. C. (2005) "The vestibular system." *Current Biology 15*, 15, R583–R586.

de Alcantara, P. (2011) *The Alexander Technique: A Skill for Life*. London: Cromwood Press.

Dieter, K. C., Hu, B., Knill, D. C., Blake, R. and Tadin, D. (2014) "Kinesthesis can make an invisible hand visible." *Psychological Science 25*, 1, 66–75.

Dowd, A. M., McGinley, J. L., Taffe, J. H. and Rinehart, N. J. (2012) "Do planning and visual integration difficulties underpin motor dysfunction in autism? A kinematic study of young children with autism." *Journal of Autism and Developmental Disorders 42*, 8, 1539–1548.

Eckberg, M. (2000) *Victims of Cruelty: Somatic Psychotherapy in the Treatment of Posttraumatic Stress Disorder*. Berkeley, CA: North Atlantic Books.

Esposito, G. and Pasca, S. (2013) "Motor abnormalities as a putative endophenotype for autism spectrum disorders." *Frontiers in Integrative Neuroscience 7*, 43. Available at http://journal.frontiersin.org/Journal/10.3389/fnint.2013.00043/full, accessed on 4 June 2015.

Feldenkrais, M. (1977) *Body Awareness as Healing Therapy: The Case of Nora*. Berkeley, CA: Somatic Resources Frog Ltd.

Feldenkrais, M. (2005) *Body and Mature Behavior: A Study of Anxiety, Sex, Gravitation, and Learning*, originally published 1945. Berkeley, CA: North Atlantic Books.

Feng, W., Stormer, V. S., Martinez, A., McDonald, J. J. and Hillyard, S.A. (2014) "Sounds activate visual cortex and improve visual discrimination." *Journal of Neuroscience 34*, 29, 9817–9824.

Fernandes, C. (2015) *The Moving Researcher: Laban/Bartenieff Movement Analysis in Performing Arts Education and Creative Arts Therapies*. London: Jessica Kingsley Publishers.

Findlay, E. (1999) *Rhythm and Movement: Applications of Dalcroze Eurhythmics*, originally published 1971. Van Nuys, CA: Summy-Birchard, Inc.

Fisher, A. G., Murray, E. A. and Bundy, A. C. (eds) (1991) *Sensory Integration: Theory and Practice*. Philadelphia, PA: F.A. David & Co.

Fitzpatrick, R. C. and Day, B. L. (2004) "Probing the human vestibular system with galvanic stimulation." *Journal of Applied Physiology 96*, 2301–2316.

Fox, N. A. (2011) "How persistent fear and anxiety can affect young children's learning, behaviour and health." *Early Childhood Matters Journal 116*, 8–14.

Freeman, C. G. (2014) *Autism and Alexander Technique: Using the Alexander Technique to Help People on the Autism Spectrum*. CreateSpace Independent Publishing Platform.

Freeman, R. D., Sultanifar, A. and Baer, S. (2010) "Stereotypic movement disorder: easily missed." *Developmental Medicine & Child Neurology 52*, 733–738.

Frego, R. J. D. (2009) "Dancing Inside: Dalcroze Eurhythmics in a Therapeutic Setting." In J. L. Kerliner and C.R. Abril (eds) *Musical Experience in our Lives: Things we Learn and Meanings we Make.* Lanham, MD: Rowman & Littlefield.

Frith, U. (ed.) (1991) *Autism and Asperger Syndrome.* Cambridge: Cambridge University Press.

Frith, U. (2008) *Autism: A Very Short Introduction.* New York, NY: Oxford University Press.

Frith, U. and Hill, E. (2003) *Autism: Mind and Brain.* New York, NY: Oxford University Press.

Gazzaniga, M. S. (1998) *The Mind's Past.* Berkeley, CA: University of California Press.

Gerber, R. (2001) *Vibrational Medicine.* Rochester, VT: Bear & Company.

Glennie, E. (2015) *Hearing Essay.* Available at www.evelyn.co.uk/hearing-essay/, accessed on 5 June 2015.

Graeff, F. G. and Zangrossi, H. Jr. (2010) "The hypothalamic-pituitary-adrenal axis in anxiety and panic." *Psychology & Neuroscience 3*, 1, 3–8.

Gran, J. A. and Brett, M. (2007) "Rhythm and beat perception in motor areas of the brain." *Neuropsychologia 29*, 893–906.

Green, D., Charman, T., Pickles, A., Chandler, S. *et al.* (2009) "Impairment in movement skills of children with autistic spectrum disorders." *Developmental Medicine & Child Neurology 51*, 311–316.

Guilliams, T. G. and Edwards, L. (2010) "Chronic stress and the HPA axis: clinical assessment and therapeutic considerations." *The Standard 9*, 2, 1–13.

Hameline, D. (1993) "Edouard Claparede (1873–1940)." *Prospects: The Quarterly Review of Comparative Education XXIII*, 1/2, 159–171. Available at http://www.ibe.unesco.org/publications/ThinkersPdf/claparee.pdf, accessed on 27 July 2015.

Hars, M., Herrmann, F. R., Gold, G., Rizzoli, R. and Trombetti, A. (2014) "Effect of music-based multitask training on cognition and mood in older adults." *Age and Ageing 43*, 2, 196–200.

Hausdorff, J. M., Lowenthal, J., Herman, T., Gruendlinger, L. and Peretz, C. (2007) "Rhythmic auditory stimulation modulates gait variability in Parkinson's disease." *European Journal of Neuroscience 26*, 2369–2375.

Heinrichs, M., Chen, F. and Domes, G. (2012) *Psychobiological Approaches for Anxiety Disorders: Treatment Combination Strategies* (ed. S.G. Hofmann). Chichester: John Wiley & Sons, Ltd.

Heinrichs, M., Chen, F. and Domes, G. (2013) "Social Neuropeptides in the Human Brain: Oxytocin and Human Behavior." In S. Baron-Cohen, M. Lombardo and H. Tager-Flusberg (eds) *Understanding Other Minds: Perspectives from Developmental Social Neuroscience.* Oxford: Oxford University Press.

Hollander, E., Wang, A. T., Braun, A. and Marsh, L. (2009) "Neurological considerations: autism and Parkinson's disease." *Psychiatry Research 170*, 1, 43–51.

Horowitz, S. S. (2012) *The Universal Sense: How Hearing Shapes The Mind.* New York, NY: Bloomsbury.

Hutchison, K. A. and Balota, D. A. (2003) "Structure vs. processing deficits in Alzheimer's disease: a matter of degree." *Neuropsychology 17*, 2, 306–309.

Janata, P. and Grafton, S. T. (2003) "Singing in the brain: shared neural substrates for behaviors related to sequencing and music." *Nature Neuroscience 8*, 682–687.

Jaques-Dalcroze, E. (1920) *The Eurhythmics Method of Emile Jaques-Dalcroze*, 3rd and revised edition, originally published 1913. Boston, MA: Small Maynard & Co., reprinted from the University of California Libraries collection.

Jaques-Dalcroze, E. (2009) *Rhythm, Music and Education*. Charleston, NC: BiblioLife Publishers.

Jaques-Dalcroze, E. (2010a) *The Eurhythmics of Jaques-Dalcroze*, first published 1913. US: Jennings Press.

Jaques-Dalcroze, E. (2010b) "Rhythm as a Factor in Education." First published in *Le Rhythme (Bale)* December 1909. *The Eurhythmics of Jaques-Dalcroze*. US: Jennings Press.

Kandel, E. R. (2007) *In Search of Memory: The Emergence of a New Science of Mind*. New York, NY: W.W. Norton & Co.

Kandel, E. R. (2012) *The Age of Insight: The Quest to Understand the Unconscious in Art, Mind, and Brain*. New York, NY: Random House.

Kraus, N. (2013) "Playing music to improve hearing in noise and tune the brain." *ENT & Audiology News 22*, 92–93.

Kraus, N., Slater, J., Thompson, E. C., Hornickel, J. *et al.* (2014) "Music enrichment programs improve the neural encoding of speech in at-risk children." *The Journal of Neuroscience 34*, 36, 11913–11918.

Kuchenbuch, A., Paraskevopoulos, E., Herhotz, S. C. and Pantev, C. (2014) "Audio-tactile integration and the influence of musical training." *PLOS One 9*, 1, 1–12.

Kwak, E. E. (2007) "Effect of rhythmic auditory stimulation on gait performance in children with spastic cerebral palsy." *Journal of Music Therapy KLIV*, 3, 198–216.

Laban, R. and Ullman, L. (1971) *The Mastery of Movement*. London: MacDonald & Evans.

Lappe, C., Trainor, L. J., Herholz, S. C. and Pantev, C. (2011) "Cortical plasticity induced by short-term multimodal musical rhythm training." *PlosOne 6*, 6. Available at http://journals.plos.org/plosone/article?id=10.1371/journal.pone.0021493, accessed on 4 June 2015.

Lathe, R. (2006) *Autism, Brain, and Environment*. London: Jessica Kingsley Publishers.

LeDoux, J. (1998) *The Emotional Brain: The Mysterious Underpinnings of Emotional Life*. New York, NY: Simon & Schuster.

LeDoux, J. (2002) *Synaptic Self: How Our Brains Become Who We Are*. New York, NY: Viking Penguin.

Levine, P. (1997) *Waking the Tiger*. Berkeley, CA: North Atlantic Books.

Li, S. C., Aggen, S. H., Nesselroade, J. S. and Baltes, P. B. (2001) "Short-term fluctuations in elderly people's sensorimotor functioning predict text and spatial memory performance: The MacArthur Successful Aging Studies." *Journal of Gerontology 47*, 100–116.

Llinas, R. R. (2002) *I of the Vortex: From Neurons to Self*. Cambridge, MA: MIT Press/Bradford Book.

Macnaughton, I. (ed.) (2004) *Body, Breath & Consciousness: A Somatics Anthology*. Berkeley, CA: North Atlantic Books.

McCleery, J. P., Elliott, N. A., Sampanis, D. S. and Stefanidou, C. A. (2013) "Motor development and motor resonance difficulties in autism: relevance to early intervention for language and communication skills." *Frontiers in Integrative Neuroscience 7*, 30. Available at www.ncbi.nlm.nih.gov/pmc/articles/PMC3634796/, accessed on 4 June 2015.

McIntosh, G. C., Brown, S.H., Rice, R.R. and Thaut, M.H. (1997) "Rhythmic auditory-motor facilitation of gait patterns in patients with Parkinson's disease." *Journal of Neurology, Neurosurgery and Psychiatry 62*, 22–26.

Mead, V. H. (1994) *Dalcroze Eurhythmics in Today's Music Classroom*. New York, NY: Schott Music Corp.

Meier, F., Theodorou, E. and Schaal, S. (2012) Movement Segmentation and Recognition for Imitation Learning. *Proceedings of the 15th International Conference on Artificial Intelligence and Statistics* (AISTATS). La Palma, Canary Islands. Volume XX of JMLR: W&CP XX.

Ming, X., Brimacombe, M. and Wagner, G.C. (2007) "Prevalence of motor impairment in autism spectrum disorders." *Brain & Development 29*, 563–570.

Moore, C. -L. and Yamamoto, K. (2012) *Beyond Words: Movement Observation and Analysis*. New York, NY: Routledge.

Mosconi, M. W., Cody-Hazlett, H., Poe, M. D., Gerig, G., Gimpel-Smith, R. and Piven, J. (2009) "Longitudinal study of amygdale volume and joint attention in 2- to 4-year-old children with autism." *Archives of General Psychiatry 66*, 5, 509–516. Available at http://archpsyc.jamanetwork.com/article.aspx?articleid=483056, accessed on 4 June 2015.

Müller, W., Haffelder, G., Schlotmann, A., Schaefers, A. T. and Teuchert-Noodt, G. (2014) "Amelioration of psychiatric symptoms through exposure to music individually adapted to brain rhythm disorders – a randomised clinical trial on the basis of fundamental research." *Cognitive Neuropsychiatry 19*, 5, 399–413.

Munson, J., Dawson, G., Abbott, R. and Faja, S. (2006) "Amygdala volume and behavioral development in autism." *Archives of General Psychiatry 63*, 6, 686–693. Available at http://archpsyc.jamanetwork.com/article.aspx?articleid=209660&resultClick=3, accessed on 4 June 2015.

Musiek, F. E. (1983) "Assessment of central auditory dysfunction: the dichotic digit test revisited." *Ear and Hearing 4*, 79–83.

Musiek, F., Guenette, L. and Fitzgerald, K. (2013) "Lateralized auditory symptoms in central neuroaudiology disorder." *Journal of the American Academy of Audiology 24*, 556–563.

Musiek, F., Shinn, J. and Hare, C. (2002) "Plasticity, auditory training, and auditory processing disorders." *Seminars in Hearing 23*, 4, 263–275.

Nacewicz, B. M., Dalton, K. M., Johnstone, T., Long, M. *et al.* (2006) "Amygdala volume and nonverbal social impairment in adolescent and adult males with autism." *Archives of General Psychiatry 63*, 1417–1428. Available at http://archpsyc.jamanetwork.com/article.aspx?articleid=209946&resultClick=3, accessed on 4 June 2015.

Nayate, A., Bradshaw, J. L. and Rinehart, N. J. (2005) "Autism and Asperger's disorder: are they the involving the cerebellum and/or basal ganglia?" *Brain Research Bulletin 67*, 327–334.

Nevid, J. S. (2012) *Essentials of Psychology: Concepts and Applications*, 3rd edn. Belmont, CA: Wadsworth.

Nolano, M., Provitera, V., Estraneo, A., Selim, M. M. *et al.* (2008) "Sensory deficit in Parkinson's disease: evidence of a cutaneous denervation." *Brain 131*, 1903–1911.

Nombela, C., Hughes, L. E., Owen, A. M. and Grahn, J. A. (2013) "Into the groove: can rhythm influence Parkinson's disease?" *Neuroscience and Biobehavioral Reviews 37*, 10, 2567–2570. Available at http://dx.doi.org/10.1016/j.neubiorev.2013.08.003, accessed on 4 June, 2015.

Nordahl, C. W., Scholz, R., Yang, X., Michael, H. and Buonocore, M. H. (2012) "Increased rate of amygdale growth in children ages 2 to 4 years with autism spectrum disorders." *Archives of General Psychiatry 69*, 1, 53–61. Available at www.ncbi.nlm.nih.gov/pubmed/22213789, accessed on 27 July 2015.

Norton, A., Zipse, L., Marchina, S. and Schlaug, G. (2009) "Melodic intonation therapy: shared insights on how it is done and why it might help." *Annals of the New York Academy of Science 1169*, 431–436.

Ogden, P. and Minton, K. (2000) "Sensorimotor psychotherapy: one method for processing traumatic memory." *Traumatology VI*, e, Article 3. Available at www.sensorimotorpsychotherapy.org/articles.html/, accessed on 5 June 2015.

Ogden, P., Minton, K. and Pain, C. (2006) *Trauma and the Body: A Sensorimotor Approach to Psychotherapy*. New York, NY: W.W. Norton & Company.

Pai, Y. -C., Wening, J. D., Runtz, E. F., Iqbal, K. and Pavol, M. J. (2003) "Role of feedforward control of movement stability in reducing slip-related balance loss and falls among older adults." *Journal of Neurophysiology 90*, 755–762.

Panksepp, J. (1998) *Affective Neuroscience: The Foundations of Human and Animal Emotions*. New York, NY: Oxford University Press.

Panksepp, J. and Biven, L. (2012) *The Archaeology of Mind: Neuroevolutionary Origins of Human Emotions*. New York, NY: W.W. Norton & Co.

Parbery-Clark, A., Strait, D. L., Hittner, E. and Kraus, N. (2013) "Musical training enhances neural processing of binaural sounds." *Journal of Neuroscience 33*, 42, 16741–16747.

Patel, A. D. (2006) "Musical rhythm, linguistic rhythm, and human evolution." *Music Perception 24*, 99–104.

Patel, A. D. (2008) *Music, Language and the Brain*. New York, NY: Oxford University Press.

Payne, P., Levine, P. A. and Crane-Godreau, M. A. (2015) "Somatic experiencing: using interoception and proprioception as core elements of trauma therapy." *Frontiers in Psychology 6*, 93. Available at www.frontiersin.org, accessed on 5 June 2015.

Perry, B. D., Pollard, R. A., Blakley, T. L. and Vigilante, D. (1995) "Childhood trauma, the neurobiology of adaptation, and 'use-dependent' development of the brain: how 'states' become 'traits'." *Infant Mental Health Journal 16*, 271–291.

Porges, S. W. (2011) *The Polyvagal Theory: Neurophysiological Foundations of Emotions, Attachment, Communication, Self-Regulation*. New York, NY: W.W. Norton & Co.

Priestley, M. (1994) *Essays on Analytical Music Therapy*. Gilsum, NJ: Barcelona Press.

Ridgel, A. L., Vitek, J. L. and Alberts, J. L. (2009) "Forced, not voluntary, exercise improves motor function in Parkinson's disease patients." *Neurorehabilitation and Neural Repair XX*, X. Available at http://nnr.sagepub.com, accessed on 5 June 2015.

Rinehart, N. J., Tonge, B. J., Bradshaw, J. L., Iansek, R., Enticott, P. G. and McGinley, J. (2006) "Gait function in high-functioning autism and Asperger's disorder: evidence for basal-ganglia and cerebellar involvement." *European Child and Adolescent Psychiatry* 15, 6, 264–266.

Rothschild, B. (2000) *The Body Remembers: The Psychophysiology of Trauma and Trauma Treatment.* New York, NY: W.W. Norton & Co.

Scheiby, B. B. (2015) "Analytical Music Therapy." In B. Wheeler (ed.) *Music Therapy Handbook.* New York, NY: Guilford Press.

Scheiby, B. B. and Pederson, I. N. (1989) "Psychodynamische Bewegung innerhalb eines musiktherapeutischen Konzepts." [Psychodynamic Movement in a Music Therapeutic Context] In H.H. Decker-Voigt (ed.) *Diplom-Aufbaustudium Musiktherapie* 3, 70–74.

Schnebly-Black, J. and Moore, S. F. (2003) *The Rhythm Inside: Connecting Body, Mind and Spirit through Music.* Van Nuys, CA: Alfred Publishing Co.

Schnebly-Black, J. and Moore, S. F. (2004) *Rhythm One on One: Dalcroze Activities in the Private Music Lesson.* Van Nuys, CA: Alfred Publishing Co.

Schneck, D. J. (1990) *Engineering Principles of Physiologic Function.* New York, NY: NYU Press.

Schneck, D. J. (1992) *Mechanics of Muscle*, 2nd edn. New York, NY: New York University Press.

Schneck, D. J. (2015) *Basic Anatomy and Physiology for the Music Therapist.* London: Jessica Kingsley Publishers.

Schneck, D. J. and Berger, D.S. (1999) "The role of music in physiologic accommodation: its ability to elicit reflexive, adaptive, and inscriptive responses." *IEEE Engineering in Medicine and Biology* 18, 2, 44–53.

Schneck, D. J. and Berger, D.S. (2006) *The Music Effect: Music Physiology and Clinical Applications.* London: Jessica Kingsley Publishers.

See, C. M. (2012) "The use of music and movement therapy to modify behaviour of children with autism." *Pertanika Journal of Social Sciences & Humanities* 20, 4, 1103–1116.

Sherrington, C. S. (1906) *The Integrative Action of the Nervous System.* New York, NY: C. Scribner & Sons.

Skoe, E. and Kraus, N. (2013) "Musical training heightens auditory brainstem function during sensitive periods in development." *Frontiers in Auditory Cognitive Neuroscience.* doi: 10.3389/fpsyg.2013.00622.

Smetacek, V. and Mechsner, F. (2004) "Making sense – proprioception: is the sensory system that supports body posture and movement also the root of our understanding of physical laws?" *Nature* 432, 21.

Smetana, J. G., Campione-Barr, N. and Metzger, A. (2006) "Adolescent development in interpersonal and societal contexts." *Annual Review of Psychology* 57, 255–284.

Spratt, E. G., Nicholas, J. S., Brady, K. T., Carpenter, L. A. *et al.* (2012) "Enhanced cortisol response to stress in children in autism." *Journal of Autism and Developmental Disorders* 42, 1, 75–81.

Stanghellini, G. (2009) "Embodiment and schizophrenia." *World Psychiatry* 8, 56–59.

Stanghellini, G. and Ballerini, M. (2002) "Dis-sociality: the phenomenological approach to social dysfunction in schizophrenia." *World Psychiatry* 1, 2, 102–106.

Stanghellini, G. and Ballerini, M. (2004) "Autism – disembodied existence." *Philosophy, Psychology & Psychiatry 11*, 259–268.

Stein, B. E. and Meredith, A. J. (2003) *The Merging of the Senses.* Cambridge, MA: The MIT Press/ Bradford Book.

Strait, D. L. and Kraus, N. (2014) "Biological impact of auditory expertise across the life span: musicians as a model of auditory learning." *Hearing Research 308*, 109–121.

Tadin, D., Nyquist, J. B., Lusk, K. E., Corn, A. L. and Lappin, J. S. (2012) "Peripheral vision of youths with low vision: motion, perception, crowding, and visual search." *Investigative Ophthalmology & Visual Science 53*, 9, 5860–5868.

Tan, H., Zhong, P. and Yan, Z. (2004) "Corticotropin-Releasing Factor and acute stress prolongs serotonergic regulation of GABA transmission in Prefrontal Cortical Pyramidal neurons." *Journal of Neuroscience 24*, 21, 5000–5008.

Tennant, V. (2005) "The powerful impact of stress and calm on health, behavior and learning." *New Horizons.* Available at www.newhorizons.org/spneeds/inclusion/teaching/tennant.htm, accessed on 5 June 2015.

Thaut, M. H. (2008) *Rhythm, Music and the Brain: Scientific Foundations and Clinical Applications.* New York, NY: Routledge/ Taylor & Francis.

Thaut, M. H., McIntosh, G. C. and Rice, R. R. (1997) "Rhythmic facilitation of gait training in hemiparetic stroke rehabilitation." *Journal of Neuroscience 151*, 207–212.

Thaut, M. H., Leins, A. K., Rice, R. R., Argstatter, H. *et al.* (2007) "Rhythmic auditory stimulation improves gait more than NDT/ Bobath training in near-ambulatory patients early poststroke: a single-blind, randomized trial." *Neurorehabilitation and Neural Repair 21*, 5, 455–459.

Tierney, A. and Kraus, N. (2013) "The ability to move to a beat is linked to the consistency of neural responses to sound." *The Journal of Neuroscience 33*, 38, 14981–14988.

Tierney, A., Krizman, J., Skow, E., Johnston, K. and Kraus, N. (2013) "High school music classes enhance the neural processing of speech." *Frontiers in Psychology 4*, 855, 1–7.

Torres, E. B., Yanovich, P. and Metaxas, D. N. (2013) "Give spontaneity and self-discovery a chance in ASD: spontaneous peripheral limb variability as a proxy to evoke centrally driven intentional acta." *Frontiers in Integrative Neuroscience 24.* Available at http://journal.frontiersin.org/Journal/10.3389/fnint.2013.00046/full, accessed on 5 June 2015.

Trevarthen, C. and Daniel, S. (2005) "Rhythm and synchrony in early development and signs of autism and Rett Syndrome in infancy." *Brain and Development 27*, S25–S34 (Supplement 1 to Vol. 27).

Trevarthen, C. and Delafield-Butt, T. H. (2013) "Autism as a developmental disorder in intentional movement and affective engagement." *Frontiers in Integrative Neuroscience 7*, 49, 1–16.

Trombetti, A., Hars, M., Herrmann, F. R., Kressig, R. W., Ferrari, S. and Rizzoli, R. (2011) "Effect of music-based multitask training on gait, balance, and fall risk in elderly people." *Archives of Internal Medicine 171*, 6, 525–533.

van der Kolk, B.A. (2014) *The Body Keeps the Score: Brain, Mind, and the Body in the Healing of Trauma.* New York, NY: Viking Press.

van der Kolk, B. A., McFarlane, A. C. and Weisaeth, L. (eds) (2007) *Traumatic Stress: The Effect of Overwhelming Experience on Mind, Body, and Society*. New York, NY: Guilford Publications, Inc.

van Vugt, F. T. and Tillmann, B. (2015) "Auditory feedback in error-based learning of motor regularity." *Brain Research 1606*, 54–67.

Wan, C. Y. and Schlaug, G. (2010) "Neural pathways for language in autism: the potential for music-based treatments." *Future Neurology 5*, 6, 797–805.

Wan, C. Y., Bazen, L., Baars, R., Libenson, A. *et al.* (2011) "Auditory-Motor Mapping Training as an intervention to facilitate speech output in non-verbal children with autism: a proof of concept study." *PloS One 6*, 9. Available at http://journals.plos.org/plosone/article?id=10.1371/journal.pone.0025505, accessed on 5 June 2015.

Warren, J. E., Wise, R. J. and Warren, J. D. (2005) "Sounds do-able: auditory-motor transformations and the posterior temporal plane." *Trends Neuroscience 28*, 636–643.

Weber, D. L. (2008) "Information processing bias in post-traumatic stress disorder." *The Open Neuroimaging Journal 2*, 29–51.

Wellman, K. (1992) *La Mettrie: Medicine, Philosophy, and Enlightenment*. Durham and London: Duke University Press.

Wright, J. (2011) "Genetics: Parkinson's disease gene linked to autism." *SFARI Simons Foundation Autism Research Initiative*; online newsletter. Available at http://sfari.org/news-and-opinion/in-brief/2011/genetics-parkinsons-disease-gene-linked-to-autism, accessed on 5 June 2015.

Wundt, W. (1902) *Principles of Physiological Psychology* (translated by Edward Bradford Titchener), originally published 1874. Available at http://psychclassics.yorku.ca/Wundt/Physio/, accessed 21 July 2015.

Yang, C. -H., Huang, C. -C. and Hsu, K. -S. (2004) "Behavioral stress modifies hippocampal synaptic plasticity through corticosterone-induced sustained extracellular signal-regulated kinase/ mitogen-activated protein kinase activation." *Journal of Neuroscience 24*, 49, 11029–11034.

Yochum, C. L. and Wagner, G. C. (2009) "Autism and Parkinson's disease: animal models and a common etiological mechanism." *Chinese Journal of Physiology 52*, 4, 236–249.

Zabriskie, N. (2010) "The hidden link between Parkinson's and Autism." Curezone message 1547894. Available at http://curezone.org/forums/fm.asp?i=1547894, accessed on 5 June 2015.

Zatorre, R. J., Chen, J. L. and Penhune, V. B. (2007) "When the brain plays music: auditory-motor interactions in music perception and production." *Nature Reviews/Neuroscience 8*, 547–558.

Zelaznik, H. N. (1996) *Advances in Motor Learning and Control*. Champaign, IL: Human Kinetics Publishing.

SUBJECT INDEX

ability, assessing 129, 172
absolute pitch 174, 176
acoustic energy 97–100
adrenal gland 72, 73–4
aging population 210–2
Alexander, Frederick Matthias 215–7
Alexander Technique 215–7
alphabet letters (vs. *solfeggio*) 175–6
amygdala 66, 68, 81
amygdala volume 81
Analytical Music Therapy 207
Angelman Syndrome 237
ankle mobility 87
anticipation 109
ASD
  diagnosis not disorder 29
  as form of PTSD 89, 206
  typical characteristics 89–91
  various theories of 77–8
assessment
  "clinical eye" case example 192
  inability not a deterrent 129, 172
assumptions, erroneous 52–3
auditory system
  central auditory processing 53, 57
  figure-ground 50, 54
  focus 50, 51, 54
  hearing vs. listening 50, 52
  memory (auditory) 54
  motor co-ordination and 54
  sound location 54
  stereophonic hearing 51
  training of 132–3
  visual-auditory integration 54
auditory-motor mapping training (AMMT) 88
autism *see* ASD
Autism and Alexander Technique 216

balance 44, 86
Bartenieff, Imgard 213–4
Basic Anatomy and Physiology for the Music Therapist 17
Basic Physiology for the Music Therapist 70
beginning the session, seated (Module 1) 117–28
behavior
  rating scale 224–5
  typical ASD 89–91
bilateral drumming 160
blindness, sense of self and 38–9
blowing long tones 119–23
Body Awareness as Healing Therapy: The Case of Nora 215
Body and Mature Behavior: A Study of Anxiety, Sex, Gravitation and Learning 214
bottom-up/top-down sequence 33–4, 58
brain
  effect of music training on 26–7
  rhythmic function of 208, 235–6
brain stem 65
breathing exercises
  blowing long tones 119–23
  rhythmic breath control 123–6
  using a kazoo 127–8
  using a recorder 117–28

case examples
  analyzing movement ability 171–3
  blowing long tones 121–2
  drumming 162–3
  hand claps 137–8
  marching "game" 149–51
  rhythmic breath control 125–6
  solfeggio 173–5
  using "clinical eye" 184–94

catecholamines (steroids) 74, 75
central auditory processing 53, 57
cerebellum 65
cerebral palsy 209–10
Claparede, Edouard 102
claps 135–8
clinical eye (case example) 184–94
closing the session, seated (Module 5) 173
Collins, Paul 77
consciousness 60
consciousness disorders 210
consistency, importance of 218–9
context, and multiple sensory inputs 21
COPING skills 79, 183
cortisol 81–3
cortisone level 75, 81–3

Damasio, Dr Antonio 19, 32, 58, 204
dementia with Lewy bodies 231–2
Descartes 130
dichotomy hearing tests 53
dimensional hearing 53–4
disorder, autism not a 29
drinking water 116
Drum Speak 157
drumming activities 156–64
duration of music class 240–1
dynamics 108–9

ear training 53–4, 103
education
    considerations for music educators 239–41
    grading progress 242
    music-based clinician as teacher 154–6
    special needs children 237–42
Einstein, Albert 59
electric keyboard 116–7
embodiment
    of musical elements 22, 23
    of rhythmic relationships 101
emotions
    definition 61
    instinct as 60
    primacy of 19
    and survival-anxiety 63
    vs. feelings 61–2

endocrine system *see* hormone production
energy, acoustic 97–100
energy cycles 97
Eurhythmics
    clinician's participation in classes 117
    definition 22, 24, 101
    history of 100–4
Eurhythmics of Jaques-Dalcroze 22
event segmentation 133
exteroception 45

fear *see* survival-anxiety
feedback-feedforward system 20
feelings, vs. emotions 61–2
Feldenkrais, Moshé 214–5, 217
fight-or-flight response 69–70, 72, 74, 79–80
    see also survival-anxiety
five senses (usually listed) 35–6
"fixed Do" system 175–6
fluorescent lighting 239
focus
    auditory system 50, 51, 54
    tactile 48
    visual 47–8
forcing function 97, 98
form (musical) 109
fornix 66
four-note improvisation 166
free drumming activity 158–9
frequency vibrations 97–8
full-body movement (Module 3) 143–52
functional adaptation 89

galloping 151–2
Gaynor, Mitchell 111
Glennie, Evelyn 22–3
globus pallidus 65
goals
    attaining functional COPING skills 183
    of treatment 180–2
graviceptive systems 44
gravity, sensing 44

hand claps 135–8
harmony 108

SUBJECT INDEX

hearing
  dimensional hearing 53–4
  vs. listening 50, 52
  as a whole-body experience 22
  see also auditory system
Hearing Essay (Glennie) 22
hemispheres, brain 69
hertz 97
hippocampus 66, 68
homeostatic set-points 19–20, 23, 62, 79, 89, 98, 200
hormone production
  adrenal gland 72, 73–4
  cortisol 81–3
  oxytocin 83–4
  pituitary gland 71, 73
HPA axis, survival-anxiety and 70–4
hypothalamus 66, 68, 71, 73
Hypothesis 1 (pervasive survival-anxiety) 79–84, 201–2
Hypothesis 2 (movement and motor-planning timing) 84–9, 202–3
hypotonia 87

illusion 32–3, 34–5
imagery 142–3
imitation/mirroring 88, 133, 141
improvisation
  four-note 166
  importance of 102, 103
  instrumental and rhythm, seated or moving (Module 4) 156–73
  kazoo-talk 168
  movement 168–9
  Q & A 164–5
  Q & A on piano 165–6
  skills in 116
  verbal 166–7
  vocal 166–7
inclusion
  of dementia patients 236
  of special needs children 237–42
inflections, tonal 165–6
information processing 64–9
instinct
  development in musical training 103
  emotion as 60
  in motor-planning 113

instruments
  effect of playing 113
  electric keyboard 116–7
  kazoo 127–8, 168
  piano 116–7
  selection for music training 241
  see also recorders
interim activities
  trampoline bounces 139–41
  "walk in the park" 142–3
  You're a mirror, I'm a mirror 141
interoception 45

Jaques-Dalcroze, Emile 100–3
jumping 152

kazoo 127–8, 168
keyboard, electric 116–7

La Mettrie, Julien Offroy de 130
Laban Notation 213
Laban, Rudolf von 212–4, 217
language development, use of kazoo for 127–8
limbic system 65–8
linear sound tracking 54
listening
  vs. hearing 50, 52
  see also auditory system
location, of sound 54
logs, tracking 178
Looking for Spinoza: Joy, Sorrow, and the Feeling Brain 61

machine, human body as 130–1
mallets (drum) 158
mammillary body 66
Man a Machine 130
marching
  "game" 145–51
  Jaques-Dalcroze on 143–4
Melodic Intonation Therapy 25, 88
melody 107–8
memory, auditory 54
Menuhin, Yehudi 96
Merging of the Senses, The 20
mirroring/imitation 88, 133, 141

Modern Dance 103
Module 1: beginning the session, seated 117–28
Module 2: rhythmic upper-body organization 134–43
Module 3: full-body movement 143–52
Module 4: instrumental and rhythm improvisations, seated or moving 156–73
Module 5: closing the session, seated 173
motor apraxia 87
motor planning deficits, hypothesis 2 84–9, 202–3
mouth instruments
  research into use of 88
  see also kazoo; recorders
movement
  deficits (hypothesis 2) 84–9, 202–3
  improvisation 168–9
  initiating instinctive 132
  segmentation 133
  sound cues for each 144–5
Moving Researcher: Laban/Bartenieff Movement Analysis in Performing Arts Education and Creative Arts Therapies 214
music
  as acoustic energy 97–100
  as mirror reflecting human behavior 99–100
  see also dynamics; form (musical); harmony; melody; rhythm; timbre
Music Effect, The: Music Physiology and Clinical Applications 17, 22, 64
'Music Soothes the Ravaged Brain' (article) 231–6
music therapy
  lack of systematic approaches in 25
  Melodic Intonation Therapy 25, 88
  Neurologic Music Therapy 25
  see also music-based treatment
Music Therapy, Sensory Integration and the Autistic Child 157
music training
  effect on brain 26–7
  positive adaptations from 98–9
music-based treatment
  definition of 29–30

Eurhythmics' suitability for 104
explaining to others 181, 183
not therapeutic recreation 182
predominant focus of 24–6
role within multi-disciplinary team 183

neocortex 68
Neurologic Music Therapy 25
neurology
  amygdala 66, 68
  amygdala volume 81
  brain stem 65
  cerebellum 65
  fornix 66
  globus pallidus 65
  hemispheres 69
  hippocampus 68, 66
  hypothalamus 66, 68, 71, 73
  mammillary body 66
  neocortex 68
  olfactory bulb 65, 67, 68
  paleostriatum 65
  parolfactory area 66
  prefrontal cortex 68–9
  rhinencephalon 65
  thalamus 66
  see also brain
nystagmus, position-related 86

objectives of treatment 180–2
occupational therapy 105
Old McDonald had a band 170–1
older clients 210–2
olfactory bulb 65, 67, 68
oral-motor therapy 88
otolith sensors 44
oxytocin 83–4

paleostriatum 65
paranoia 208
Parkinson's disease 209–10
parolfactory area 66
perfect pitch 174, 176
peripheral vision 47
physiologic psychology 58
physiology, individuality of 32–3, 78
piano skills 116–7

pituitary gland 71, 73
Polyvagal Theory 206
position-related nystagmus 86
post-traumatic stress disorder (PTSD)
    ASD as form of 89, 206
    distorted sensory information in 75
    Eurhythmics for treatment of 205–7
practice, repetition of 46, 218
predictability 80
prefrontal cortex 68–9
prescriptions, treatment 180–1
progress
    grading of special needs children 242
    rate of 129
    tracking 178, 222–3
proprioception
    importance of music-based clinicians' awareness of 40
    interaction with vestibular and visual systems 44–6, 85–9
    overview 36–42
psychodynamic therapy 204–9
psychoticism 208

Q & A improvisations 164–6
quick response reactions 103

reality, illusion as 32–3, 34–5
recommendations for a client (sample) 226–30
recorders
    use real instruments (not toys) 129
    using for breathing exercises 117–28
relationship, client-clinician 219
relaxation, importance of 101, 117
report of clinical work (sample) 226–30
resistance 219–20
reticular formation 67
Rett's Syndrome 138
rhinencephalon 65
rhythm
    function of brain 208, 235–6
    overview of 106–7
    training in 102–3
Rhythm and Movement: Applications of Dalcroze Eurhythmics 154–5
Rhythmic Auditory Stimulation (RAS) 209

rounds (canons) 124
running 152

Saint-Exupery, Antoine de 179
schizophrenia 207–8
seating arrangements (in music class) 240
senior population 210–2
senses *see* auditory system; five senses (usually listed); proprioception; "sixth sense"; tactile system; vestibular sensory system; visual system
sensorimotor deficits 104–5
Sensorimotor Psychotherapy 205–6
sensory integration 20–1, 23
sight-singing 173
sing-reading 167
"sixth sense" 38
skipping 151–2
solfeggio 103, 173–7
sound cues, for movements 144–5
sound discrimination 54
Sound of Music, The 177
space walk 169–70
special needs children 237–42
Spinoza, Baruch 218
square peg/round hole analogy 77, 78
stereophonic hearing 51
stereotypic movement disorders (SMDs) 87
steroids (catecholamines) 74, 75
stroke 209–10
structure of treatment sessions
    Module 1: beginning the session, seated 117–28
    Module 2: rhythmic upper-body organization 134–43
    Module 3: full-body movement 143–52
    Module 4: instrumental and rhythm improvisations, seated or moving 156–73
    Module 5: closing the session, seated 173
    overview 114–7
    see also interim activities
survival, focus on 19, 58

survival-anxiety
  continual sense of 20
  definition 63
  and fear 63
  from inaccurate sensory processing 64
  and HPA (hypothalamus-pituitary-adrenal) axis 70–4
  pervasive (hypothesis 1) 79–84, 201–2
  see also fight-or-flight response
Synaptic Self: How Our Brains Become Who We Are 60
synesthesia 23

tactile system 48–9
teacher, music-based clinician as 154–6
tempo, selection of 132
terminology 29–30
thalamus 66
therapeutic relationship 219
therapy *see* music therapy; music-based treatment
"three-drum plus game" 164
timbre 107
toe-walking 87
tracking progress 178, 222–3
trampoline bounces 139–41
treatment prescriptions 180–1

'Understanding the Included Special Needs Child in Music Classes' (article) 237–42
upper-/lower-body organization (Module 3) 143–52

upper-body organization (Module 2) 134–43

vegetative/minimal states 210
verbal improvisation 166–7
vestibular sensory system
  balance function of 44, 86
  interaction with proprioception and visual system 44–6, 85–9
  overview 42–6
Vibrational Medicine 22
visual impairment, sense of self and 38–9
visual system
  focus 47–8
  interaction with proprioception and vestibular system 44–6, 85–9
  overview 47–8
  peripheral vision 47
  proprioception and 41
vocal cords, lengthening 127
vocal improvisation 166–7

"walk in the park" 142–3
walking
  learning 43–4
  space walk 169–70
  see also marching
water breaks 116
Waterman, Ian 40
whole-brain-whole-body experience 21–2, 23, 113
Wundt, Wilhelm 32, 58

You're a mirror, I'm a mirror 141

AUTHOR INDEX

Abercrombie, H. C. 82
Abril, C. R. 212, 213
Alberts, J. L. 200
Alexander, F. M. 29, 216
Alexander, G. E. 86
Altenmüller, E. 200
Amaral, D. C. 80
Amos, P. 85
Atigh, A. 85

Baer, S. 87
Ballerini, M. 208
Baloh, R. W. 44
Balota, D. A. 200
Baron-Cohen, S. 77, 132, 133
Beck, D. L. 53
Bellis, T. J. 53
Berger, D. S. 15, 20, 22, 24, 25, 34, 35, 37, 44, 53, 59, 63, 64, 65, 66, 68, 80, 82, 97, 98, 116, 122, 132, 133, 140, 147, 157, 161, 178, 181, 182
Beringer, E. 214
Biven, L. 62
Blasing, B. E. 133
Blumenthal, A. L. 34
Bradshaw, J. L. 87
Brennan, J. 130
Brett King, D. 130
Brett, M. 199
Brimacombe, M. 87
Bundy, A. C. 34
Buzsaki, G. 34, 208

Campione-Barr, N. 37
Chen, F. 83
Chen, J. L. 200
Cohen, D. J. 77

Collins, P. 78
Corbett, B. A. 80, 82
Crane-Godreau, M. A. 200
Cytowic, R. E. 23

Damasio, A. R. 24, 34, 37, 59, 61, 86, 87
Daniel, S. 87
Davidson, R. J. 82
Day, B. L. 44
de Alcantara, P. 216
Delafield-Butt, T. H. 87, 132
DeLong, M. R. 86
Dieter, K. C. 41
Domes, G. 83
Dowd, A. M. 89

Eckberg, M. 200
Esposito, G. 87

Feldenkrais, M. 214
Feng, W. 55
Fernandes, C. 214
Findlay, E. 22, 154
Fisher, A. G. 34
Fitzgerald, K. 53
Fitzpatrick, R. C. 44
Fox, N. A. 83
Freeman, C. G. 216
Freeman, R. D. 87
Frego, R. J. D. 213
Frith, U. 77

Gazzaniga, M. S. 59
Gerber, R. 22
Glennie, E. 22

Graeff, F. G. 83
Grafton, S. T. 200
Gran, J. A. 199
Green, D. 89
Guenette, L. 53
Guilliams, T. G. 83

Hameline, D. 102
Hare, C. 53
Hars, M. 211
Hausdorff, J. M. 209
Heinrichs, M. 83
Hill, E. 77
Hollander, E. 200
Honrubia, V. 44
Horowitz, S. S. 24
Hsu, K. -S. 83
Huang, C. -C. 83
Hutchison, K. A. 200

Janata, P. 199
Jaques-Dalcroze, E. 208, 211

Kalin, N. H. 82
Kandel, E. R. 59
Kraus, N. 23, 26, 50
Kuchenbuch, A. 23, 26
Kwak, E. E. 200

Laban, R. 212
Lappe, C. 113
Lathe, R. 24
LeDoux, J. 19, 24, 34, 59, 60, 63, 80, 82
Levine, P. 200, 206
Li, S. C. 200
Llinas, R. R. 34, 59
Lombardo, M. V. 77

McCleery, J. P. 87, 88
McFarlane, A. C. 200
McIntosh, G. C. 200, 209
Macnaughton, I. 200
Maurer, R. G. 86, 87
Mead, V. H. 22
Mechsner, F. 37, 38, 40, 41, 42
Meier, F. 133
Meredith, A. J. 20, 24, 25, 34, 35, 179

Metaxas, D. N. 87
Metzger, A. 37
Ming, X. 87
Minton, K. 200, 205
Moore, C. -L. 212
Moore, S. F. 22
Mosconi, M. W. 81
Müller, W. 208
Munson, J. 81
Murray, E. A. 34
Musiek, F. E. 53

Nacewicz, B. M. 81, 83
Nayate, A. 87
Nevid, J. S. 37
Nolano, M. 200
Nombela, C. 200
Nordahl, C. W. 81
Norton, A. 25

Ogden, P. 200, 205

Pai, Y. -C. 200
Pain, C. 200
Panksepp, J. 34, 62
Parbery-Clark, A. 26, 50
Pasca, S. 87
Patel, A. D. 200
Payne, P. 200
Pederson, I. N. 207
Penhune, V. B. 200
Perry, B. D. 207
Porges, S. W. 34, 77, 206
Priestley, M. 207

Rice, R. R. 200
Ridgel, A. L. 200, 209
Rinehart, N. J. 87, 89
Rothschild, B. 207

Schaal, S. 133
Scheiby, B. B. 207
Schlaug, G. 77
Schnebly-Black, J. 22
Schneck, D. J. 17, 20, 22, 24, 25, 34, 35, 37, 44, 53, 56, 59, 63, 64, 65, 66, 68, 70, 80, 82, 83, 97, 98, 140, 181

Sherrington, C. S. 38
Shinn, J. 53
Skoe, E. 26
Smetacek, V. 37, 38, 40, 41, 42
Smetana, J. G. 37
Spratt, E. G. 82
Stanghellini, G. 208
Stein, B. E. 20, 24, 25, 34, 35, 179
Strait, D. L. 50
Strick, P. L. 86
Sultanifar, A. 87

Tager-Flusberg, H. 77
Tan, H. 83
Tennant, V. 181
Thaut, M. H. 25, 200, 209
Theodorou, E. 133
Tierney, A. 23, 24
Tillmann, B. 201
Torres, E. B. 87
Trevarthen, C. 87, 132
Trombetti, A. 211

Ullman, L. 212

van der Kolk, B. A. 200, 206
van Vugt, F. T. 201
Viney, W. 130
Vitek, J. L. 200

Wagner, G. C. 87, 200
Wan, C. Y. 77, 88
Warren, J. D. 200
Warren, J. E. 200
Weber, D. L. 200
Weisaeth, L. 200
Wellman, K. 130, 164
Wise, R. J. 200
Woody, W. 130
Wright, J. 200
Wundt, W. 24, 34, 204

Yamamoto, K. 212
Yan, Z. 83
Yang, C. -H. 83
Yanovich, P. 87
Yochum, C. L. 200

Zabriskie, N. 200
Zangrossi, H. 83
Zatorre, R. J. 200
Zhong, P. 83

Made in the USA
Coppell, TX
13 April 2025

48246706R00148